The Rise and Fall of an Economic Empire

The Rise and Fall of an Economic Empire

With Lessons for Aspiring Economies

Colin Read

First published 2010 by
PALGRAVE MACMILLAN

Palgrave Macmillan in the UK is an imprint of Macmillan Publishers Limited, registered in England, company number 785998, of Houndmills, Basingstoke, Hampshire RG21 6XS.

Palgrave Macmillan in the US is a division of St Martin's Press LLC, 175 Fifth Avenue, New York, NY 10010.

Palgrave Macmillan is the global academic imprint of the above companies and has companies and representatives throughout the world.

Palgrave® and Macmillan® are registered trademarks in the United States, the United Kingdom, Europe and other countries.

ISBN: 978-0-230-27370-2 hardback

This book is printed on paper suitable for recycling and made from fully managed and sustained forest sources. Logging, pulping and manufacturing processes are expected to conform to the environmental regulations of the country of origin.

A catalogue record for this book is available from the British Library.

Library of Congress Cataloging-in-Publication Data

Read, Colin, 1959–
    The rise and fall of an economic empire : with lessons for aspiring economies / Colin Read.
        p. cm.
    ISBN 978–0–230–27370–2 (hardback)
    1. Economic history. 2. Commerce – History. 3. United States – Economic conditions. I. Title.
HC21.R39 2010
330.9—dc22   2010027555

A catalog record for this book is available from the Library of Congress.

10 9 8 7 6 5 4 3 2 1
19 18 17 16 15 14 13 12 11 10

Printed and bound in Great Britain by
CPI Antony Rowe, Chippenham and Eastbourne

This book is dedicated to my wife, Natalie, mother, Gail, and daughter, Blair. These three women keep me grounded and offer me wonderful balance in my life.

Contents

Illustrations

Tables

Figures

Preface

For most of the span of human civilization, economic development appeared to move at a snail's pace. Economic empires came and went, but at a rate much slower than the span of a human life.

The forces that foster the rise of an economic empire, and subsequently bring about its decline, are universal. More than two millennia ago, the same forces brought Greece to its apex, and then Rome. Meanwhile, China was progressively developing and exerting its economic power over the last 3000 years. In the latter half of the last millennium, Spain and Portugal, Italy, the Netherlands, England, and, finally, the United States, vied for global economic supremacy. Yet, despite this more rapid pace of economic ascendancy over the past five centuries, citizens of each of these nations would not witness a rise and fall of their economies within the span of a single human lifetime.

Now, for the first time, economic change is occurring at a pace that can be observed within one's lifetime. In less than a century, we will have seen England, then the United States, and soon China each hold the mantle as the world's largest economy.

We will see that part of the reason for accelerated economic dominance is the rapid pace of information transfer. Those elements that allow one nation to succeed economically can now be easily observed and imitated by other competing nations. And, with few impediments to discourage the flow of financial capital across borders, economic resources can rapidly follow opportunity.

The ease at which innovations can spread, financial resources can move across borders, and global consumers can seek out the better mousetrap anywhere in the world means that economic success can be rapid. However, economic power is now more transient than at any other time in human history. If economic supremacy can occur rapidly, likewise can economic decline. And, if economic supremacy is a goal, constant monitoring of those vying to knock an economic empire off of its pedestal has become a necessity.

Throughout this book, I document the various forces that give rise to economic supremacy, and the subsequent forces that make it impossible to retain economic supremacy indefinitely. I document these forces not because I subscribe to a fatalist view of the transience of economic power. Rather, I remain hopeful that knowledge of the forces that give rise to the creation of an economic empire will allow nations to more carefully and sustainably plot their economic trajectory and mitigate their ultimate decline. If we can better understand the forces that eventually cause an economic empire to become less organized, less powerful, and destined to economic decline, we can better manage our economic destiny and maintain our economic power.

In the analysis, I focus on the economic ascendancy of the United States over the last century and a half. I do so not because the U.S. economic superpower is ubiquitous or its destiny predetermined. Rather, the rise of the U.S. economy was most rapid, and occurred at a time in our history in which development of competing economic powers could not be contained. We are living in a laboratory and observing the grand economic experiment in the United States that appears to be entering a nascent maturation.

However, while we can observe the forces that give rise to the U.S. economic superpower, and the forces that lead to its decay, we can just as readily see how these same forces are imitated and usurped by other nations no more likely to avoid the same inevitable destiny. Perhaps by recognizing the dismal prophecy of economic rise and fall, we can foster a more sustainable economic system that will some day foster longer-term, if less spectacular, growth. In doing so, we may also offer a prescription of all peoples and nations to discover an economic affluence that is sustainable and less prone to the gyrations brought on by economic competition between nations.

About the Author

Colin Read is a professor of Economics and Finance, former dean of the School of Business and Economics of the State University of New York College at Plattsburgh, and a columnist for the *Plattsburgh New York Press Republican* newspaper. He has a Ph.D. in Economics, J.D. in Law, M.B.A., Master's of Taxation, and has taught economics and finance for 25 years. Colin's recent books include *The Fear Factor: What Happens When Fear Grips Wall Street*, *Global Financial Meltdown: How We Can Avoid the Next Economic Crisis*, and a book on international taxation. He has written dozens of papers on market failure, volatility, and housing markets, and appears monthly on a local PBS television show to discuss the regional and national economy. He has worked as a research associate at the Harvard Joint Center for Housing Studies and served the Ministry of Finance in Indonesia under contract from the Harvard Institute for International Development. His consulting company can be found on the Internet at www.economicinsights.net. In his spare time, he enjoys tending to his vineyard and floatplane flying from the home on Lake Champlain that he shares with his wife, Natalie, daughter, Blair, and dog, Walter.

Introduction

The year 1776 was one of profound innovations: Adam Smith published *The Wealth of Nations*, a book that remains the definitive treatise on the workings of markets; the United States declared independence from Britain on the decidedly economic premise of life, liberty, and the pursuit of happiness; and British parliamentarian Edward Gibbons published his first volume of *The Decline and Fall of the Roman Empire*. These three events documented the advantages of a new system of economics, the creation of a nation based on economic premises, and the reasons why a mighty and robust system can come to an end. The year also marked the beginning of an empire that now finds itself struggling to maintain its relevancy and its once-assumed dominant global economic position.

Less than a century later, an insight from the realm of science cast light on the dynamics of complex systems. Just as Adam Smith motivated a paradigm shift in our understanding of markets, Charles Darwin's publication of *On the Origin of Species* in 1859 further contributed to our understanding of how species may evolve to better adapt to their environment. The phrase "survival of the fittest" is not only used to describe a biological organism within its environment, but can also be used to describe any complex system – from military empires to political empires. This profound tenet of biology is no less profound when applied to economies.

The Law of Diminishing Returns proves that no institution can grow too big. At some point, greater size inevitably introduces inefficiencies. The very forces that ensued ensured growth and dominance of an institution in one era can contribute to its decline in another. History has demonstrated this phenomenon over and over. From the extinction of the dinosaurs and the fall of the Roman Empire, to the transformation of the United Kingdom from an entity that dictated foreign policy to one that dealt in foreign policy, the eventual downfall or the surrender of dominance by the largest and most powerful military empires seems to be inevitable.

Economic empires are no different. Just like the dinosaurs, economies evolve and are governed by the harsh Darwinist law of survival of the fittest. This book documents the creation and evolution of economic empires and their eventual demise.

Of course, economics and politics are inextricably linked. With the rise of economic power comes political influence, at both the national and international level. Though it would be impossible to document the rise and fall of an economy with global reach without also treating political dimensions, this book does not emphasize the politics that arises when a nation enjoys a dominant economic position. Nor do I discuss dominance that flows from military prowess. Although most books on the rise and fall of empires focus on military might, militarism is treated here as in support of broader economic principles, and not the root of economic power. Instead, we will discover how an economy can establish itself and develop the institutions that drive it toward its apex. I also document the forces that eventually cause an economic empire's decline, only to be replaced by yet another economy that ascends its own apex.

The example drawn upon for this book will be the U.S. economic system, not because we live in an era in which the dominance of the American economy has been challenged definitively. Rather, it is because the U.S. economy is the first in this modern era that was born of an economic ideal, epitomized an economic model that was replicated almost everywhere, assisted in the dismantling of competing political-economic systems, and was at the root of a global financial meltdown that arose precisely because of its economic might.

Unlike Gibbons' documentation of the decline and fall of the Roman Empire, the concluding chapter of this story cannot be written for perhaps another century. In the ensuing century, we will discover whether a dominant economic system can avoid demise through the process of reinvention, or whether the now familiar economic cycle will repeat itself elsewhere. Meanwhile, aspiring nations are reinventing themselves along economic lines, with an almost patriotic zeal to replace the United States as the pinnacle of economic might.

I present this book not as a critique of a system pioneered by a nation in its infancy and brought to fruition over more than two centuries. Rather, my goal is to treat the various and complex economic issues so the reader can comprehend the theories that will ultimately dictate the final outcome. As our economic fate unfolds, its history will determine which of these factors will decide our economic future.

Part I

From 10,000 B.C. to 1776 – The Discovery of Economies of Scale

We begin by describing the importance of markets and the creation of economies of scale. These early markets were able to motivate production and channel consumption with great efficiency, especially compared with the command and control system usually employed by emperors who relied on a more hierarchical economic model. We also describe how markets could support much larger levels of production that would bring costs down and increase the surpluses earned by the producing class. We show that, by the end of the First Industrial Revolution, markets and economies of large-scale production became the prevailing economic model.

Those readers well versed in markets, the roots of economies and diseconomies of scale, and the role of colonialism in fueling demand in the First Industrial Revolution may wish to skip Part I and proceed to Part II.

1
An Economic Prehistory to Economic Emperors

> (Agriculture)...was a complex process and can now be viewed more legitimately as the paragon of evolutionary process that Darwin originally recognized. There are many interacting factors involved that we know about operating on a wide range of levels from the gene to the farmer and climate – the challenge is to integrate them into a single story.
>
> (Robin Allaby, research scientist who discovered the first known examples of an agrarian economy, 2008)[1]

The simple innovation of agriculture sprung upon the world a sequence of innovations that remain with us today. Perhaps the most important of all is the creation of economic systems that allowed us to manage the surpluses of agriculture to meet human needs and wants more than 23,000 years ago.

All economic systems share one important aspect. They provide incentives to produce, or disincentives not to produce, and divide the spoils of production among various participants. Beyond these simple roles, each economic system imparts its own flavor on the ultimate fairness and efficiency of the production and distribution of goods and services. While each system inevitably has its own coercive aspects, none demonstrates "survival of the fittest" as well as the primitive command and control economy practiced before the formation of markets.

As it turns out, the very strengths of a command economy to control all aspects of production give rise to human desires to create some economic autonomy through underground markets.

Agrarian society and the dawn of history

Economies arose with the development of humankind. In fact, all sentient beings practice economics. The word "economy" can be traced back to its

Greek roots: "oikos," meaning "house," more metaphorically alluding to our environment, and "nomics," referring to "management." Humans, from the beginning have studied and learned to manage our environment to satisfy our wants and needs. Motivated to meet our needs and self-interest, we differ little from other species in this most essential aspect.

In fact, other living beings have developed controlled and systematic economies that allow them to survive and thrive long before humans developed even rudimentary economies. Ants and bees are considered social animals because they maintain strong and systematic hierarchies in the greater interest of the colony and the queen. In the absence of markets, there are obvious exchanges of services, essential roles for each participant, and an advanced system of specialization, all through mechanisms of genetics and brute force, and all functioning seemingly in concert.

Ants and bees had one advantage over early humans, though. Their interactions have been benefitted by their fixity. The royalty, their primary authority, remains stationary in a shelter in a heartland called the hive. The hinterland on its periphery provides the hive with the food resources that support its survival.

Millions of years of evolution have perfected the command and control economy for these social animals. Such a heartland/hinterland model, in which the queen and elite remain stationary and the worker ants and bees harvest a broader environment, has allowed these economies to remain incredibly robust. However, humans would eventually take such equal advantage of permanent shelters and the harvest of sustainable and local sources of food only with the invention of agriculture.

Agriculture is thought to have developed in Syria 23,000 years ago. These humble beginnings initiated a series of economic innovations that would provide spectacular economic growth in the ensuing millennia.[2] Humans moved from a nomadic hunter-gatherer society, in which they were forced to travel from place to place in search of sources of food, to a system based on agriculture and animal husbandry. No longer were humans uprooted constantly in permanent pursuit of migrating animals. Freed from the need to chase their food sources, humans could now co-locate their crops with their shelters. That made all the difference, as this agrarian focus completely revolutionized humankind and acted as the precursor to the modern economic empires.

Before this revolution, humans could only organize in relatively small tribes, predominantly along family lines. The nomadic tribes had to be relatively mobile, making scale a disadvantage. With a premium on mobility, these nomadic clans could neither invest in nor plan for permanent shelter and large stores of food. They also expended a great amount of energy migrating and transporting rather than producing.

Whereas the agricultural revolution permitted permanent settlements, and habitation evolved, once built, these settlements freed their inhabitants to devote more time to other pursuits.

Similarly, agriculture allowed a subset of the tribe to feed many others. Humans were liberated from a regime in which a couple of hunters could provide for only themselves and a few others to one in which a few could feed many.

This agrarian revolution instantly created a surplus of labor. With a few planters and harvesters able to feed many, and a few builders able to shelter many, the remainder of the tribe could concentrate on other pursuits such as the creation of more elaborate tools, the development of the written word and sophisticated language, and the first opportunity to record history.

This demarcation between prehistoric and historic humankind coincided with a period of economic development that was unprecedented. For the first time, a species learned to dominate and control its environment rather than live within it. Humans learned to develop economies that were fueled by and, in turn, controlled the environment in ways that satisfied human wants and needs.

Command and control

While the innovation of markets that serve and adapt to human needs has obvious implications on the growth of the modern economy, it was not immediately obvious that markets should be free and decentralized. The harsh reality of prehistoric societies is that only those who had the most scarce and valuable resources held the most economic power in society. With scarcity came power.

In the earliest economies, it was likely that the most powerful and prolific hunter was also able to garner the most social and economic power. The politics of human organization and the economics of wealth were likely as linked then as they are now. There is something timeless about the association of power with wealth for those who command the scarce resources that satisfy human wants and needs.

One way to translate this political power arising from control over important and scarce resources is in the creation of an economic dictatorship. Command over important resources endowed on some the power to dictate the actions of others wanting to attach themselves to the fortunes of the economically powerful. Wealth and privilege in these early settlements could purchase power and influence in ways that were much more significant and grander than any hunter-gatherer society could have contemplated.

This ability to control resources and command the actions of others is of incredible significance – in both the creation of new economic wealth and in its subsequent distribution. Undoubtedly, many resources had to be devoted to the maintenance of this power. As empires grew, far-flung military supply chains had to be supported physically, and cadres of surrogate leaders had to be supported economically. These legions could also extend the reach of the powerful and could expand the hinterland that could serve the heartland.

A system constructed by and for the controlling elite, and the peasantry that fulfilled the role of production, was a precarious one. It was always vulnerable to a stronger army from the outside or a cunning political aspirant from within. Cycles of dominance, intrigue, strife, and discipline have prevailed ever since. These empires were successful in using their might to expand hinterlands. However, such an economic model of command and control was also vulnerable because more effort was devoted to the maintenance of control rather than to the creation of new production and wealth.

Flawed omniscience

Compared to our lives with diverse choices, brought on by the modern market economy, bees and ants lead simple economic lives. The preordained ways in which the bees and ants serve the colony is determined genetically before birth. The hive must satisfy the basic needs of each set of its members. These needs are well-defined. For instance, satisfaction of the simple needs of the production group, known as worker bees or worker ants, are coordinated by the elite that control the hive. However, satisfying such needs is relatively simple when the producing group is homogeneous, both genetically and socially, and when all understand, and no one challenges, their relative positions in the socioeconomic order.

Unlike the bees and ants, the diversity of choices that humans enjoy is almost infinite. The motivation and control of humans have no such preordained subservience. Perhaps no species demonstrates as much diversity of expression and wants as we humans do. This diversity increases with the expansion of our intelligence and awareness. It is influenced profoundly by the aspirations and realizations of others. We are motivated not only by what we have, but also by what others have amassed for themselves.

Conspicuous consumption

While Thorstein Veblen popularized the term "conspicuous consumption" in his seminal 1889 book *The Theory of the Leisure Class*,[3] measuring one's wealth relative to another's was not a new concept. When agrarian surpluses satisfied the most basic human wants and needs, humans were motivated to focus their attention on novel ways to satisfy their higher wants and needs. Wealth creation for its own sake became a distinctly human foible.

Our economic leaders understood that the satisfaction of basic human needs was a necessary ingredient for an orderly society. The leaders needed order and predictability to retain their grip on power. They ignored the basic needs of their peasantry at their own peril. They had to strike a balance between the needs of the elite and the needs of the peasantry that tolerated the elite's control.

Just as the queen bee and her courtesans control the hive, the elite must command and direct production and dictate the distribution of goods. Such command and control emerged as the essential ingredient in the art of economic power. Failure to understand the subtleties of this responsibility opened opportunities for overthrow from within or from worker revolt. A strange mix of benevolence and ruthlessness, and a new political cunning of previously unprecedented proportions became the characteristics that fueled the success of dictators.

The precarious perch

The responsibility of economic power is a precarious balance. The wealth of the elite necessarily insulated emperors from the potentially riotous peasantry. This isolation made it difficult over time for the elite to discern the evolving needs and the prevailing satisfaction of the peasants. As the isolation inevitably increased, the increasingly out-of-touch dictator became vulnerable to overthrow by the much more numerous peasantries, or to overthrow from an aspiring contender who had a greater sense of the needs of peasants, or their greater loyalty.

As economic leaders tried to avoid overthrow and maintain the reins and shackles of economic control, they also had to direct the tools of economic production that would create and amass the production to perpetuate this delicate economic balance. Production had to be organized in functional units that were of optimal size and that contained the proper mix of skills. Workers had to be coordinated and motivated to produce, either through a sense of the common good or for fear of punishment otherwise.

It would take hundreds of generations before there emerged viable substitutes for this model of a command and control economy. Once the substitute of the free market caught hold, there was no going back. Before then, this command and control model of economic order through coercion remained relatively robust.

These earliest production-oriented economies grew in power proportional to the resources the empire commanded and the economies of scale their economic discipline created. The robustness of these empires was also proportional to the ability of their economic leaders to effectively command and maintain economic production relative to the abilities of potential adversaries.

Looks like we have a failure to motivate

All successful economies have some common characteristics. They must send out signals of what to produce when and where, and they must subsequently distribute the spoils of this production in sufficient proportion to motivate those who toil to produce. Market economies coordinate through free markets and the invisible hand, which we will describe later. However, a benevolent dictator could, in theory, be equally effective in allocating production. Through the effective distribution of the fruits of workers' production, a benevolent economic leader with sufficient understanding of the needs of the economy can effectively distribute production to mimic a free market. However, history suggests that few dictators have the skill and the omniscience of the needs of the working peasantry to maintain economic efficiency and order for long.

The inevitable failure of a centrally planned command and control economy is that its initial expediency and efficiencies bred greater scale and rapid economic growth. This greater scale made it increasingly difficult to stay in touch with the needs of individuals within a vast and growing economic empire. This theme that reoccurs over our economic history leads us to observe that economic success eventually sows the seeds of its own demise.

Some features shared by all economies are as follows: They provide the incentive to produce or disincentives for refusal to produce, and they direct a share of production to workers who are also consumers. Consumers could at times be the producers themselves, or could earn a share of the production, with another share of production going to those that distribute the goods, command their production, or otherwise enjoy the fruits of wealth creation.

The subtleties of this arrangement are not lost on a worker toiling day in and day out to produce the goods and services that fuel this elaborate economic system. They voluntarily accept membership to the economic system if they receive a quality of life no worse than what they could receive if they were to do it alone without the advantages the greater economy can offer. Those unwilling to trade their economic freedom for their share of a larger economic pie may nonetheless be forced into economic servitude. However, the price of holding workers in servitude is the devotion of greater resources to coercion.

We will see later how market economies assist in the coordination function. In the meantime, let us look at the correlation between incentives and effort.

Incentives to cheat

The command and control economy compels and directs the production process. However, while one can lead a horse to water, one cannot necessarily make it drink.

Individuals can be coerced to produce. A greater investment in coercion can even achieve some success in inducing workers to produce at an optimal level. However, such a coercive system is not sustainable. Rather, to be effective, it requires constant effort and monitoring, and a wide range of motivational tools.

To police a command and control economy, economic authorities must extract maximum effort with minimum monitoring costs. The optimal level of monitoring, motivation, and effort is difficult to achieve. This optimum becomes increasingly difficult as the scale of the enterprise increases. As increased monitoring and control efforts consume a greater share of available resources, inefficiencies inevitably rise with scale, and ultimately frustrate greater economic scale.

Shirking is the Achilles heel of the command and control economy. As the size of any organization increases, economic commanders have an increasingly difficult task to align the goals of the organization with the efforts of the individual.

Of course, a company of one individual has no such problem. The sole proprietor well understands the relationship between effort and aggregate organizational production. Even an organization with a few participants is better able to align effort and production. Shirking of any member of a smaller unit is obvious to those who must take up the slack.

However, as early command and control organizations increased in size, there emerged reduced alignment between those who produced, those who policed production, and the political elite at the top who enjoyed and redistributed production. Efficiencies that arose from increased organizational size were eventually overwhelmed by the inefficiencies that were incurred as energy was devoted to hold the organization together.

Not all jobs are created equal

There are alternatives to brute economic force and workers held in servitude. Some tasks require greater skill and training. Such producers can be motivated by appeal to worker pride and by the opportunity for advancement to less monotonous or menial work, or by the reward of greater prestige and privilege.

Such motivations were not bestowed on those who could be easily compelled to produce, or whose production was not sufficiently individualized to engender a sense of scarcity or pride of workmanship that would justify an elevated status in society. Farming, hard or unskilled labor, transportation of goods, military service, and basic retailing demanded less training and afforded few opportunities for diversion of production. Such production could be policed with little effort. Output per worker can be monitored relatively easily, and workers who do not work out can be replaced with relative ease. So long as the scale of the operation is not too large, shirking can be prevented, to a point.

Workers with scarcer talents were able to extract greater rewards and more autonomy. These workers may have had unique skills and may have belonged to exclusive clubs or guilds that police themselves. In this case, a share of the savings in external monitoring could be retained instead by the tradesperson.

Beyond unskilled workers and skilled tradesman are the technocrats and aristocrats who are closely aligned to the wealth of the elite and governors. As the organization grows, these technocrats and aristocrats could act on behalf of the ruling elite. Their unfailing loyalty to the ruling elite allowed the economy to increase in scope. However, if the scope of the empire became too expansive, this system of technocrats and aristocrats too had to grow. And, in the process, the allegiance to the ruling elite inevitably weakened, and the opportunities to foment adversaries and contenders for power naturally grew.

A system that divided producers into various functional groups that must be closely monitored and policed could not be replicated indefinitely. Ultimately, it became increasingly difficult to direct production in a way most advantageous for the ruling elite. Consequently, the size of a command and control economy became constrained, and the growth of the empire created ever-growing pathways to its own demise.

While the difficulty in monitoring almost everything nearly everywhere exposed the weakness, and was the limiting factor of the command and control economy, the decentralized marketplace knew no such limitations.

Fruit of the rise becomes the seed of decline

The agrarian revolution and early barter economies allowed for a dramatic expansion in the scope of goods that humans could produce. It also allowed humans time to pursue higher-level activities beyond the mere maintenance needs of food and shelter. The resulting economic bounty produced huge incentives to organize into larger groups and tribes, with some of the spoils diverted to maintaining a ruling elite that fomented this organization.

However, the greater scale of economic organization illustrated that ever more expansive economic empires become increasingly vulnerable to contenders for power and increasingly corruptible as power is amassed.

2

Barter, Economic Emperors, and the Decentralized Marketplace

> The propensity to truck, barter and exchange one thing for another is
> common to all men, and to be found in no other race of animals.
>
> (Adam Smith, 1776)[4]

The most basic markets are as old as agrarian economies themselves. It is agrarian surpluses that motivated the creation of market economies. We will consider the source of these surpluses in the next chapter. We first address the role of markets themselves.

By creating efficiencies so that one person could feed or shelter many, we simultaneously created an avenue for trade. When individuals' production exceed their basic needs, they seek out avenues to trade their excess for a higher want or need.

Surpluses not devoted to the economic commander find their way into markets, sanctioned or not. These markets compete with, and sometimes challenge, the authority of the economic commander.

The role of trade

Before the creation of a common currency, trade would inevitably require someone with a surplus in one good and a desire for another good to seek out someone with a converse demand for one good and need for the other. To solve this "double coincidence of wants" was both time consuming and inefficient. Nonetheless, it provided each individual with an avenue to trade something of surplus, and thus of little value to them, for something scarce, and of great value to them. Such "gains from trade" are the innovation of the agrarian economy and of markets everywhere since the agrarian revolution.

A barter economy is cumbersome and inefficient in more ways than just the challenges in meeting the double coincidence of wants. If there were only two individuals willing to trade with each other, the surpluses of a good for one individual would be traded for the surpluses of the other. It is impossible to establish any comparative value to these surpluses because the surpluses add only value in the time each producer devoted to their production. If both individuals devote almost the same amount of time to produce the surpluses, it is likely that these surpluses would be valued identically.

For example, let us say one farmer can easily produce and mill ten excess bags of flour beyond the household's needs and there was one potential trading partner who can easily produce ten dozen extra hen's eggs. The "price" for one bag of flour would equal a dozen eggs. In essence, these two traders would barter away their surpluses, and, in doing so, would formulate a price that balances the supply and demand for each good. If at the end of the day, the trades are consummated and the surpluses are consumed, we say that the markets for eggs and flour have cleared.

However, the number of participants or traders will affect this "market-clearing price." Let us assume that traders expand the market for goods. Now, in the above example, let there be one farmer producing an excess of ten bags of flour and another ten farmers each producing an excess of ten dozen eggs. If there are no other trading possibilities, the price of a bag of flour would go up, from the dozen eggs in the previous scenario, to ten dozen eggs.

This new price of flour relative to eggs can influence the decisions of the various market participants. Some hen growers may decide to go into flour production, and the flour miller may try to make even more flour. Either way, sellers and buyers will adjust their production and consumption needs to suit the market dynamics. The markets will then evolve to produce a long-run equilibrium mix of each of the goods.

This principle of groping toward a market-clearing price for two goods becomes more complicated when applied to more goods and more traders. Let us say that a couple of potters are willing to trade surplus pots for flour and eggs. Now, a potter might exchange pots with a miller, and in turn exchange the flour for eggs with the hen grower. Eventually, this elaborate set of trades will establish relative values for flour, pots, and eggs. The situation is complicated significantly, though, because a trader had to produce and sell pots to get the flour that he could in turn trade for eggs. The double coincidence of wants had become a triple coincidence.

One way to simplify this complex chain of actions would be to have all traders exchange their surpluses for something they each value equally: a common currency. This would facilitate all kinds of trades. Producers can then sell their goods for money, which they in turn use to buy goods of their choice, without having to track down a trader who would satisfy their double coincidence of wants. In essence, money allows every transaction to satisfy the double coincidence of wants because all transactions involve either giving up or receiving the common currency called money.

This money can take on many forms. The most essential requirement is that all market participants acknowledge its mutual value. This value is typically in the recognition that the currency can be exchanged for goods valued by buyers. A currency can also have intrinsic value because it is either a rare and scarce metal or a commodity that all need and hence the value.

The most efficient form of money is one that does not spoil, is easy to transport and exchange, and does not divert a valuable commodity from its purpose to function as a medium of exchange. Various ancient forms of money, such as grain or rare metals such as gold or silver, violate some of these criteria. As a consequence, state-issued paper forms of money that were made scarce by a state's promise to limit their supply emerged as the predominant form of money for the last millennia.

What's it worth to you

With the innovation of a common currency came "liquidity" that enabled a high level of trading activity. No longer was value solely in the eyes of a beholder. Sellers were not beholden to the double coincidence of wants, and they could readily value their goods based on a well-understood and well-communicated market price at any time. This price could be denominated in dollars or pounds, euros, or renminbi, or whatever currency that was commonly accepted in the region.

Even trades between regions could then be consummated by determining the amount of trade offered up in one region's currency compared to the amount of trade offered in return in another's currency. This supply and demand for different currencies determined an exchange rate, just as the exchange rate for flour and eggs was determined.

Unfettered and perfectly functioning markets determined the relative value of each good to another, or of every good in terms of the currency. These valuations determined a correct set of prices across all markets. The first fundamental theorem of welfare economics states that, if we get all these prices right in a world of perfect markets, the economy would attain its optimum efficiency and the resulting price equilibrium will lead to efficient use of available resources.

A double-edged sword

Markets can fail for various reasons, but even a world of partially failed markets probably performs better than a world in which economic dictators command all production decisions. Nonetheless, the creation of a monetary system likely created a quandary.

The very creation of a monetary system facilitated trade, participation in markets, economic efficiency, and, ultimately, taxation. Rather than a share of production for the emperor, the economic commander could take his share in cash. However, it was also easier to hide cash than bags of flour, dozens of eggs, or boxes of pots.

By coordinating and facilitating trade itself, those who commanded and controlled distribution found it easier to tax. However, by empowering consumers to circumvent the command and control economy in favor of free, and less fettered, markets, individuals could undermine the very economic system that economic commanders-in-chief worked so hard to create. The monetary system, and the markets it facilitated, was precisely the mechanism that undermines the brute force, command, and control empire.

Even an emperor cannot reverse the tide

While even Jesus Christ would not challenge the power of the Caesars to produce and to tax, the command and control of even the mightiest economic empire breaks down under the sheer pressure of millions of individuals doing whatever they can to advance their own economic interests. Consequently, markets are inevitable, whether or not they are condoned.

The very forces that gave rise to economic empires based on command and control caused their demise. These early command and control economies depended mainly on the ability to monitor and encourage production, based on the economic preferences of those who plot the growth of the economy. In essence, a command and control economy could grow only if an increasing number of individuals aligned their goals with that of the central authority. Expansion of a command and control economic empire required a greater number of workers, but most critically required a proportional increase in the number of loyal overseers, with the interest of the central authority at heart.

However, just as a growing number of workers made monitoring more difficult and shirking easier, it became increasingly difficult to find a growing cadre of enforcers who would relegate their self-interest to that of the emperor and the state.

Most command and control economic empires eventually recognized the folly of organizing all activity everywhere, and accepted this inevitability of side markets, at a price. Such alternative markets formed in which some production bypassed traditional channels and traded were relatively free of command and control interference. Those who traded in these markets were taxed, with the success of the tax collectors tied to their ability to monitor and enforce these extensive and increasingly ubiquitous markets.

Emperors could learn to harness the ambitions of emerging markets. A growing empire might have one Caesar but had to tolerate many local governors, lords, or land barons. These propertied locals had every incentive to extract agricultural surpluses and to keep its peasants in subsistence. They also had some incentive to hide these feudal surpluses from their emperor, and thus were, in some sense, in competition with the emperor of the economic empire.

Free marketeers also competed for surpluses. Likewise, they, too, were in competition with their feudal land barons and the emperor. So long as they paid their taxes to the state, they offered a limit to the power of the land barons, and somewhat rebalanced power in favor of the state. This system of markets was tolerated, at least as long as they paid the taxes due to the emperor.

The difficulty of free markets, though, is that while a worker producing on behalf of an emperor had an incentive to shirk, the free marketeer had every incentive to work harder and to hide gains from the tax collector.

This reality is as fundamental as self-interest. Even today, the crusade to hide gains from the tax collector is almost considered an economic sport in many economies. A tax collector must monitor every transaction to ensure that taxes are properly paid. Failing that near impossibility, the free marketeer has a decided advantage in diverting production from the command and control economy to a parallel underground economy driven not in the interests of the state but by the self-interest of myriad enterprising individuals.

A command and control economy thus required an unsustainable effort to coerce all participants to tolerate its centralized economic decision-making. Individuals would do so only if the predictability and the diversity of their share of production were equally valuable as the alternative, perhaps underground, free market economy.

Economic fine-tuning

The damning disadvantage of the centrally planned economy was that it could distribute production more coarsely than a market could provide. Let us assume the centrally planned economy orders production of ten bags of flour and ten dozen eggs. A central authority cannot possibly anticipate the wants and needs of each participant. Even assuming the central authority does not divert some of this production for the emperor, each producer is forced to consume five bags of flour and five dozen eggs, regardless of whether they like bread or omelets. No central planner could be sufficiently omniscient to anticipate every consumer's needs, much less each producer's abilities. Therefore, inefficiencies would become unavoidably rampant and increasingly worsen as the producing and consuming population grows in size and diversity.

On the contrary, a free market system with low transactions costs and efficient transportation networks musters a level of efficiency that cannot be surpassed by any other economic system, in theory.

However, even an unfettered system is not perfectly efficient. Markets require continuous vigilance to ensure they remain uncorrupted.

The taxman commeth

What differentiates a command and control economy from a mixed economy with both private production and free markets, and a command economy funded by taxes paid to the state?

Individuals value economic autonomy just as they value participation in any system that can provide advantages with low risk and high predictability. The unfettered free market offers high rewards, but with equally high risks, whereas the command and control economy provides high predictability and greater inefficiencies because individuals cannot fully realize their preferences.

Participants in an economic system will sacrifice some efficiency in return for either autonomy or predictability. Either the free market system, the command and control system, or a mixed economy combination of the two can satisfy one or the other of these twin goals of economic autonomy and predictability. A mixed economic system can be maintained only if the inefficiencies that arise in the command economy sector do not out-swamp our valuation of its predictability or violate our desire for economic autonomy.

A mixed economy

When these underground economies emerge, they are most often rationalized by participants as a way to overcome the inefficiencies of a bloated command economy. Of course, no economy is truly free. Every economy with a taxation system has some government sector that provides goods or services to its residents in ways that substitute for markets.

For instance, recent reports reveal that, in Greece, the world's twenty-seventh largest economy, 40% of the gross domestic product is in the public sector.[5] This combination of a command economy and a free market economy frustrates taxpayers who believe that they are getting insufficient governmental service for the taxes they pay. Consequently, some estimate that 25% of the private economy is an underground economy hidden from the tax authorities and maintained without the use of receipts.[6]

Empirically, we see that no strict command and control economy has been sufficiently robust to succeed in a world of free market and mixed economies. This then poses the question: What are the hurdles that a command and control economy must overcome to succeed?

Central planners of mixed and command and control economies eventually discover what Arthur Laffer, the economic advisor to U.S. president Ronald Reagan, knew in the 1980s, and John Maynard Keynes, the noted Depression-era economist, postulated in the 1930s. On one hand, if the central authority extracts no taxes, it cannot raise revenue to provide for the infrastructure that will promote economic growth. On the other hand, if the central authority extracts a 100% tax and leaves nothing for producers and workers, no person will choose to work for free . Therefore, a rate, somewhere between a 0% and a 100% tax rate, has to be fixed that can yield the highest revenue and can still maintain a high level of economic activity.

As Laffer himself stated[7]:

> The Laffer Curve, by the way, was not invented by me. For example, Ibn Khaldun, a 14th century Muslim philosopher, wrote in his work The Muqaddimah (that)...at the beginning of the dynasty, taxation yields large revenue from small assessments. At the end of the dynasty, taxation yields a small revenue from large assessments.

Laffer attributed this incredible insight to Khaldun, who almost seven centuries ago recognized that an increasingly burdensome central authority taxes its way toward its own demise. In a desperate attempt to fuel the needs of a political aristocracy, producers are burdened to the point that they either reduce their efforts or find alternative pathways for producing outside of the coercive control of the central authority.

Keynes expressed a similar sentiment even more starkly:

> When, on the contrary, I show, a little elaborately, as in the ensuing chapter, that to create wealth will increase the national income and that a large proportion of any increase in the national income will accrue to an Exchequer, amongst whose largest outgoings is the payment of incomes to those who are unemployed and whose receipts are a proportion of the incomes of those who are occupied...
>
> Nor should the argument seem strange that taxation may be so high as to defeat its object, and that, given sufficient time to gather the fruits, a reduction of taxation will run a better chance than an increase of balancing the budget. For to take the opposite view today is to resemble a manufacturer who, running at a loss, decides to raise his price, and when his declining sales increase the loss, wrapping himself in the rectitude of plain arithmetic, decides that prudence requires him to raise the price still mor – and who, when at last his account is balanced with nought on both sides, is still found righteously declaring that it would have been the act of a gambler to reduce the price when you were already making a loss.[8]

It seems inevitable that greed, complacency, and the lack of discipline in achieving efficiency often leads tax authorities to extend beyond an economy's capacity to pay. In turn, they sow the seeds of their own demise.

A caveat on Laffer

A subtlety lost in our Laffer curve discussion is that the optimal level of taxation is not fixed. The economic psychology invoked in this principle is the balance between taxes paid, capacity to pay, and the perception of value. For instance, if the taxed revenue was used to purchase and disperse goods and services precisely as taxpayers would have chosen themselves, there would be no effective burden. Dissatisfaction rises in proportion to the gap between what taxpayers would have bought and what politicians chose on their behalf.

Taxpayers can be educated about the value in the investment of economic infrastructure that none would sponsor individually. If it is apparent that the investments made by the taxing central planner produces an equivalent long-run value for workers and producers, the burden is not substantial.

However, taxpayers are most diverse. For instance, those nearing the end of their lives may not see the return in infrastructure investments. The number of economic decisions is as diverse as the number of taxpayers themselves. To defer individual control to even a benevolent dictator or to a democratically elected group that would make spending decisions on behalf of us all diverts economic autonomy to others in proportion to the tax rate. In the extreme, a high tax rate forces all to consume based on political pandering to the median voter-taxpayers. Such a regime is bound to frustrate almost all taxpayers, in one way or another.

Are markets self-policing?

Central tax collectors can also argue that they facilitate the very creation, maintenance, and policing of markets. Beyond a legitimate role in diverting private production to build infrastructure for the public good, such as policing, roads, and fire protection, the economic authority can also regulate and police markets to ensure they function in the public interest.

While some would argue that markets are inherently self-policing, with access to good market information, suppliers and demanders can themselves make informed decisions that best suit their interests.

The latter argument assumes that market prices reflect all information. Certainly, there is more information available to market participants today than at any time in the past. Yet, even Alan Greenspan, the former chair of the U.S. Federal Reserve that first brought celebrity to central banking, recently confessed that his undying faith in the self-policing of free and unfettered markets is an assumption that is no longer valid.

Greenspan testified, on October 23, 2008, before Henry Waxman's Congressional House Committee on Oversight and Government Reform: "Those of us who have looked to the self-interest of lending institutions to protect shareholders' equity, myself included, are in a state of shocked disbelief..."[9]

When a committee member asked whether Greenspan still believed that markets are self-correcting and self-regulating, he replied:

> The evidence now suggests, but only in retrospect, that this market evolved in a manner which if there were no securitization, it would have been a much smaller problem and, indeed, very unlikely to have taken on the dimensions that it did. It wasn't until the securitization became a significant factor, which doesn't occur until 2005, that you got this huge increase in demand for subprime loans, because remember that without securitization, there would not have been a single subprime mortgage held outside of the United States, that it's the opening up of this market which created a huge demand from abroad for subprime mortgages as embodied in mortgage-backed securities.

In his typically obtuse manner, Greenspan admitted that a lack of oversight of the marketplace could create problems that could bring down the markets themselves. He was also concluding that markets are more fragile than he imagined, and more prone to damage caused by widespread fraud and deception, poor information, lack of faith, and unenlightened greed. When markets break down, there is an increasing recognition of the need of a central authority to police markets in an ever-vigilant manner to ensure market participants maintain their confidence in the institution.

Fruit of the rise becomes the seed of decline

Markets were an innovation that fostered growth in production and distribution of goods. This growth fueled economic empires that diverted a share of production to the ruling class. This diversion, through taxation, subsequently undermined the economic democracy inherent in markets. By offering an avenue for markets and income outside of the planned economy, a parallel underground economy will emerge that challenges, and eventually frustrates, the command and control economy.

The underground economy remains robust because it is adept in satisfying the diversity of wants and needs of an increasingly complex market economy. Its superiority in better satisfying human preferences ultimately challenges the ability of an economic emperor to command the economy.

3
Specialization and Surpluses

I have seen a small manufactory (of pins) where ten men only were employed, and where some of them consequently performed two or three distinct operations. But though they were very poor, and therefore but indifferently accommodated with the necessary machinery, they could, when they exerted themselves, make among them about twelve pounds of pins in a day. There are in a pound upwards of four thousand pins of a middling size. Those ten persons, therefore, could make among them upwards of forty-eight thousand pins in a day. Each person, therefore, making a tenth part of forty-eight thousand pins, might be considered as making four thousand eight hundred pins in a day. But if they had all wrought separately and independently, and without any of them having been educated to this peculiar business, they certainly could not each of them have made twenty, perhaps not one pin in a day.

(Adam Smith, *On the Causes and Consequences of the Wealth of Nations*, Book 1, Section 1.2, 1776)[10]

Just as the advantages of markets cannot be denied or contained, humans in the pursuit of their own self-interest inevitably discovered the advantages of specialization. Our time and effort are perhaps the most precious resources of all, and each of us strives to use our endowed resources most efficiently to produce that which will best sustain us. We naturally gravitate to an economic system that best caters to our desire to use our endowed resources most efficiently.

For centuries, the brute force, command and control economy was the dominant form of human organization. Power was proportional to the number of subjects serving the emperor, the geographical scope that an army could maintain, and the power amassed and attributed to the political elite.

This system was amazingly robust, primarily because no alternative system had yet emerged. However, while the system of royalty governing the peasantry preserved the economic order, for a time, every example of such empires proved unsustainable. At some point, the needs of the empire clashed with needs for efficiency and economic relevancy.

Empires follow the same script

This book derives its name from a genre that described empires over the ages. From Edward Gibbon's *The History of the Decline and Fall of the Roman Empire*[11] to Lawrence James' *The Rise and Fall of the British Empire*,[12] William Shirer's *The Rise and Fall of the Third Reich*,[13] and Paul Kennedy's *The Rise and Fall of Great Powers*,[14] authors have documented how power has been maintained through the use of force, armies, and wars. Military dominance, first by land, then by sea, and finally through one of the first applications of the modern military-industrial complex, took their cues from regimes before them. Each shared an amplified sense of their own destiny and perceived greatness, regardless of the fate meted out to previous dictators who had expressed the same arrogance.

All economic empires share these qualities.

To better understand this universal quest for empire, we must first understand the great acceleration of wealth that accompanies the formation of an economic empire.

Adam Smith and a new political economy

Adam Smith's great works, beginning in 1776, initiated the study of economics, as we know it. His insights were most instructive in describing the process by which fantastic surpluses were created. In the seminal book *An Inquiry into the Nature and Causes of the Wealth of Nations*,[15] Smith described a process by which economic empires could be formed.

Smith studied and postulated economic principles even before economics emerged as a stand-alone discipline. Rather, he was appointed as a lecturer and chair in moral philosophy. Early in his career, his academic vocation competed for his attention to service to the church. Indeed, his research was not constrained to the understanding of the creation of wealth, but rather was a treatise on the evolution of humankind throughout the millennia.

Smith's first two books in the five-book series that constituted "An Inquiry into the Nature and Causes of the Wealth of Nations" were philosophical, anthropological, sociological, and economic analyses of the transition away from the brute force economy that predated the Middle Ages, and toward an era of mercantilism that emerged alongside the Industrial Revolution.

Smith was the first to create a treatise on the creation of new and vast wealth. Writing at the onset of the Industrial Revolution, he was chronicling a transition from political-economic models of feudalism, military dominance, and colonialism. He was writing as a British subject as his nation was reaching the apex of its colonial dominance.

While his treatise is commonly known as "The Wealth of Nations," his reach is much more thoughtful. He was documenting the causes of the creation of an economic empire. The First Industrial Revolution was built on economies of scale that arose because of the hybrid of colonialism maintained through military might.

Smith understood the significance of the economic phenomenon that he was describing. In the eighteenth century, he had analyzed the forces that induced the rise of an economic empire. Even now, more than two centuries later, scholars still refer to the economies and diseconomies of scale he described in the economic empire-building of the First Industrial Revolution.

We have so far discussed the limitations of an economy based on brute force. We will discuss later the advantages, and subsequent disadvantages of colonialism. We begin by introducing a central tenet to the creation of a modern economic empire.

Economies of scale and the pin maker

Smith's often-quoted story is of the pin manufacturer who could make ten pins a day. The product of this single laborer could be stretched to two hundred pins a day if the laborer employed the "utmost industry."

However, if the process of pin manufacturing could be broken into upwards of eighteen separate stages of pin production, a team of ten specialists, each devoted to between one and three of these operations, could produce forty-eight thousand pins per day if they exerted themselves.[16] This production would work out to a pin every twelve seconds per worker, over an eight-hour day.

In this example, production could increase twenty-four fold over the best example of a pin maker working alone and performing all pin-making operations in succession rather than ten makers each devoted to a single or a few operations. This model is different from that of the hunter or gatherer who must necessarily complete all steps of a successful hunt.

The efficiencies of this new industrial model was capable of creating vast surpluses of production. These surpluses go well beyond the by-then familiar advantage of specialization of labor and the concomitant concentration of skill such specialization garners.

In fact, this new model of industrialization documented by Smith was the antithesis of our previous understanding of specialization of labor. By dividing manufacturing up into a number of simple operations, an individual laborer could become extremely specialized in his task in a very short time. These early industrialists could invent machines that will perform complex functions, with the craftsmen relegated to operators. There would soon be little need for the skill of these artisans and craftsmen.

Three centuries later, we all understand such mechanization accompanied by little need for skill or artistry. In my first summer job after high school, I discovered this industrial approach to a product once made by skilled artisans. After an interview of no consequence, I was hired to carve wooden owls. I was hesitant as I had no carving experience. The proprietor assured me that experience did not matter. A skilled artisan was employed to make the first wooden owl. It was then attached to a carving machine that would trace out the artisan's cuttings and carve out ten owls at a time.

I was asked to place ten blocks of wood in the assigned locations on the machine, center a smooth metal pointer on the original carved owl, and simply guide the pointer along the carving. As I did so, cutters moved in parallel, cutting the wooden blocks at the equivalent points as I traced. When I had traced along the entire carving and no more wood came off the blocks, new ten owls had been "carved."

With no experience, I could produce ten carved owls in perhaps half an hour; and each of them resembling the original hand carved owl. I could reduce the time to carve an owl to an average of three minutes. In reality, I am sure I could not carve an owl myself if I were given three days, three weeks, or even three years.

After watching many episodes of the popular Science Channel television show *How It's Made*, I am sure a carved owl every three minutes or a straight pin every twelve seconds would be considered primitive in the twenty-first century.

The disassembly line

You may be familiar with the ubiquitous folklore of Ford Motor Company. While Henry Ford was credited with the creation of the assembly line, this innovation was actually applied by many others before his first foray into assembly lines in the early twentieth century.

The term "assembly line" can be traced back to the meat packers of Chicago. The city was an economic hub of a new hinterland-heartland model: taking farm animals transported whole from across the Midwest to Chicago, and then processing them into meat before icing and transporting them elsewhere for consumption.

The disassembly line broke butchering up into a number of processes. The butchers disassembled animals into a number of constituent parts, much like in the example of the production of pins, but with a stark difference. In this meat manufacturing process, the work was brought to individual workers rather than having the workers move to the workproduct. Animals were gradually disassembled as they moved down a line at a steady speed.

There were numerous refinements in this approach. First, the work moved along a line at a steady speed that was as fast as feasible, to maximum the production rate. This steady movement required individual tasks to be broken up in a way so that each task took the same amount of time as all others.

However, a pre-requisite for this elaborate system to work was that each station must complete its task in concert with, and at the same rate as, all other stations. This synchronization provided the second innovation. No single worker could slacken off or shirk without delaying the entire line and suffering the wrath of management and other stations alike. If workers were paid in proportion to their collective rate of production, the person who slowed down the flow, and the pay of his colleagues, was most notorious indeed. Assembly lines ultimately used peer pressure to prevent shirking and maximize effort.

Obviously, the emphasis on speed was a strong motivator. The other aspect of this extreme specialization was that tasks must necessarily be reduced to the most basic elements. Speed substituted for skill.

While speed became the essential criterion to keep the disassembly line running in concert, the skill necessary to master one single operation was minimal. While the design and management of the entire line may be as critical as the skill once required of a highly experienced guildsman, any single operation could be mastered in very short order.

The emphasis of speed over skill, and a process that actually made skill unnecessary, was also a far-reaching innovation in itself. By making every job so basic that any worker could be easily replaced, the balance of power shifted from artisans and craftsmen to management that could then hire unskilled labor.

Henry Ford took this technique to new heights with the production of the Model T automobile. By using this technique in which unfinished cars were brought to the worker stations rather than have the stations travel to different cars, Ford's factories could dramatically increase the rate of car production. In doing so, he could also decrease the labor costs that represented the single largest component of manufacturing costs. He could manage do so even after paying his workers an amount larger than the prevailing wage in the automobile manufacturing industry at the time.

Economies of scale

The assembly line can also demonstrate an important concept in economics. Let us assume that we lay out an assembly line throughout a factory floor to ensure workers have a workspace that is efficient and uncongested. Given this investment in a factory floor, an assembly line, and the necessary tooling, the actual cost per car manufactured will depend primarily on the wages paid to the assembly line workers and the rate at which the assembly line operates.

Consider the cost efficiency of such an assembly line. Let us assume that the daily cost of paying the mortgage for the land the factory is on, the loans for the factory and machinery, and the wages for the workers for the day comes to $100,000. Let us also assume that each car requires labor and materials at a cost of $500. If the assembly line moves so slowly that only a single car is produced each day, that car would be priced at $500 for materials and $100,000 for fixed overhead costs.

However, if the assembly line could run quickly enough that 100 cars are produced per day, the average cost per car would fall to $1,500, and for a thousand cars a day, the cost would fall to $600 per car.

This process allowed Henry Ford to sell Model T Fords for just over $800 in its debut in 1908, and below $600 just a few years later as the process was perfected.

This increasing efficiency or economy rises as the production rate increases, to a point. Economists call this decreasing average cost phenomenon the "economies of scale." If there were no other factors at work, the cost of producing a good would continue to fall to a value close to the cost of labor and raw materials employed in production.

However, efficiency cannot be improved indefinitely. In the previous example, the cost of a car could fall to $600 if the assembly line could be speeded up to 1,000 cars per day. If the shop floor manager tried to increase the speed of the assembly line further, diseconomies of scale began to set in.

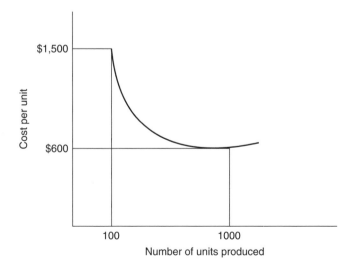

Figure 1 Increasing economies of scale

For example, if the assembly line went too swiftly, one station or another may not be able to complete their task before the unfinished car moved to the next station. This failure usually requires the tripping of an alarm that freezes an entire assembly line built up on the sequential completion of various tasks. This delay costs not only that station a few precious seconds, but taxes each station, upstream and downstream, with the same delay.

Using this analogy, the efficiency of the entire assembly line begins to decline rather dramatically. Rather than driving increasing economies of scale, an attempt to produce more than the most efficient number of units of production per day actually slows production and raise costs. Economies of scale and decreasing average costs per unit of production give way to diseconomies of scale and increasing average costs of production. The most efficient level of production maximizes efficiency without incurring the penalties of diseconomies of scale.

All production processes will benefit from some efficiencies as production is increased. The reasons for these efficiencies are varied. One efficiency is in the ability to spread those fixed costs of factory construction and equipment installation over more and more units produced. Economists label these efficiencies "declining average fixed costs" because the advantage of spreading fixed costs over more and more production is ongoing.

Another economy of scale arises from the increased symbiosis of the production team. An assembly line that moves more rapidly pushes each operation to be completed more quickly. The careful design and evolution of the assembly line optimizes the advantages of effective teamwork and handoffs along the assembly line.

The cost of materials may also demonstrate some economies of scale. Those that supply the various component parts used by the assembly line may offer quantity discounts because larger orders to satisfy the assembly line may allow the suppliers too to optimize their production rates.

Balanced against these economies of scale are diseconomies that actually increase costs with production increased beyond a point. We already noted the diseconomies of scale that result if the assembly line moves too rapidly. In addition, beyond a certain point, suppliers may require even greater prices for the raw materials as their factors of production become scarce due to increased demand. Similarly, increased production requires more workers. A greater number of workers will be forthcoming only if a higher wage is offered. Ironically, these new and more costly workers will not typically be of the same high quality of the previously employed and experienced workers.

In addition, beyond a certain optimum point, increased production rates may result in an increase in the rate of product defects. These product defects become even more problematic if they force the recall of a large number of units.

If an assembly process finds that it is pushing itself beyond that efficient scale that minimizes production costs, it is unwise to push production still further, at least if competitive markets would not support the concomitant increase in costs. One strategy might be to produce a second or third shift on the production line, or to produce another factory or assembly line entirely.

However, while the strategy of multiple shifts or multiple factories may prevent the increased costs of pushing one assembly line too quickly, it still introduces a completely new set of fixed costs. While a second plant may well allow production to be doubled while keeping costs as low as possible, the market must be able to absorb twice the production. In addition, suppliers must be able to ratchet up their supply of materials and labor.

Entrepreneurs put up the financial capital to purchase the factory and machinery, buy more raw materials that become increasingly scarce with each purchase, and find additional workers, but at a higher wage. They must weigh these various diseconomies of scale against the revenues they can expect from increased production. However, their revenues per last unit sold will necessarily drop with increasing production. If overproduction creates a glut in the market place, capitalists suffer both from diseconomies of scale and decreased market prices for their goods.

This phenomenon of decreasing returns to scale is actually an implication of a broader economic principle called the Law of Diminishing Marginal Returns. This law states that the efforts in any activity eventually reach a point of reduced effectiveness. For instance, the diseconomies of scale in production lead to growing inefficiencies that outweigh the original efficiencies of economies of scale. The Law of Diminishing Marginal Returns explains why one industrialist cannot dominate all manufacturing, or, for that matter, why one economic empire cannot subsume the entire global economy.

Not too small, not to big

Like all industrialists, Henry Ford was acutely aware of these economies of scale and the eventual diseconomies of scale as enterprises become too large. Just like the emperors before them, entrepreneurs come to realize that their managerial brilliance is also in short supply.

Increasing the scale of an industrial empire may induce the same inefficiencies that arise when an economic empire is expanded. Managerial expertise is spread too thin, the left hand does not know what the right hand is doing, loyalties are divided, and it becomes increasingly difficult to manage the increasing diversity, and the diverse needs they demand, as the scope of any enterprise increases beyond a point. Just as there is an optimal size of an empire that is fueled by a shared vision and mission, so is there an optimal size for any economic enterprise.

Industrialists know that diseconomies of scale can come on in dramatic fashion. Too rapid expansion can overextend an enterprise to the point where it breaks under its own weight, its inability to satisfy its capital needs, or even its ability to recover from minor glitches compounded over major production runs.

For these reasons, large enterprises sometimes break themselves up into smaller, more nimble, and more efficient units. A high degree of corporate centralization is sometimes followed by bouts of decentralization and corporate breakups. For instance, the breakup of a monolithic company like American Telephone and Telegraph (AT&T) in the United States resulted in a number of smaller companies that could be more nimble and innovative in a more competitive environment.

The extent of the market

These economies of scale arising from increasing returns are also limited by the ability of the market to absorb them. Let us use a simple example. An economy made up of fabled Robinson Crusoe and his man Friday cannot support the product diversity and low costs as could a larger economy. Each could specialize in one enterprise, with Robinson perhaps charged with food production and Friday with shelter construction. An economy in search of greater product diversity would need a wider pool of available workers to produce efficiently this wider diversity of products. This diversity of production must also be supported by a broader pool of consumers able to absorb these products.

A larger market can support greater diversity and greater efficiency both in production and in consumption. In addition, trade between nations permits additional gains in diversity and efficiency, as we shall see.

Fruit of the rise becomes the seed of decline

Economies of scale are a driving force that encourage size. However, like the dinosaurs, any enterprise can become too large to support their organizational mass. Once economies of scale decline to the point that they are balanced by growing diseconomies of scale, optimal scale is reached. Any further growth simply drives up costs, reduces enterprise coherence, and forces an empire nearer to the point where it breaks under its own weight. While most operations recognize that growth for growth's sake is sheer folly once minimum efficient scale is reached, empires often know no such bound. Consequently, empires and enterprises alike often grow beyond the onset of diseconomies of scale.

Empires begin to expect growth as a measure of continued success. Encouraging and forcing growth beyond the point for which increased scale is effective simply make an empire more vulnerable and less nimble. It is these invulnerabilities and inflexibilities that can eventually bring down even the mightiest empires.

4

The First Industrial Revolution

> It is known, to the force of a single pound weight, what the engine will do; but, not all the calculators of the National Debt can tell me the capacity for good or evil, for love or hatred, for patriotism or discontent, for the decomposition of virtue into vice, or the reverse, at any single moment in the soul of one of these its quiet servants, with the composed faces and the regulated actions.
>
> (Charles Dickens, *Hard Times*, 1854)[17]

It was not until relatively recently that the advantages of markets, specialization, and the innovation of power and transportation came together to produce new goods and wealth unprecedented in ten thousand years of human history. We have become accustomed to the fast pace of progress and the amazing efficiencies of production. We forget that if human history were a kilometer long, this modern era of economic bounty merely represents the last few paces.

This rapid evolution of modern economies and modern government has created new wealth, new public institutions, and new solutions to new problems. The laboratory of the modern economy is still experimenting.

Generations of wealth

Comfort and a modicum of wealth are relatively modern concepts that are currently enjoyed broadly within the club of developed nations and among the elite of the rest of the world's nations.

The developed nations, formerly part of a political coalition aligned with the United States and Western Europe over the duration of the Cold War, would have once been called the First World. With the collapse of the Cold War–era Iron Curtain, these nations should be more accurately called the First Economic World, a term that replaces a more dated term "the developed nations."

This First Economic World is a relatively new phenomenon. For millennia, there have been a small minority of the human population who have enjoyed a level of economic security well beyond subsistence. Only over the past few centuries have a majority of the citizens of any single nation achieved wealth beyond subsistence. For the first time in human history, we can now imagine that, within our lifetimes, a majority of the world's population may be able to enjoy a level of consumption greater than mere subsistence.

The creation of a middle class

Ever since surpluses were made possible with the Agrarian Revolution, there has been a class of individuals who have accumulated more than they could consume. With this accumulation of surpluses came new challenges. The surpluses created the need to protect property from those who find it easier to usurp the product of others, rather than produce themselves.

Those individuals who could maintain order and protect their property have held an esteemed position in our civilizations. Their contribution was not just in governing the citizenry. They also protected public and private property so that individuals would covet less and produce more. They quickly learned to understand the importance of an emerging working class. Through these protections came civilizations as we now know them.

The origins of civilization were indeed profound. Freed from nomadic ways and able to settle, enjoy permanent structures, and accumulate surpluses, there emerged the elite, and their entourage, with the peasantry constituting the vast remainder.

This economic system prevailed for millennia, and has only recently been discarded by the majority of the earth's human population. Over the course of little more than two centuries, a new and dominant economic class has emerged, enabled by new rights and the protection of their property. Since the creation of civilization itself, there has been no revolution like the formation of the middle class.

The reason was the First Industrial Revolution.

Freed from toil

The concept of economies of scale is not new. Surely, since the dawn of civilization, enterprising farmers, potters, and generals, Caesars, Kings, and Khans understood the value of labor divided up by and devoted to individual tasks. For instance, military leaders understood defense in economic terms. A colonel determined the optimal size of his brigade, made up of several battalions, which, in turn, were made up of companies, platoons, and squads. Each had specialties and tasks, and each was of a size that could be led by lieutenant colonels, captains, lieutenants, and sergeants. The optimal size depended on the capacity of its leaders to maintain order and efficiency and their members to develop some allegiance, camaraderie, and teamwork.

Such a model of optimal organizational teams would remain unchanged as long as humankind's capacity to lead and coordinate remained unchanged and individual team members were yet to take advantage of labor saving devices.

All that changed with the creation of new forms of power of a capacity many times that of a human and many times greater than ever contemplated before.

A new source of power

Humankind had harnessed the power of animals ever since the wave of shepherding and agriculture in our prehistory. In these early days, animals were primarily employed as labor saving tools that would only modestly multiply the power capacity and stamina of humans. Animals, would require significant human intervention to be coerced to produce their advantage in power and stamina.

Two innovations early in the Industrial Revolution changed it all: first, the water wheel and second, the steam engine.

On first blush, the water wheel seems like a modest innovation. While it may have been evolutionary in the creation of power, it was revolutionary in the ways it changed how humans organized to produce.

Some of the first applications of water wheels were in the milling of flour and the turning of looms. Before the application of water wheels, cottage industries was formed for skilled guildsman and the semi-skilled apprentices and weavers. There were few economies of scale because one to two people had to power and operate a single loom.

There was also no division of reward between physical capital, the machines of production, and labor. The cottage weaver owned the loom and used it to augment the fruit of his labor. The owner of the physical capital and of the human capital was one in the same. Physical capital was interwoven, if you will, with human capital and was not a factor distinct and separately rewarded over the income earned by the craftsman.

With the invention of the water wheel, a craftsman could attach many looms to a single power source. This necessitated a new design for looms that was freed from the model of one operator who was also the power source. The operator could then run many looms with a much greater capacity to weave and an ability to produce orders of magnitude larger than a single skilled worker powering a small loom could produce.

Obviously, the economies of scale that could be extracted from this simple innovation of large-scale power were substantial. However, the innovations did not stop there.

A paradigm shift

Before large-scale power, looms were located where the skilled craftsmen chose to live. Cottage industries were run out of private homes and cottages and were extended family affairs. There was little economy of scale from having a hundred looms in a room compared to just one or two looms. Production was distributed across the countryside and was performed parallel to and in conjunction with the other enterprises that supported the rural economy.

Certainly, in this model, most all production was local, including the product of these looms. Specialization provided only modest surpluses. Because goods were distributed locally, there was no ready market for dramatic surpluses anyway. The skilled artisans in each community could easily meet the weaving, potting, milling, and blacksmithing needs of the village.

Once waterwheels harnessed power sufficient to run a hundred looms, the potential economies of scale expanded dramatically. Waterwheels created an advantage to having a hundred looms in one large room, with the capacity to produce at a scale a thousand times larger than could be produced by even the most sophisticated and extensive cottage manufacturer. However, every village may not have ideal river power, and ideal river stretches may not intersect villages.

It would be difficult to convince a sufficient number of skilled weavers to set up shop in one central location, perhaps tens or hundreds of miles from his or her village. Even if such a cooperative could be formed to collectively tap the power of the waterwheel, they would likely prefer to operate with some autonomy rather than as an entity making a single product line in large scale. Guildsmen were unaccustomed to the subjugation of their autonomy to a larger entity. They would rather forgo the economies of scale created by this new organizational structure if they could retain their economic autonomy.

Instead, one enterprising individual could build the water wheel, buy or lease the looms, and hire the workers to staff the looms. Rather than deal with the strong personalities of guildsmen, this factory owner could design the factory floor, the looms, and the tasks so an unskilled operator could produce successfully.

Large-scale power changed our economic model. The real innovation of the water wheel was that it induced a new organizational structure, created factories, and, most profoundly, redesigned work optimized for unskilled labor rather than the skilled craftsmen who had dominated production for millennia. The combination of greater economies of scale and lower labor and power costs revolutionized production. In turn, vast surpluses of production were created. It also forever disrupted the model of rural peasants and the elite who governed the district.

Meet the new boss

Before this revolution of centralized power, and the wave of urbanization it created, emperors and peasants were separated only by local lords and by the merchants who served all. The peasantry disliked the landlords who kept them at the bare level of subsistence. Royalty had a greater allegiance to the peasantry because both groups shared a mistrust of the occasional upstart lord who controlled local production.

In the shared governance system of England during this First Industrial Revolution, the House of Lords shared in the responsibility of local governance. The opportunity for chicanery was rampant, though, and the royalty well understood the need to protect the peasantry, without whom there would be no production. Industrialists would soon challenge this proven balance.

The model of emperors, feudal lords, and peasants was well understood for millennia. Once some factory owners began rewriting the models of production and amassed huge production surpluses, these industrialists lodged between the royalty and the peasantry began to grow and to rival the power of feudal lords.

This emerging middle class both joined and rejuvenated the merchant class and began to command unprecedented wealth. While this new class was made up of commoners, their newfound status in a rapidly growing economy gave them growing political influence. They were soon granted membership to a new House of Commons in England that supplanted the authority of the House of Lords.

At the same time, workers were moving into growing urban areas, leaving fewer in the countryside. While the draw of the emerging cities was strong and the work plentiful, the economies of scale of the new organizational structures did not necessarily make for higher quality of life.

As we have discussed, factories created such specialization of tasks that skilled labor was unnecessary. Consequently, anyone who complained about the working conditions or pay could easily be replaced by another. Some work required so little skill that even children were hired as laborers. The rural poor soon became the urban poor.

Meanwhile, huge surpluses of goods and wealth created by these economies of scale were increasingly concentrated in the new power brokers, a nouveau riche. The nouveau riche was all too happy to pay its fair share to the royalty if only it would be given the status it sought. Royalty was happy to oblige because these nouveau riche industrialists were the engines of growth for a rapidly expanding economic empire. Moreover, the industrialists were far more interested in making money than were the lords, whose primary enterprise was to divert the surpluses that would go to royalty or extract the surpluses that held the rural poor in poverty.

The dramatic growth in the economic fortunes of England at the time was not without its social critics. While Adam Smith was extolling these virtues in "The Wealth of Nations," other social critics were increasingly concerned about the growing gap between an urban poor and the nouveau riche capitalists. For millennia, all understood the wealth gap between royalty and the rural poor. Never before had economies encountered a growing income gap between the new urban poor and the nouveau riche capitalist commoners. New social distinctions were necessary.

These new income gaps between emerging classes would be a continuing challenge thereafter.

John Stuart Mill and Karl Marx

So concerned was the ruling elite about this growing tale of two citizenries, confined shoulder to shoulder in growingly congested cities, that the subject was the talk of social, political, and economic philosophers.

Two economist philosophers epitomized radically different approaches to the new problem of the distribution of societal wealth. Karl Marx claimed that there was a fundamental flaw with the new and prevailing economic model. He suggested these new capitalists that owned the means of production and, hence, extracted the lion's share of newly created surpluses, should be stripped of what he perceived as ill-gotten gains. He argued that those who do not produce by the sweat of their brow ought not to be afforded such sway and power in the new economy. Marx' solution was to confiscate the means of production and return them to the working class.

Just as government has for millennia held the responsibility of establishing the rules that provide for economic growth, a new form of government would be necessary to effect the requisite change. Marx argued that a revolution might even be necessary because the nouveau riche capitalists would not willingly give up control of a nation's productive capacity.

Karl Marx was not a revolutionary by nature. He was first an economist, and was advocating political reform only to enable what he saw as necessary economic change. Indeed, Marx was a leading thinker and researcher in economic growth in his time at the middle of the nineteenth-century England.

On the other hand, John Stuart Mill, an equally well-educated person who, like Marx, was also a product of the middle class, was advocating a less revolutionary approach. He envisioned the development of a vast middle class within which a large share of the fruits of economies of scale could be retained. He saw the need to raise the status and economic power of the urban poor, not through revolution but through education.

This, too, would require a much more significant and activist government to provide the infrastructure and institutions for such a transformation to happen. Mill postulated that a workforce of increased education and skill would generate increased production and value to employers. Mill's middle class would thus extract greater income commensurate with their greater worth to capitalists, and this increased economic influence would redress the wealth imbalance that the industrial revolution brought on.

Fruit of the rise becomes the seed of decline

The developed economic world would be forever changed. It is remarkable what such a small technological innovation could set in motion. It is even more amazing that humankind was able to adapt to this rapidly changing social landscape over just a dozen generations.

The water wheel, then the steam engine, economies of scale and capitalism, a new inequality of wealth, an urban poor and nouveau riche, combined to compel a greater role of government to resolve a heightened tension between the rich and the poor.

Only in a handful of times in the history of civilization has something come along that forever changes social balances developed and sustained over centuries. In the case of the First Industrial Revolution, dramatic economies of scale created growth and wealth that has been unprecedented in the course of the human experience. Like most all social and economic innovations, these fruits were not distributed evenly. When prevailing groups in society had seen their position and economic status shift, greater resources needed to be devoted to redress such imbalances, in part, for fear of the repercussions if left alone.

This dynamic is not unfamiliar. It is clear that developed nations have gone, for the most part, down the path advocated by Mill. Even countries like the former U.S.S.R. and China, constituted under the theories of Karl Marx, have since recognized both the necessity of free markets and industrialization, along with a redirection of resources on behalf of the working class.

However, in the absence of an organizational model that would create partners of those who own the financial and physical capital and those who own their own human capital, government is necessarily injected in between the two groups. The greater the economies of scale, it seems, the greater the size or footprint of government needed to redress the imbalances.

Unfortunately, we will discover that the role of government, not as producers but as redistributors on behalf of the middle class, ultimately limits the efficiencies of industry and leads to a decline in competitiveness of an economic empire.

5

Colonialism Puts Sugar in Our Tea

So they began to think how they might raise as much corn as they could, and obtain a better crop than they had done, that they might not still thus languish in misery. At length, after much debate of things, the Governor (with the advise of the chiefest among them) gave way that they should set corn every man for his own particular, and in that regard trust to themselves; in all other things to go in the general way as before. And so assigned to every family a parcel of land, according to the proportion of the number, for that end, only for present use (but made no division for inheritance) and ranged all boys and youth under some family. This had very good success, for it made all hands industrious, so as much more corn was planted than otherwise would have been by any means the Governor or any other could use, and saved him a great deal of trouble, and gave far better content. The women now went willingly into the field, and took their little ones with them to set corn; which before would allege weakness and inability; whom to have compelled would have been thought great tyranny and oppression.

(William Bradford on the movement from cooperative farms at the Plymouth Plantation to individual plots)[18]

The inviolate Law of Diminishing Marginal Returns explains why growth cannot be maintained forever. A corollary of this law is the need for a growing homeland to expand its hinterland to allow the homeland to continue to grow.

Emperors have long understood that an expanding hinterland could bring back riches and products otherwise unattainable by the elite of the homeland. The Aztecs and Mayans understood this principal advantage of empire building, as did the Romans, the Spanish and Conquistadors, and numerous others who plundered in the interests of their emperors.

The First Industrial Revolution put an entirely economic spin on this well-worn phenomenon. However, while it was able to create surpluses never before seen, its economic commanders could not resist distorting the terms of trade that had frustrated habitants of the hinterland in empires past, as we shall see. This tendency to redefine terms of trade to the advantage of an economic empire seems to be an inevitable action of all empires.

An ever-thirsty industrial complex

Great surpluses arose from the economies of scale that flowed from mass power sources and greater mechanization at the onset of the First Industrial Revolution. To fuel these surpluses, there had to be a proportionate increase in the raw materials consumed by these new factories.

For instance, mechanized weaving looms powered by water wheels could increase yarn and weave production by many orders of magnitude. This scaling up of production in turn required a supply of sheep wool that must also be increased in the same dramatic proportion. It also required a greatly expanded market for these huge surpluses, and transportation networks to get the goods to market.

Any domestic economy at the onset of the First Industrial Revolution could neither fuel the input needs of these new factories, nor absorb the greater production made possible through the economies of scale.

These new economic empires needed both a larger hinterland from which to draw raw materials and the expanded consumer markets that these hinterlands could provide. The industrial revolution required a new form of globalization.

Mercantilists and a new globalization

Until the First Industrial Revolution, an expanded global footprint was viewed as a measure of nautical superiority and as an opportunity to bring home the riches and diverse goods produced elsewhere. The emerging theory of mercantilism was not to exchange factors of production and final goods with others. Instead, mercantilism required trading partners to buy the goods of the homeland in exchange for gold and silver that could be used to support their navies. The industrial revolution created a new urgency for expansion of product markets and the discovery of sources of precious metals and wealth that could fund global expansion.

This expansionary colonial model did not begin with the First Industrial Revolution. The Greek metropolises portended to a colonial model, with the word metropolis translated as "the mother city." Similarly, the term colony was derived from the Latin word "colonia," meaning a place for agriculture.

The Romans spawned the first empire of the modern era. Indeed, the word empire is derived from the Latin word "imperium," which means an expanse of humanity under military command. At its peak, the Roman Empire controlled a region that encompassed an area from what is now known as Iraq in Asia, through Egypt and northern Africa, Morocco, Spain, France, and Great Britain, much of Western and some of Eastern Europe, and through Greece and Turkey. This empire, administered from Rome, lasted for hundreds of years, and even continued from a throne in Constantinople (now known as Istanbul) beyond the onset of the Age of Discovery in the fourteenth century.

The Roman Empire was controlled through legionaries who would protect the extent of the empire in return for payments from the Roman Treasury. At the same time, the loot and taxes collected from the hinterland provided a source of revenue to compensate the legionaries. The empire was sustained through brute force and the ability of the hinterland to fuel the wealth of Rome. Other areas of the empire would serve to feed the nation and its armies. For instance, grain production from what is now Egypt was essential to feed Rome and its armies.

An expansion of the empire not only provided a ready supply of new wealth and food but also innovated by allowing a diversity of religion. The Roman Empire tolerated this diversity that arose through the conquering of new lands. The prevailing Roman practice of religion worshipped multiple gods, so the new forms of worship in faraway lands was not particularly problematic at first. However, the diversity of thought, faith, and values did make for a less homogeneous and cohesive empire.

In turn, this empire left an indelible mark on all economic empires that followed it. While Latin, the language of Rome, is no longer a national language, it was the basis of the Romance languages of Italian, Spanish, French, Portuguese, and others. Indeed, the Roman Empire left behind institutions and contributions that are embedded across global cultures. For instance, *National Geographic* magazine noted:

> The enduring Roman influence is reflected pervasively in contemporary language, literature, legal codes, government, architecture, engineering, medicine, sports, arts, etc. Much of it is so deeply imbedded that we barely notice our debt to ancient Rome. Consider language, for example. Fewer and fewer people today claim to know Latin – and yet, go back to the first sentence in this paragraph. If we removed all the words drawn directly from Latin, that sentence would read; "The."[19]

This political and economic conquest demonstrated that geographical expansion was not without its challenges and compromises. As with all empires, the Roman Empire could not prevail. It was forced to defend its advantages on all fronts, whereas a contender must only challenge Rome's dominance on any single front. The Roman Empire eventually contracted, and had lost its

Western dominance in over the first 500 years of the modern era. In 1453, it sacrificed dominance in its Eastern frontiers with the fall of Constantinople at the hands of the Ottomans.

The Age of Discovery

An Age of Discovery and Exploration overlapped the end of the Roman Empire and predated the First Industrial Revolution. This era arose because improvements in navigation, map making, and ship building allowed the Portuguese and Spanish empires to reach around the world. From the fourteenth to the seventeenth century, these explorers "discovered" the Americas and established trade routes to Asia and Africa. By the early seventeenth century, the Dutch, having recently been declared independent from Spain, explored Australia and New Zealand.

These explorations were pursued not merely for the esoteric value of discovery. Motivated in part to extend military reach and control and to create opportunities for accessing new sources of gold, silver, and spices, these early explorations were designed to be exploitive rather than symbiotic. There was little sense that indigenous populations would create a ready market for European goods. Nor was there a sense that the taking of land and property were subject to negotiations with the indigenous populations. Empire expansion remained primarily military and exploitive, in sharp contrast to an emerging model of economic colonialism.

A new economic colonialism

The traditional military motivation for colonial expansion was discarded for a much more pragmatic principle. A growing capacity for domestic production demanded a greater supply of factors of production and a ready market for finished goods.

The expansion of the Roman Empire embraced a diversity of cultures, religions, and peoples, as it expanded from the peoples of Southern Europe to parts of Asia, Africa, and Northern Europe. The expansion of an empire motivated by geographical conquest and enforced by military might was less concerned about growth of factor markets and markets for finished goods.

Similarly, the Age of Discovery was driven by new navigation technologies, brought diverse finished goods to the heartland, and allowed the treasuries of Spain, Portugal, and the Netherlands to replenish their stocks of gold and silver. However, these bounties were for novelty and convenience rather than for the sheer necessity of economic growth.

English explorers also participated in the Age of Discovery. While they did not quite challenge the explorations of the Spanish, Dutch, and Portuguese at the time, their explorations did help support the First British Empire over the Age of Discovery. Their discoveries also created a greater thirst for novel consumption, and an appreciation for potential trading partners that had been previously unknown.

However, the changes induced by the exploration of trade routes and the expansion of trade alone would pale in comparison to the changes induced by England's Industrial Revolution. The potential of the First Industrial Revolution could not have been realized, though, were it not for the new colonies formed through Britain's expansion in its age of discovery.

New technologies motivated this necessity for economic growth and expansion with the onset of the Industrial Revolution. Without a ready supply of raw materials, the only innovation of the First Industrial Revolution would have been a displacement of some of the rural poor into the cities, and a further creation of rural unemployment as the cottage industries were displaced by urban factories owned by newly moneyed industrialists. Industrialists had to create new markets if they were to thrive.

A precarious revolution

The potential for dramatic production expansion through the First Industrial Revolution could be frustrated in two ways. The first bottleneck could be shortage of raw materials. The former surpluses and wealth that was once rural bound would soon be concentrated in this nouveau riche class of industrials. Surpluses would no longer be going to the displaced cottage industry guilds, and reduced rewards would be going to unskilled labor who displaced semi-skilled labor. Consequently, large surpluses were accumulated by nouveau riche capitalists. However, these capitalists did not have sufficient appetite for the consumption of their own products. How many sweaters can a capitalist wear?

Hence economic innovation had to find new markets for their products proportional to the dramatic expansion of factor markets, for agricultural products, wool, the metals to build the machines, and the surplus of labor arising from increased industrial efficiency.

The small island of Britain that was the hotbed for this First Industrial Revolution simply could not meet the ever-growing needs for these factor and product markets. Nor would enhanced trade with traditional enemies in France or Spain offer a solution. These rival countries would prefer to expropriate or imitate the economic and industrial innovations of Britain, rather than purchase them.

Instead, the heartland British Empire needed hinterlands with a well-defined set of essential characteristics. There would need to be good land to produce the agricultural products that allowed the empire to expand. And, there must be an opportunity for English families to migrate to the hinterland to coordinate hinterland production and offer a distinctively English market for the goods emanating from British factories.

Any economic empire would prefer this expansion to be primarily based on mutual advantage rather than forced by military reach. Economic expansion does not need to be troubled with political, military, and cultural complications. It would rather expand through enlightened self-interest and with a velvet glove rather than an iron fist.

Through colonization of English men (mostly) and women in America and Canada, India, and, a little later, Australia and New Zealand, and Eastern and Southern Africa, the United Kingdom created ideal opportunities for economic expansion without inordinate cultural challenges. Britain could expand first by forging avenues of trade for raw materials, in exchange for finished goods, and then through the settlements that could provide a long-term opportunity for stable trade.

The flavor of this expansion is also illustrated by the names of the major players in this colonial expansion, especially in the Americas and Canada. The Hudson's Bay Company, the Northwest Trading Company, the London and Bristol Company, the Virginia Company and the Plymouth Company, the Society of Merchant Venturers, and the Dorchester Company were some of the economically interested groups that sponsored colonization in the Americas.

These companies and colonies came to provide fish, beaver furs and skins, tobacco, rum, timber products, coal, and other raw materials, foodstuffs, and stock for the textiles industries. In exchange, they received profits for the investors and domestic goods that could fill the resource-laden ships when they turned around and headed to the Americas.

This relationship was decidedly symbiotic, with both the heartland of Britain and the hinterland of the colonies benefiting from the mutually advantageous trade. However, the system clearly was in the control of companies, royalty, and legislators in Britain. These terms of trade, naturally, were defined to maximize the value to Britain while still providing a sustainable and ongoing relationship with the settlers and the indigenous groups with whom Britain had to trade.

A new life in indentured servitude

Not all participants in this new symbiotic relationship came to new lands under unfettered free will. To be transported across open ocean a century or two after Columbus or Cabot was reserved for adventurers or for those who had little else to lose. If an analogy to the colonial economy was the company town, even the cost of transportation to the new town would be provided, in the interest of commerce, for a price.

Most of those who accepted the bargain were males who were young and indentured.[20] Many were skilled, and were obligated to work for the enterprise that sponsored their trip to the New World. Four years' indenture was common, depending on the supply and demand for able-bodied men and women willing to serve the enterprise of Mother England. This indenture was the only way, for most, to make it to a new land that would otherwise cost a year's working wage.

However, once the indenture contract was satisfied, these new inhabitants were free to explore new economic arrangements and new markets. This combination of free marketeers, indentured servants, sharecroppers, and slaves made for an explosive mix of classes, tensions, and envy. Meanwhile, those who profited from these differential prices of labor would naturally exploit it for what it was worth for as long as they could.

Monopsonies and monopolies

As an analogy, consider the classic company town. It employs most workers in the town, at either the mine, factory, or the company store. Because workers in the town have no choice but to work for the sole employer, they lose their ability to bargain aggressively for higher wages. Because they have no place to spend their wages but at the company store, they must endure the price the company store demands for finished goods.

Of course, workers are free to leave town. They will not stay unless they are offered a package of wages and goods prices that allows them to subsist. If they are attracted to the town with false promises and have to borrow from the company to pay for the move, they may be captive in the town, unable to save to pay off the loan and unable to get ahead.

Let us take this model and compare it to the arrangement of some colonists who were promised a land of milk and honey. The ultimate terms of trade that would determine a colonist's very survival were dictated by the heartland company. The company dictated compensation for the colonist's services or products and the company's price for the finished goods needed by the colonist but not produced locally.

At this point, we must take a little time to describe some economic theory that explains how firms determine the wage they offer their workers and the price they charge for their product.

If a single buyer wants to contract with an additional supplier who would provide one more unit of its factor inputs, it will have to offer a better deal not only to the new (and presumably higher priced) supplier, but also to other suppliers. This pushes up the marginal cost of a buyer's factors of production. The buyer will equate this cost of increased supply from its various suppliers to the price it can garner in employing the factor in its production process. Because expanding supply requires it to set a new terms of trade for like-positioned suppliers of all sorts, it will tend to reduce the level of buying but will still offer a price to all that equals their (common) supply price, not the value to the sole buyer.

By pursuing this policy, the buyer reduced the benefits to the colonial sellers and kept this surplus for itself. Economists label these sole buyers as monopsonists.

On the product side of the market, a monopoly seller could set terms of trade for final goods for consuming colonists by reducing output in an effort to artificially raise prices. The benefit to colonists again faltered, with the heartland sellers pocketing the difference.

Either way, the colonial power reserves all the gains from trade for itself and keeps the colonists beholden, with no opportunities to sell to any other but the colonial power, and with no opportunities to buy finished goods from any other but the colonial power.

By extracting much of the gains of trade for itself, the colonial power grows ever stronger, while the colonists are kept barely above subsistence.

A colony as a company town also runs the constant frustration of shifting terms of trade. Just as a colony begins to figure out a way to advance its own lot, terms of trade may be renegotiated unilaterally to keep the colonists subservient and dependent.

A noble monopoly?

Monopolies and monopsonies are familiar institutions to economists. An organization that has invented a better mousetrap should inevitably be rewarded with the fruits and surpluses commensurate with that innovation. One who would buy when no others could should be rewarded in equal measure. However, economists abhor the monopolist or monopolist that retains its economic strength by fiat or regulation alone. The company that maintains its monopoly surpluses, or, what economists call "rents," simply because it pleases the colonial power to subjugate the colonists, does not promote economic power or grow the economic pie.

A profitable franchise maintained solely because it perpetuates an economic imbalance will not be sustainable. If better mousetraps could be had, but an empire in a faraway land prevented its subjects from enjoying the innovation, frustration is fomented and sustainability is threatened.

Economic theory tells us that the monopolist or monopsonist is an economic blight. By offering a reduced supply of goods in the hopes of driving up their price, or by limiting purchases of factors with the goal of driving down prices, these exploiters sacrifice surpluses. Some that would have bought cannot, and some that would have sold will not. Generous profits are earned for the heartland because profits are prevented in the hinterland. This model is fragile, awaiting only a trader who can offer a better deal. An empire that offers nothing but monopolies and monopsonies are doubly damned.

However, from the perspective of the heartland, the profits of the monopoly are almost irresistible. These compelling monopoly profits were indeed the source of its inevitable demise.

Fruit of the rise becomes the seed of decline

The model of economic colonialism differs substantially from the model of military dominance that it replaced. By providing a ready market that a colony can provide for the factors of production and by offering a steady demand for the finished goods of the heartland, the colonists of the hinterland contributed to substantial economic growth for the colonizing power.

This economic model of symbiosis permits rapid growth for a heartland struggling to find factor markets and ready markets for their finished goods. However, the gains from trade are often lopsided. The colonies that serve the empire gain little, while the empire gains a lot. By manipulating the terms of trade over time, the empire extracts the maximum possible surplus.

Just as emperors gradually increased taxes to maintain their quality of life when their empire subsided, the worsening terms of trade for colonists often festered as an issue of colonist disenfranchisement and eventually fomented declarations of economic independence. With the loss of its hinterland, the heartland's growth was stalled. With the notorious breakup of England and the New World, hinterlands willing to let the economic empire continue to thrive began to dwindle.

Part II
A Second Industrial Revolution

The year 1776 introduced the world to a new economic world and a new economic empire. A new constitution, vast natural resources, and a dream that attracted talented human capital from around the world permitted the United States to forge a Second Industrial Revolution. However, while this new land of opportunity created great economic wealth and power, its early economic evolution was not without some fits and starts.

6
A Declaration of Economic Independence

I must study politics and war that my sons may have liberty to study mathematics and philosophy. My sons ought to study mathematics and philosophy, geography, natural history and naval architecture, navigation, commerce and agriculture, in order to give their children a right to study painting, poetry, music, architecture, statuary, tapestry, and porcelain.

(American Revolutionary and its second President, John Adams, letter to Abigail Adams, 1780)[21]

The original seafaring nations of Spain, Portugal, and Italy were able to monopolize their established trade routes between Europe and Asia. These seafaring nations with a sufficiently powerful military force to protect their nautical supply chains could grow from expanded diversity of trade itself. Without the same ready access to these trade routes, an industrial nation like Britain could fuel economic growth only by expanding the hinterland of resource markets and the market for their final goods. Their hinterlands had to grow in proportion to their increased productive capacity. If hinterlands could not continue to grow, or if productive capacity could not ratchet up accordingly, a nation had to rely on more coercive terms of trade to fuel expansion.

Britain's colonial model would inevitably fail if it could not provide a robust and sustainable military presence that would allow it to permanently coerce colonies to serve the mother country. One former colony, still in its infancy, would soon challenge Britain's global empire.

The United States of America was the first country with access to gigantic resources and with the goal of defining itself not only on a new premise but also as a reaction to an old premise. The Revolutionary War was indeed revolutionary in ways that even its founding fathers could not have imagined. By founding a nation on a new and previously untested economic and political proposition, the first nation based on the free markets and the protection of property created a concept that has since swept the world.

This new country was going down the path of a novel economic paradigm because of a weakness in the then dominant economic model.

An invitation to a tea party

The settlers of the New World were decidedly different from the cross section of citizens that populated Mother England. The homeland had a mix of royalty, elite, and clergy, entrepreneurs, an emerging middle class, and the urban and rural peasantry that provided the vast majority of the labor. However, the New World was more diverse and divisive.

There were a small number of elite and moneyed in the British North America colonies. They were either appointed by Mother England, represented companies from the heartland, or were self-made. The peasant stock was, for the most part, either indentured, previously indentured, descendants of the indentured, or slaves. While the lower class of England had accepted their place, the vast majority of those in the New World carried with them a culture developed from the receiving end of exploitation.

Even the wealthy felt exploited. If they made their living in import-export, they were entirely dependent on the price set by the mother country for their imports, or the price stipulated for their exports. Neither market catered directly to nor reflected the strength or preferences of traders in the colonies.

Those who were economically independent, and did not suffer disadvantageous terms of trade set forth by the mother country or its companies, nonetheless remained vulnerable to the whims of changes in trade terms. The difference between the price at which a good is sold and the revenue that the producer received is the tax that must pass to the governor through the customs houses. Just as earlier empires fell into the trap of increased taxation to fuel an ever-expanding nation or support increasingly inefficient economies, these taxes imposed by Mother England were viewed as increasingly burdensome by the colonies.

Combine the perception of increased economic burden designed solely to fuel the needs of a distant and increasingly resented motherland, and a culture often on the wrong side of labor exploitation, and an environment ready for revolt is created. And revolt they did.

There had been escalating squabbles in the middle of the eighteenth century in New England and British America. The most notorious was the Tea Act of 1773, passed by the British Parliament in an effort to raise additional revenue for Britain and protect the profits of the East India Tea Company. New World colonists at the time argued that such revenue generation schemes were unjust as they amounted to taxation without representation.

Some colonies resisted this new tax by simply refusing to accept delivery of the taxed tea at harbor side. The colonists of Massachusetts had what they thought was a better idea. In a fit of pique, they overpowered the ship containing the tea and dumped the tea chests overboard into the Boston Harbor.

This simple act of defiance of English authority was met with even harsher reaction from their Parliament. A year after the Tea Act of 1773, the Parliament in London passed the Coercive Acts of 1774. This legislative act included a provision that there would be no further commerce in Boston until the British East India Company was compensated for its lost tea. The escalation of legislation was met with protests, additional acts of defiance, and, most significantly, the convening of the First Continental Congress.

This new political entity purported to represent the colonies to Mother England and petitioned for repeal of the Tea Act of 1773, the Coercive Act of 1774, and the resolution of other grievances. Sides were galvanizing in this rapidly escalating trade and taxation dispute. However, the protection of a monopoly based in motherland began a decade earlier.

A familiar story – just the names have changed

One of Britain's most successful set of economic ventures, for a time, was the granting of monopoly franchises to British companies that would bring new wealth, resources, and exotic goods to England from its colonies. In return, the colonies would receive finished goods.

The new wealth of England arising from its industrialization in the seventeenth century created a penchant for spices and tea. At the turn of the eighteenth century, the East India Tea Company was granted a monopoly to import tea from India. In exchange for this concession to the East India Tea Company, parliament extracted a 25% tax on the wholesaling of tea once it arrived on England's shores. In addition, the government levied an additional sales tax on retail tea. These taxes were not only lucrative for the government, but also created incentives to smuggle tea from nearby Netherlands, where taxes were minimal.

The East India Tea Company was losing thousands of pounds annually from the smuggling of untaxed tea both across the North Sea from the Netherlands and by merchant ships into the colonies. To halt this smuggling, Parliament reduced taxes on tea retailed in Britain and offered the East India Tea Company a rebate on wholesale taxes for tea re-exported to the Colonies.

This reduction of taxes on those in the motherland by further taxing those forging new lives in the hinterland fomented revolt. These early acts of taxation, most notoriously the Townshend Acts of 1767, were argued as unconstitutional by the Whigs, a new political group of colonists. Whigs argued that the constitution required taxes to be levied only with the consent of the elected representatives of British subjects. As the colonists in spite of being British sub-jects did not have representation in Parliament, they challenged these acts and similar acts to follow.

The argument that only colonial assemblies could tax led to some new reforms in Parliament, including repeal of the Stamp Act – a piece of legisla-tion that raised taxes still further and was highly resented by the American colonies.

However, the dual necessity to expand government revenue from the col-onies to reduce smuggling and taxation at home, and the growing sense that colonists must be put in their place, resulted in a wave of increasingly coer-cive acts from a parliament bent on crushing colonial foment. Their determin-ation resulted in the Declaratory Act of 1766 that simply stated that parliament reserved the right to legislate in the colonies in "all cases whatsoever."

Obviously, battle lines were being drawn. There were skirmishes, boycotts, a growing number of smugglers, and other gestures of economic empowerment from the 13 colonies. There were even some appeals of coercive laws, but these repeals proved only temporary in nature. Each time a law was recalled, another more coercive law replaced it.

Clearly, Britain's policies were fluid. The British parliament recognized that it had to not only offer some limited empowerment of assemblies in the colonies, but also had to retain the loyalty of the governors and customs duty officials who served as its eyes and ears in the colonies. Some taxation to support the assemblies, to pay and keep the loyalty of their governors, and to assert parliament's dominion over the colonies was viewed as neces-sary. To turn taxation over to the emerging colonial assemblies would ultim-ately disempower the homeland's parliament and its dominion over the New World.

Parliamentary pique required the empire to maintain the coercive taxes, and, in some cases, to escalate taxation. Hubris and a stubbornness to retain the power and dominion of the British Empire overtook any sentiment of a long-term relationship built on mutual advantage and symbiosis. It was diffi-cult to give up the hard-won privilege of an empire.

In fact, by the Boston Tea Party Revolt of 1773, some of the more onerous taxes had been repealed, and the price of tea imported from Britain had actu-ally been coming down. This did not bode well with smugglers and their merchants. Indeed, the die had been cast, and a diverse group of importer-exporters, Whigs calling themselves the Sons of Liberty, smugglers, and revo-lutionaries caught word of a new shipment of tea coming from England.

Mass protests and demands for the resignation of appointed representatives of the King had been mounting over the fall of 1773. Of the seven ships of tea that had traveled to the colonies that fall, the revolts turned back most. However, a steadfast Governor Hutchinson of the Colony of Massachusetts refused to turn the Boston-bound ships back, perhaps because his sons were importers of tea to the colonies.

With the arrival of the tea ship *Dartmouth*, Whig leader Samuel Adams called for a town meeting. The meeting passed a resolution demanding the *Dartmouth* to turn back without unloading the tea and paying the customary duty. Soon, three ships were in harbor and thousands of Bostonians were amassing in the streets. Following another town meeting, scores of men left to overtake the ships docked at Griffin's Wharf and unloaded 342 tea chests into the harbor, without paying the taxes due to Governor Hutchinson and Mother England.[22]

This act of defiance and revolt was met with horror and derision by the British. Some parliamentarians, and even some colonists, most notably founding father Benjamin Franklin, stated that the lost tea must be repaid. Merchants fearful of a trade war even offered to repay the amount themselves. The House of Lords refused such settlement as battle lines stiffened on some quarters. Indeed, the main parliamentary antagonist of these recalcitrant colonists, Lord North uttered:

> The Americans have tarred and feathered your subjects, plundered your merchants, burnt your ships, denied all obedience to your laws and authority; yet so clement and so long forbearing has our conduct been that it is incumbent on us now to take a different course. Whatever may be the consequences, we must risk something; if we do not, all is over.[23]

The beginning of the end – the seeds of another empire

Growing resolve in Parliament resulted in a series of sweeping reassertions of power. In their pique, the British parliament passed a series of regressive acts in 1773 and 1774.

For instance, the Boston Party Act of 1773 closed the port of Boston until the East India Company was repaid for the lost tea. Not surprisingly, this act was viewed by Bostonians as overreaching broad persecution for the acts of less than 200 men.

In addition, the Massachusetts Government Act forced governance on the colony under the direct control of the King, and limited the revered town meetings of its colonists. The Administration of Justice Act of 1774 allowed the governor to move trials of the accused to venues where they would not be judged by their peers. This act was commonly regarded as a mechanism to limit witnesses who would appear on behalf of the defense of colonists.

In addition, the Quartering Act of 1774 allowed the government to house British soldiers in commandeered buildings if local residences refused to respect a request to house the soldiers. And, the Quebec Act of 1774 enlarged the boundaries of the Province of Quebec, under British Rule. This ultimately deprived some colonists of their land and was viewed cynically as an attempt to curry favor with French Canadian settlers who may subsequently sympathize with the British should there be war. The Act had religious overtones as well, fomenting some resentment of traditionally Protestant colonists by favoring Catholic French Canadians.

We will see how these reassertions became tenets to be challenged as the colonists declared their economic independence and constructed their own constitution.

Revolution and war are costly, especially at the geographic limits of far-flung empires. To appease the colonists, Britain followed the Coercive Acts of 1774 with the Conciliatory Resolution of 1775. The latter resolution stated that a colony that would provide for the defense of imperial authority could assume their own taxation regime and suspend taxes diverted to Mother England.

By 1778, the last vestiges of the Tea Act were repealed through the Taxation of the Colonies Act. By then, though, there was no turning back the clock.

Protection of property

While there certainly were tensions arising from heavy-handed British rule, and there were resentments over harsh or exploitative treatment of indentured servants, the concerns of the colonists were decidedly economic. Colonists wanted more of the fruits of their labor and the purchasing power of their income to stay at home.

On the other hand, what good is a colony to an empire if it cannot provide a new source of wealth for the ruling elite? Gone were the days of simple empire-building for power's sake. Even the Caesars of the Roman Empire accepted a modicum of pragmatism in its governance so long as order was preserved and there was something for the Caesar.

However, as we have seen time and again in empire after empire, the very desire to expand creates an empire too far-flung. The increasing diversity of peoples and interests in a far-flung empire led to management problems. It became increasingly difficult to share a vision and a centrality of mission. Too many became interested in protecting the fruits of their labor. Meanwhile, the empire strove to tax some of these fruits in support of loftier goals that were not valued by those who considered themselves oppressed.

At some point in the decline of an empire, there is a shift away from the shared value that made the empire strong and toward a more individualistic subculture. Just as Protestants took back God from the Catholic Church hierarchy, economic revolutionaries grew suspect of decisions made purportedly on their behalf and funded with their hard-won earnings.

Therefore, it seems natural that individual property would become the central tenet of such an economic revolution.

Economic empowerment

Britain was walking a fine line. While it asserted its authority and offered concessions to colonists that would isolate the radicals among them, it had the great challenge of appearing moderate in polarized times. However, Britain's definition of moderation was substantially different from the moderation proposed by the new Continental Congress of the 13 colonies.

Meeting in Philadelphia in 1789, this first Continental Congress advocated economic independence from Britain. It formed an association of the colonies designed to boycott British finished goods. By doing so, it encouraged exports to Britain but sought alliances with other nations with whom it could conduct trade. It also asserted greater self-sufficiency in the production of goods and items to satisfy colonists' needs. However, by offering defense for Massachusetts in the event of hostilities with Britain, the Congress was ultimately sowing the seeds of economic independence even at great human cost.

Fruit of the rise becomes the seed of decline

An empire could be viewed as a contract. The empire provided security, prosperity, access to markets, and the protection of property to its citizens, in return for a share of the economic pie. If citizens of an empire perceived that these returns exceed the cost of membership to the empire, they are content to support the economic system.

All economic systems have winners and losers. If the health of any economic system requires that citizens voluntarily support the system, the converse may also be true. A healthy empire contains those who benefit a lot and those who benefit just enough from their membership to continue to support the empire.

If the citizens most immediately associated with the empire are the likely big winners, the more marginalized citizens are more likely to challenge the economic system.

It is these marginalized citizens, who are disaffected by the system, or who feel abused by the system, who are the harshest critics of an empire.

In a more geographically compact and homogeneous economic system, these have-nots can be isolated by a sense of nationalism and by a prevailing mood of the culture to support the prevailing economic system. In a far-flung empire that typically remains most responsive to the citizens closest to the heartland, the marginalized residents are those who may have least access to the immediate privileges of the heartland. The distant colonies are by their very nature marginal and often marginalized economically. This is a natural consequence of the colonial model that is very difficult to avoid.

Some colonial systems offer sufficient benevolence toward the hinterland to avoid this natural tendency to disaffection. Most empires, though, meet the sense of marginalization from its far-flung participants as a sign of disloyalty and a lack of appreciation and character. The issue becomes one of political pique and hubris rather than a natural tension between differing economic interests and perspectives.

This fatal flaw in an empire that becomes too diverse to support a common economic vision is almost inevitable. When the inevitability is combined with an inability to mount sufficient coercive force to maintain the empire, revolution is unavoidable.

The American Revolution was not the first challenge to the authority of an empire. However, it was the first to forge a new political system on decidedly economic grounds rather than on the principles of power and politics. This innovation, the creation of a nation in opposition to an outdated colonial and mercantilist economic model, was the spark that revolutionized capitalism and constitutions worldwide over the next two centuries.

7

An Economic Bill of Rights

To renounce liberty is to renounce being a man, to surrender the rights of humanity and even its duties. For him who renounces everything no indemnity is possible. Such a renunciation is incompatible with man's nature; to remove all liberty from his will is to remove all morality from his acts. Finally, it is an empty and contradictory convention that sets up, on the one side, absolute authority, and, on the other, unlimited obedience.

(Jean Jacques Rousseau, *The Social Contract*, Book I, Chapter 4 – Slavery, 1762)[24]

If the First Industrial Revolution was centuries in the making, the economic revolution was almost instantaneous. The period running from 1762 to 1787 may well be the most profound quarter century in the history of political and economic philosophy and thought. It culminated in a grand experiment that is only now reaching its conclusion.

The amazing quarter century began with Jean Jacques Rousseau's publication of *The Social Contract* in 1762. This influential doctrine extended the "quid pro quo" nature of economic contracts to social contracts. From the Latin and from contract law dating back to the Caesars, quid pro quo literally means "something for something." Rousseau argued that citizens would give up some autonomy to the state in return for an environment created by the state that allowed its citizens safety and an opportunity to thrive.[25]

This social contract is not static, but can rather evolve with changing needs. By arguing that the state's relationship with its citizens is bilateral and dynamic, a traditional economic convention of "something for something" had been extended to government and politics. It was the responsibility of elected representatives in a republic to allow this social contract to evolve over time in the interest of a productive and harmonious society.

The concept of a social contract was, in itself, responding to a tide of change. The dominant economies of the world in the eighteenth century were slowly coming out of feudalism. This system had lords and their vassals, to whom they granted land, provide the resource by which rural peasants could practice farming or pursue their livelihood. These lords and vassals were both land capitalists and governors of the economy. They would conduct trade with other lords and would guarantee military security for the region. Peasants certainly did not have economic freedom. The vast majority of citizens lived in servitude to the lords and vassals of these medieval empires.

With the rise of the First Industrial Revolution and the creation of the machines and factories that produced vast new types of physical capital, the traditional rural feudal balance was disrupted. For the first time, large numbers of peasants could be freed of the economic toil in the countryside, only to replace rural toil with the toil in new urban centers. While they may have been freed from being bound to land that they could not own, they were not freed from exploitation in the city.

The new capitalists had devised a system of production that needed few highly skilled laborers and a plethora of unskilled labor. In this new economy, it was still difficult for unskilled labor to gain economic freedom.

The New World offered the freedom to own land and to create surpluses one could sell; at least once the debt to travel to the New World had been repaid and the contract for indentured servitude had been released. With the cost of one way transportation to the new world equivalent to one to two years' wages for urban peasants, very few went to the new world with either property or economic autonomy. Those that had would rather stay in England and continue the activities that made them successful. Consequently, the vast majority of those who traveled to the New World worked in either indentured servitude or were under the employ of the King or an English company.[26]

Once the indentured servitude contract expired, the most industrious of these new settlers could develop for themselves a modicum of economic security. The goal of many of these new entrepreneurs was to gain financial autonomy while at the same time try to avoid the oppressiveness of the King's governors and the King's taxes.

Such entrepreneurs were all too keen to create any underground and self-sufficient economy they could muster. This overarching drive to create economic independence, obtain and protect property, and escape economic oppression was central in their declaration of economic independence. In the first region where European traditions were combined with New World resources and open land, this New World was the first world where such a declaration of economic independence by this class of people could actually succeed.

To best understand the important role of property in the formation of the United States, it is helpful to go back to the deliberations of those who would create the Bill of Rights, and to those economic philosophers that preceded them. Even the notion of "life, liberty, and the pursuit of happiness," while profound then, was neither entirely new, nor universally embraced.

Life, liberty, and the pursuit of happiness

In the summer of 1776, various colonies were producing declarations of rights. The most notable precursor to a 13-colony declaration of independence was the Declaration of Rights offered up by George Mason and approved by the Virginia Convention of Delegates, less than a month before the colonies declared independence. Mason wrote:

> That all men are by nature equally free and independent, and have certain inherent rights, of which, when they enter into a state of society, they cannot, by any compact, deprive or divest their posterity; namely, the enjoyment of life and liberty, with the means of acquiring and possessing property, and pursuing and obtaining happiness and safety.[27]

It is clear from his writing that the *commonwealth* was concerned about property and its role in fostering prosperity and economic independence. From liberty and property could flow happiness.

This notion of life, liberty, and the pursuit of happiness was advocated much earlier by the English philosopher John Locke, who in 1690, almost a century before the Declaration of Independence, wrote in the second of Two Treatises of Government:

> But though this be a state of liberty, yet it is not a state of licence: though man in that state have an uncontroulable liberty to dispose of his person or possessions, yet he has not liberty to destroy himself, or so much as any creature in his possession, but where some nobler use than its bare preservation calls for it. The state of nature has a law of nature to govern it, which obliges every one: and reason, which is that law, teaches all mankind, who will but consult it, that being all equal and independent, no one ought to harm another in his life, health, liberty, or possessions: for men being all the workmanship of one omnipotent, and infinitely wise maker; all the servants of one sovereign master, sent into the world by his order, and about his business; they are his property, whose workmanship they

are, made to last during his, not one another's pleasure: and being furnished with like faculties, sharing all in one community of nature, there cannot be supposed any such subordination among us, that may authorize us to destroy one another, as if we were made for one another's uses, as the inferior ranks of creatures are for ours. Every one, as he is bound to preserve himself, and not to quit his station wilfully, so by the like reason, when his own preservation comes not in competition, ought he, as much as he can, to preserve the rest of mankind, and may not, unless it be to do justice on an offender, take away, or impair the life, or what tends to the preservation of the life, the liberty, health, limb, or goods of another.[28]

In his treatise, Locke argued that all are subordinate to one maker, and that made all humans equal to one another. From that equality flows a right, and perhaps even an obligation, to preserve oneself and to not impair "the liberty, health, limb, or goods of another."

The revolutionary colonist John Adams was influenced by Locke's writings. More than a decade before the writing of the Declaration of Independence, Adams wrote a pamphlet entitled "Thoughts on Government: Applicable to the Present State of the American Colonies." He included in these writings:

We ought to consider what is the end of government, before we determine which is the best form. Upon this point all speculative politicians will agree, that the happiness of society is the end of government, as all divines and moral philosophers will agree that the happiness of the individual is the end of man. From this principle it will follow, that the form of government which communicates ease, comfort, security, or, in one word, happiness, to the greatest number of persons, and in the greatest degree, is the best.

All sober inquirers after truth, ancient and modern, pagan and Christian, have declared that the happiness of man, as well as his dignity, consists in virtue. Confucius, Zoroaster, Socrates, Mahomet, not to mention authorities really sacred, have agreed in this.

If there is a form of government, then, whose principle and foundation is virtue, will not every sober man acknowledge it better calculated to promote the general happiness than any other form?

Fear is the foundation of most governments; but it is so sordid and brutal a passion, and renders men in whose breasts it predominates so stupid and miserable, that Americans will not be likely to approve of any political institution which is founded on it.[29]

Adams appealed to earlier philosophers in his argument for economic freedom and the freedom to pursue happiness. From these beginnings, on

October 14, 1774, the First Continental Congress passed a resolution penned by Major John Sullivan, delegate from New Hampshire. It read in part:

> That they are entitled to life, liberty, and property, and they have never ceded to any sovereign power whatever, a right to dispose of either without their consent.[30]

A new world was witnessing a dramatic shift in the philosophy of government, from a nation of laws to a nation of people as well as the principle of property and the right to pursue and preserve property, articulated as an inalienable right.

However, while Adams was tipping his hat to Locke and others, he was also opening up the debate on the pathway to happiness and economic fulfillment. More than a decade later, Thomas Jefferson was working with Adams, Benjamin Franklin, Robert R. Livingston, and Roger Sherman on a committee charged with writing a Declaration of Independence. Jefferson, as chief author, chose a phrase borrowed from the sentiment, if not the words, of Locke, but without the word "property." Instead, the Declaration of Independence adopted by the Second Continental Congress on July 4, 1776 read:

> We hold these Truths to be self-evident, that all Men are created equal, that they are endowed by their Creator with certain unalienable Rights, that among these are Life, Liberty and the pursuit of Happiness.[31]

Other countries would subsequently adopt their own versions of this three-part declaration. For instance, France subsequently emphasized liberty, equality, and fraternity in their motto "liberté, égalité, fraternité." Meanwhile, Canada proclaimed the right to "peace, order, and good government." In addition, the Universal Declaration of Human Rights, adopted by the United Nations General Assembly in 1948, declares in Article 3 that "Everyone has the right to life, liberty and security of person." It goes on to state in article 17[32]:

> *(1) Everyone has the right to own property alone as well as in association with others.*
> *(2) No one shall be arbitrarily deprived of his property.*

It is well understood today that humans have rights to life, liberty, the security of person, and property, and a government has an obligation to protect these rights. This concept had become universal 258 years after John Locke wrote that a government should preserve the life, the liberty, health, limb, or goods of another. After more than two centuries of familiarity with a constitution for the people rather than for the ruling elite, it is easy for those of the First Economic World to take for granted this radical departure from the status quo.

Certainly, the preservation of safety was an aspect of government well understood even in feudal times. Without a secure populace, there can be no prosperity. However, by the time of the American Revolution, it was becoming increasingly apparent that the protection of property was an equally important element in promoting economic development and prosperity.

A social experiment

Some have argued that the founding fathers were mere political opportunists. Made up of lawyers, publishers, merchants, doctors, plantation owners, and military men, these economic revolutionaries would certainly benefit from an economic system freed from British taxation and onerous terms of trade. However, they would also formulate a new economic system that would foment an American Dream in which any one of its citizens will have an equal opportunity to prosper.

Certainly, the Declaration of Independence and a new economic constitution would well serve the citizens of a new nation. The fascinating aspect of this new economic order, though, was the degree to which it also fostered new prosperity, based not on privilege but rather on a preference toward wealth production. The founding fathers were more privileged than all but the representatives of the King were. Yet, they strived to produce a constitution that eschewed privilege for plain old hard work.

There are two competing perspectives on economic wealth. One perspective is that wealth is meant to be redistributed. This is the constant sum, economic pie model. Those who subscribe to this model view politics as a worthwhile activity. After all, politics is the system that decides not what is produced but for whom it is produced. Most treatises that deal with the rise and fall of empires are in this camp. The military invariably plays a central role in defending the surpluses of the empire and in expropriating the surpluses of less powerful empires.

The alternative world-view believed in the positive sum, growing economic pie concept. The founding fathers were decidedly skeptical of this theory of production and politics. Many had been strongly influenced by the multi-volume treatise of Adam Smith that began publishing in 1776.

Smith argued against an old-fashioned mercantilism, of which monopolies such as the British East India Company was the classic example. Instead, Smith advocated for free markets. He also introduced his readers to the concept of the "invisible hand," the force of self-interest that ensures enough sellers produce what buyers want or need.

The invisible hand and enlightened self-interest

The notion of an invisible hand works best when politics does not interfere. Unless there is some sort of fundamental failing in a market, producers' self-interest induces a producer to make more of those things that are in high demand, and hence of high price, and produce less of those items that have falling prices because of waning demand. Politics cannot add to this dance of self-interest, and indeed would likely detract from its efficiency.

Production based on self-interest is motivated, entrepreneurial, and efficient. A system that can foster and harness this creative and self-interested energy can produce a bigger economic pie. If politics gets in the way of this process, the economic pie will not grow to its full potential, and may even decline as too many individuals strive to usurp the production of another rather than produce themselves.

In other words, the founding fathers believed in enlightened self-interest that recognized the true dynamo of individual energy was the path to prosperity. Once an empire was on this path, there would be more bounty for all, the privileged included.

The founding fathers also hoped that an economic constitution would allow it to heal itself from costly wars and British blockades. They realized they did not have the ready markets and protectionism that British rule afforded. Moreover, they could not afford to mount a navy that could prevent the piracy and plunder that threatened American commerce. They were willing to put privilege aside to create a prosperous nation. They could not have foretold just how successful this new political experiment, based on the ideas of Locke, Rousseau, Smith, and others, would be.

Two economic regimes

Economists differentiate between two alternative economic approaches through the labels "rent production" and "rent seeking." The term "rent" is used to describe the surplus or profits of an activity. Rent is the difference between the value an individual or market places on an item and the costs incurred to produce the item. These surpluses, or "rents," offer an incentive to produce, with the largest rents going to the most scarce or most valued activities. Seeking the rents of others thwarts this important process by diverting human energy to distribution rather than production.

Economists well understand the folly of rent seeking in the world viewed as a constant sum game. Rent seeking is seen as the counterproductive effort to extract the surpluses of others, leading some to conclude that mere theft is even preferred to fraud. Both theft and fraud cause a transfer of wealth from one entity to another. However, the problem with fraud is that too much effort is devoted to it. If the chattels could be taken without such effort, at least the fraudsters' time would be freed to pursue some more productive activity.

Of course, the problem with both theft and fraud is that they require people to devote even more energy into preserving and protecting wealth rather than in producing in the first place. An important element of the social contract requires government to render unnecessary individual justice and protection of property so that the citizens are freed to produce and prosper.

The founding fathers of a new United States were determined to keep government out of the rent-seeking business as much as possible. Their economic optimism took as an act of faith the assumption of a world that was a positive sum, growing economic pie. This optimism may have been as much a matter of convenience as idealism. Certainly, the decimated markets of revolutionary America had little capacity to support a British style government.

Nor would the newly empowered population tolerate the trade of one oppressive regime for another. While there was a strong sense of a uniting of the various states, they were ever wary about a federal government that placed too strong a hand on state sovereignty.

Fortunately, the founding fathers took time to think through their revolutionary economic philosophies. Had they rushed into a social contract according to Rousseau in which government offers order, infrastructure, and prosperity in return for its citizens' support and taxes, they would not have fully absorbed the messages of Adam Smith. While the Declaration of Independence was an important step toward a loftier socioeconomic goal, it was not sufficient, and may even have proven to be counterproductive, in itself.

Over the 15 years between the Declaration of Independence and the Bill of Rights that were the first amendments to the Constitution, the founding fathers created a blueprint for an economic union that none had invented to that date, and few have failed to imitate since. They created a model that managed to preserve limited government for more than a century.

The great debate of rights and privileges

One of the most telling battles in the forging of a more perfect economic union was in the separation of rights and privileges. The sentiment was not to create a nation of privilege and entitlement. Rather, it was to foster industriousness and production. While few would argue that government could supplant the private sector as the economic engine that fuels society, the careful balance between a right and an opportunity was debated.

John Adams and Thomas Jefferson, two of the members of the First Continental Congress charged by their colleagues to pen the document for the declaration of independence committee, took seriously the responsibility for defining the words that would set a new nation down the path of economic independence. These founding fathers would, in turn, become the second and third presidents of the nation, would become political rivals in their middle years, and would die on the same day, July 4, 1826 as the best of friends. In 1776, however, they were collaborators, that agreed on the essential importance of individual pursuit of life, liberty and happiness.

Economic aspects of the Constitution

The Constitution and its first ten amendments provided the foundations for a new economy. None of these innovations was entirely novel or revolutionary in themselves. Moreover, many of these innovations took years, decades, or a century to implement. In total, though, they sent a message to a new nation that it was ready for business. This model has since been replicated numerous times by other nations.

The constitutional provisions included the power to tax and to control the money supply. While the treasury was a necessary tool to pull a new nation out of debt and to finance a subsequent war in 1812 with Britain, the power of the bourse was seen as an essential tool to maintain confidence in a common currency. In reality, this power was not fully understood or exploited until the Great Depression in the 1930s. However, the U.S. constitution, in Article I, Section 8, was the first that delineated and enshrined the role of monetary policy as a tool of prosperity.

The article also confined the powers reserved by the federal government to those necessary to promote and regulate trade, with the goal of fostering economic growth.

The constitution went on to protect the right to private property in a several ways, as we will describe later.

Finally, the constitution set up a system of checks and balances, with a House representing the people by population; a Senate offering regional representation to each State; an executive branch that was considered the co-equal of the Congress; and an independent judiciary, called the Supreme Court, that would go on to define itself as the entity that ensures the other branches do not exceed their constitutionally limited powers.

These checks and balances were defined to ensure that government could not grow in scope by fiat. Indeed, John Adams had argued fervently for the need of any constitution to include a provision that enshrined the power of individuals to rebel against government no longer by the people and for the people. These balances, including the right to rebellion, were essential to offer a check against a government that turned to rent seeking and privilege rather than rent production.

Two provisions of the Bill of Rights and the Amendments to the Constitution stood out, especially in light of a wariness of the founding fathers. These were the actions of privilege and rent seeking that so infuriated these early revolutionaries. Amendment 5 of the Bill of Rights, called the "due process clause," stated that those charged with a crime must be accused by a grand jury of their peers. No individual could be tried twice for the same offense, a person may not be compelled to testify against himself and in opposition to his own self-interest, and no person shall be deprived of life, liberty, or property without due process of law. The "takings clause" went on to elaborate that, should private property be taken for public use, just compensation must be paid. This takings clause is often known as the law of imminent domain.

We will see later that the takings clause, and others, was subsequently relaxed.

An amendment to the constitution that did not appear until 70 years after the Civil War went on to strengthen the due process clause by declaring that all those born or naturalized in the United States are citizens of the United States. These federal citizens could not have their constitutional rights of the protection of life, liberty, and property abridged by any state without due process of law.

Fruit of the rise becomes the seed of decline

Other countries, most notably England, had established through Common Law or civil codes some of the protections afforded to all citizens by the U.S. Constitution. However, no country had written down these rules for healthy commerce as a set of founding principles and afforded the individual all the protections of an independent judiciary. There was tremendous economic value to the private sector in these words because, for the first time, property was enshrined as an individual right. There was even greater symbolic value to state that:

> We hold these truths to be self-evident, that all men are created equal, that they are endowed by their Creator with certain unalienable Rights, that among these are Life, Liberty and the pursuit of Happiness. That to secure these rights, Governments are instituted among Men, deriving their just powers from the consent of the governed, That whenever any Form of Government becomes destructive of these ends, it is the Right of the People to alter or to abolish it, and to institute new Government, laying its foundation on such principles and organizing its powers in such form, as to them shall seem most likely to effect their Safety and Happiness.[33]

This grand statement held that there are certain truths held to be self-evident – that all men are created equal and have an inalienable right to life, liberty, and to the pursuit – for the first time offers the opportunity, and the responsibility, to create one's own happiness. A new nation even offered protection from an oppressive state by granting the right to bear arms in the interest of a well-armed militia.

It is apparent in even a cursory reading of the Declaration of Independence, the U.S. Constitution, and the first ten amendments to the constitution comprising the Bill of Rights that a new economic order was formulated based on not only what it was and could be but also by what it would not become.

Some of these most strident declarations of individual sovereignty over an oppressive state would be eroded under the constant and unrelenting force of new and special interests, as we shall see later. A quarter century of brilliant insights into and protections from human nature could not be expected to anticipate every possible scheme designed to separate fair-minded women and men from their property. Laws would need to develop to prevent, or at least ameliorate, every conceivable abuse of an evolving economy.

It is also interesting to note that the very sentiment of economic individualism would fall victim to the same sort of market failures and monopolizations that gave rise to revolutionary fervor in the first place. The British East India Company, and similar price riggers in factor and goods markets of the eighteenth century, were replaced by railroad tycoons and rigged financial markets in the nineteenth century. Not much had changed. Not even a commandment from the gods could prevent politicians and industrialists alike from coveting the chattels of another as an easier path to amass great wealth than through production.

8
Dominance through Economics

No country can be well governed unless its citizens as a body keep religiously before their minds that they are the guardians of the law, and that the law officers are only the machinery for its execution, nothing more.

(Mark Twain and Charles Dudley Moore,
The Gilded Age – A Tale of To-day, 1873)[34]

More than anything else, this New Economic World was in the right place at the right time with the right document to truly open up commerce. The new nation also had room to expand and was instantly freed from the monopolized trade routes that so restricted colonial mercantilist powers in England, France, and Spain. The new United States heralded in a freewheeling economic style where anything was possible. A Second Industrial Revolution would soon take hold and would attract people from around the world who valued economic freedom and had little to lose.

An economic system that could create and amass economic power with breathtaking speed and efficiency made obvious that economic power creates political might. However, with political potency comes the pursuit of power rather than the pursuit of production.

New industrialists

One primary reason for a U.S.-style Second Industrial Revolution was that this new economic world held great tracts of land and huge resources. Its immigrating inhabitants, for the most part, moved from one of the most developed and congested empires in the world to the least populated potential empire. It also managed to attract those who had nothing to lose and every incentive to work hard to create a new life. Finally, while it may not have been the beacon of high culture, it was the beacon of economic vitality, with bragging rights of the first constitution for a modern era.

There were a number of bumps along the road before the United States could enjoy the fruits of its economic seeds. A new Gilded Age had to wait until the completion of the War of 1812, and resolution of the divisive issue of slavery through a civil war. With the conclusion of the Civil War, a reunified country could begin empire building in earnest. And begin it did. By the time it was finished, it had eclipsed Great Britain as the world's largest economy – just a little more than a century after it declared its independence from the tiny island that ruled a vast empire.

A century of empire building

Almost every economic empire goes through similar cycles of steady-state economic stagnation until some sort of spark is lit, a period of reshuffling that sets the stage, and then a period of prolonged, spectacular, and seemingly endless growth that follows. This period of endless growth may be called a gilded age in any economy, and has become known as that in the United States post–civil war era.

While the U.S. Gilded Age in the post–civil war period is attributed to an immense industrialization process, all gilded ages share a number of features. There must be a nascent untapped potential for dramatic growth. Such economic success requires an aligning of the stars, with each precondition satisfied.

The most important condition is in a lack of constraints to growth. Dramatic increases in productive capacity can be likened to a six-cylinder economic engine. The first cylinder is human capital. There must be a sufficient supply of unused or underutilized human capital that can be deployed in industrialization without creating needs elsewhere. An underemployed rural population made industrialization possible in industrializing England. Migration from the world over made it possible in the nineteenth century United States. Over time, immigration or dramatic procreation is necessary.

The second cylinder is the investment necessary to purchase innovative physical capital. Industrialization in any sector requires technologies that can augment human capital and leverage that scarce resource to the highest possible degree. Such investment requires a shared optimism for the future, and some early successes that will convince all that the economic engine is firing successfully.

The third cylinder is an adequate supply of natural resources, such as land, minerals, water, energy, agricultural land, and the other items necessary to feed the industrial machine. Each industry needs a different mix of these resource factors. The economies of the nineteenth century needed vast amounts of all these factors. Fortunately, land and resources were abundant in the vast new country of the United States.

The fourth cylinder is a supply chain that can move these factors and the resulting goods and services around to be sure bottlenecks in any single factor supply will not gum up the works. Ways to move people and raw materials to the industrial machines, and finished products to the output markets, are essential if dramatic growth is to occur.

The fifth cylinder is entrepreneurship and effective management. Individuals must be responsible for ensuring that all these factors are brought together in the same place at the same time and in the most effective manner. There need not be a large number of such entrepreneurs. However, without a sufficient number of conductors, the concerted transformation of resources and creativity into products and profits degenerates into chaos.

Finally, a nation must ensure that economic leadership keeps the tracks greased, the engine oiled, the markets working, and the entrepreneurs rewarded. Without this sixth cylinder of a legal and economic framework that rewards or, at the very least, does not inhibit innovation, this high performance engine cannot run on all cylinders.

Indeed, the double-digit levels of growth experienced in the United States in the nineteenth century and elsewhere now can be possible only if each cylinder of the economic engine is firing efficiently and evenly. When that happens, anything will seem possible. Few can imagine anything but sustainable economic growth in perpetuity.

A Gilded Age

However, just as there cannot be a perpetual motion machine, there cannot be perpetual spectacular growth. Although this book is a study of the forces that give rise to dominating economic development, and the causes of economic trials and failure, there are some peculiar examples from the Gilded Age that offer important lessons in economic history.

The term "Gilded Age" was attributed to Mark Twain and Charles Dudley Warner from their book *The Gilded Age: A Tale of Today* that was published in 1874.[35] Mark Twain was a humorist and social commentator with an uncanny ability to put a light but most effective touch on uncomfortable human circumstances. These authors took the name from a line in William Shakespeare's play *King John* (1595): "To gild refined gold, to paint the lily... is wasteful and ridiculous excess."

Twain and Warner raised awareness of inevitable class struggles through humor just as other writers of the era such as Karl Marx and John Stuart Mill treated class struggles from more scholarly perspectives. These writers were certainly cognizant of the amazing ability of the modern economic machine to create immense wealth and surpluses. In fact, few failed to marvel at such newfound wonders. However, some, including these four writers and economic philosophers, were concerned about the destabilizing effects of such dramatic wealth creation. They concerned themselves about the ability to manage growth without social upheaval, and perhaps even revolution.

As we have seen, political revolution often follows a change in economic circumstances. Humorists like Mark Twain used their stories to offer parables about what could happen when cultures clashed. Meanwhile, economists like John Stuart Mill recommended accommodations that could prevent clashes that would derail the economic engine. Still others, like Karl Marx, advocated a new economic system that shifted the balance entirely from one privileged class to another. Obviously, sustained economic growth had to avoid numerous landmines if it is to stay on course.

England had to come to terms with such an accommodation earlier in its history, as it faced the consequences of the First Industrial Revolution. America did not yet have the advantage of a hinterland that could fuel growth and maintain profits in the homeland sufficient to keep the public content.

In this Second Industrial Revolution coincident with the Gilded Age, a newfound country built on a new economic premise began in earnest, first on the eastern seaboard of the United States. Each of the original 13 colonies touched the sea and each had a port that offered a gateway between the resources of the vast interior and the markets abroad. Each had shipbuilders, water and then steam-driven mills, experienced free tradesmen, eager entrepreneurs, and a large and continuous stream of immigrants landing on its shores each year.

The eagerness of every newcomer to cast off the memory of indentured servitude and plug in to this vast economic machine helped create fortunes for some. While the labor force was diverse in skills, ambitions, and races, the elite group of new industrialists that harnessed their skills was decidedly homogenous.

This club of the wealthy industrialists in the Gilded Age included names that remain familiar even today. Cornelius Vanderbilt, J.P. Morgan, Andrew Carnegie, John Rockefeller, Henry Ford, and Andrew Mellon created the capital upon which great wealth was built. They then redirected this great wealth into ever-increasing levels of capitalization. In the process, they built the railroads, the stock markets, the oil pipelines, the banks, cars, and factories that fueled a level of modernization and expansion never before seen.

This nouveau riche also built great temples to their wealth in opulent luxury befitting kings and queens. Their indulgent display of wealth and their willingness to advance their own interests in a vacuum of governmental intervention or oversight let their critics coin a new term: "robber baron."

The first robber barons

Concentration of the fruits of economic output in the hands of a few was not new. After all, the feudal system concentrated agricultural production with land barons and lords, in exchange for subsistence living and military protection.

What was new in the Second Industrial Revolution, however, was the immense scale and pace of seemingly accelerating wealth. Never before had the fruits of such enormous production so rapidly generate wealth for so few who had not been granted their elite status by heritage, military, or political prowess.

There is a stabilizing effect on elitism when it was the product of heritage or military conquest. All participants born into their roles must spend a lifetime living in their own skin. In contrast, this nouveau riche came from backgrounds not unlike those who toiled in the factories, on the rail beds, in the mines, or at the oil wells that created immense wealth. These industrialists were earning such wealth, and were so visibly manipulating markets, to enhance their wealth, simply because they were in the right place at the right time. The workers took notice and began coveting the wealth of these new elites.

Recognizing the explosive danger of opulent wealth when others are working hard to barely hold on to the American Dream, some like Andrew Carnegie actually espoused a responsibility that went along with richness. His philosophy of philanthropy was not only noble in gesture but also pragmatic. His "Gospel of Wealth" called for industrialists like himself to endow hospitals, museums, universities, and libraries.[36] The institutions sponsored by Carnegie and others like him allowed ordinary citizens to enjoy a framework that would keep them healthier, enlightened, educated, and literate on a sustainable basis. It also created the sense of sharing the wealth, without any government entity called to force such sharing.

New organizational models

Dramatic growth in this Second Industrial Revolution can be attributed to experimentation with new institutions and organizational models previously untried.

The first organizational model was a new nation's constitution that protected property from overreaching government. The constitution delimited the power of government to tax and protected property from takings and unreasonable search and seizure. It also maintained the right of the people to overthrow an oppressive government, and created a supreme court that would independently protect and mete out these rights so that new commercial innovations could flourish.

The second organizational innovation was a new legal fiction called a corporation. Corporations were not an entirely new invention. They had been very effective in mobilizing the capital in the First Industrial Revolution that swept through Britain. However, the employment of new organizational models reached unprecedented heights in the Second Industrial Revolution that swept through the United States in the Gilded Age.

A corporation is novel and effective in a number of ways. First, it creates a legal entity, with the right to contract and to sue. It allows protection of passive investors behind this corporate shield. In the event that a corporation is sued or otherwise is obliged to pay a debt in excess of its assets, the investors are liable only to the extent of their investment in the corporation. This policy allows investors to limit their investment exposure on the downside, but at the same time enjoy all the benefits of a successful venture.

Investors also have the ability to sell their shares of ownership of a corporation. If the corporation is publicly listed, these sales of shares, and the purchases by another investor, are facilitated in stock markets. The resulting liquidity of corporate ownership ensures that the owners of corporations can easily match the combination of expected return and risk to suit their investment preferences.

Finally, a corporation is free to focus on the collective goals of the shareholders. Under the preceding proprietorship model, an enterprise had competing goals. One goal was to return profits to the owner in return for the owner's investment and toil. Another goal was to meet owner's other needs. These could range from providing the owner and her family with employment or a place to live, or even an outlet for philanthropy or community charity.

These self-interested goals of the proprietorship model are deemphasized in the corporate model. Because a great diversity of shareholders own a corporation, the prevailing corporate motive is profit. Even the most diverse shareholders can share this singular goal. The corporation may also have goals of charity, community goodwill, etc., but these goals are typically secondary.

The ability to trade shares, to engage professional management to run corporations, to shield owners from recourse should the venture fail, and to maintain a focus on profits means that corporations have a real advantage in capital formation and growth. Without question, the corporate form is the prevailing form of all large enterprises, almost without exception.

This organizational structure was invaluable in facilitating the dramatic capital formation and economic growth of the Gilded Age. Without it, the financial surpluses that were forming would not have found a home for reinvestment and subsequent growth.

And grow they did. Corporations grew larger than any private organization but perhaps the Catholic Church. A century and a half after the onset of the Gilded Age, Wal-Mart, the largest corporation, was generating revenue of $243 billion. This production would place it larger than any but the top 16 nations in the world. In 2000, Wal-Mart would generate revenue just behind the gross domestic product of Russia, the center of an empire that vied with the United States for global supremacy throughout the Cold War.

A new tension between the private and public sectors

The mammoth size and monopolization of corporations soon became an affront to good public policy. Government responded to the growing power and influence of corporations by curtailing their potential size and influence.

In the interest of sound public policy, government began to regulate ways in which corporations could conduct their business and cooperate with each other in their efforts maximize their joint profits. Government also began to tax the profits of corporations before these profits were subsequently paid out to shareholders, and then would tax shareholders again at the personal level.

Government was succumbing to a pressure arising from the growing imbalance between corporations and the rest of the population. The corporate model was becoming so strong that it began to eclipse the power of other owners of factors of production. In the capitalist model, the providers of financial capital decide how the other factors, such as human capital, physical capital, resource capital, and managerial capital, are combined to produce profits. These huge financial capitalists had the capacity to pull all the strings and keep the greatest bulk of the surpluses that had formerly accrued to the other factors of production in more equal measure.[37]

As government regulations tried to limit the power and scope of corporations to extract ever-increasing surpluses and greater shares of production through monopolization, corporations quickly figured out ways to continue to grow and to circumvent the regulations designed to constrain their growth. Just as closing a door to block nature will only force nature through the window, corporations invariably found ways to go around any obstacle. Even today, it is said that whenever hundreds of legislators pass laws to correct market failings, thousands of a country's brightest lawyers immediately begin work to find ways around these laws.

A classic example is the response to trusts. Good public policy mandated that individual markets be protected from the monopolization of one large corporation. The government of Gilded Age America did not want to see corporations controlled, for instance, by a handful of railroad barons dominating interstate commerce. When regulation and statute prevented them from doing just that, the corporations instead formed "trusts," which provided an overarching coordinating body to allow many corporations with shared interests to act as one.

While not a monopoly in the legal sense, these trusts nonetheless coordinated their activities and otherwise acted like monopolies in every other way. Because of these clever ploys, a new form of regulation called "antitrust" regulation was created. From then on, the mergers and actions of corporations came under waves and waves of additional scrutiny. At times, the government would go to extreme measures to prevent certain proposed organizational structures to form.

Despite the government's antitrust regulations, increasingly powerful, resourceful, and well-capitalized corporations were able to create economies of scale and managerial efficiencies that simply could not be replicated by other organizational structures or by smaller companies. Mammoth corporations began to dominate the most lucrative and richest forms of commerce.

Untold economies of scale

These large corporations enjoyed a number of advantages of economies of scale.

First, they had much more influence in factor markets and could demand more favorable terms of trade for their factors and resources.

Second, they could produce more efficiently because they were able to invest in all the various stages of production rather than having to contract-out parts of their production.

Third, the innovations and economies of scale they enjoyed in one production category also gave them an advantage in another.

Fourth, they could market and distribute these various products simultaneously and at lower cost than their smaller corporate cousins could muster.

Finally, they could develop vast, well trained, and efficient managerial networks to govern effectively these long supply-and-production chains. The economies of scale they could generate so easily could not be replicated by smaller, less advantaged firms.

So long as they did not get too big and suffer countervailing problems of inefficiencies that usually come with size, the mega-corporations could grow and could either swallow up lesser competitors or put them out of business.

These corporations have been called ruthless in their pursuit of greater profits and in their exploitation of every possible advantage or cost savings. To call a corporation ruthless is perhaps to call a lion ruthless. It is simply in the nature of a corporation to pursue profits by any legal means. If this unfailing pursuit of profit required a corporation to extract surpluses from other forms of capital, or put other companies out of business, it was quite natural to do so as it was a "survival of the fittest" in an economic sense.

The way they succeeded certainly bordered on or crossed the line of criminality at times. Even if a corporation did not cross the line, it could still be labeled as immoral or unethical in its actions. This imposition of human values on a corporation is awkward, though. For, while the corporation is considered a legal person, its sole purpose is to make profits for its shareholders. Corporations do not participate at church on Sunday or engage in the talk around town like their organizational predecessors may have.

The corporate form, the trusts, and the innovations in scientific management and production efficiencies were dramatically changing commercial America. Private fortunes never before seen were being amassed by a few. Meanwhile, the commoditization of labor was either preventing the working class from sharing this fortune or making them poorer. By the beginning of the twentieth century, little more than a generation into the Gilded Age, the United States had overtaken every country but Britain in its per capita industrial production. A few years later, the United States would eclipse its former colonial power, too. Never before had a country amassed so much economic power so quickly.

Workers strike back

Barely two decades into the Gilded Age, human capital struck back. In 1886, the American Federation of Labor was formed. The approach was, by definition, confrontational. If the lumbering giants of financial capitalist-owned corporations were becoming too powerful relative to other forms of capital, human capital could organize itself to rival the power of financial capital. Rather than the creation of a symbiotic organizational structure that rewarded all its capital contributors, the new model would be one in which titans, representing financial and human capital respectively, would fight it out. The noted Depression-era economist John Kenneth Galbraith would later label this new model "countervailing power."[38] The era of special interest economics and politics was formed.

It should have been expected that there would be a societal response to burgeoning corporations. Whenever there is change, positive or negative, some group will likely be disadvantaged. It is also highly unlikely that all groups in society will benefit equally. When combined with corporations' unyielding drive for profits, naturally and by design, a societal reaction seems inevitable.

Corporations could, of course, recognize that their long-term profits and viability demands a measure of social responsibility. Indeed, closely held corporations owned by just a handful of individuals often recognize this responsibility. However, a large corporation representing thousands of diverse shareholders often focuses on the one thing all agree upon – profits. Even long-term profit considerations are less likely goals when thousands of shareholders are clamoring for short-term rewards. A corporation in a very fast moving and dynamic environment either cannot afford to divert its attention to long-term sustainability, or will fail to see stability as important when things are moving so rapidly.

There were a number of social innovations that could have ensured a smoother and more efficient path to prosperity. While the corporations were working diligently on the one hand to lower costs, their efforts to raise revenue on the other hand often came by monopolizing markets. Recognition early on of the need for competitive markets would have avoided some of the early pitfalls of American-style capitalism. However, solutions to the market failures that result from monopolization were as elusive then as they are now.

The other major market failure that raised public hackles was a concern over a viable, sustainable, and contented long-term labor force. Human capital is unique among the various forms of capital. Though the corporation is considered a legal person, it cannot vote. And, while natural resource capital, entrepreneurial capital, and financial capital are also important, these forms of capital are owned by few people who, presumably, vote for their interests and the protection of their assets.

It is only human

Human capital has a unique role in society. If the vast majority of voters in a democracy are also human capitalists, a political system that does not favor this sector, at least to some degree, functions at its own peril. Even dictatorships recognize this reality, unless they are able to bleed off sufficient revenue to maintain an army that can successfully coerce and control the unhappy masses.

Satisfaction of the wants and needs of human capital is also unique. Human capital is most productive when it is well trained and educated. One may argue that the machines used in factories are also more productive when they are well maintained and well built. However, employers are more reluctant to invest in training and education of their employees for fear that in a free country they may subsequently offer those newly acquired skills to the highest bidder. Alternatively, an investment in an innovative machine is not as risky because the employer knows a machine will always work at the will of its owner.

Consequently, when employers cannot enforce long-term exclusivity contracts with their employees, there is a bias toward increasingly sophisticated machines and less sophisticated workers. While corporations can benefit from highly trained and educated workers, they would prefer to bid for those talents in the marketplace rather than train potential workers early on. Whether they bid for talent in the labor market place, or train their own employees, they will inevitably pay the same price for the workers. Therefore, unless there is a shortage of public investment in education, employers leave the augmentation of the value of human capital to some other segment in society.

Similarly, employers recognize that individual members of a mobile labor force are easily replaced. One of the managerial innovations of the Gilded Age was the scientific model of production. Into what economists call the production function go the various forms of capital – human, resource, financial, physical, managerial, and entrepreneurial. And out comes the product.

Frederick Taylor, a Gilded Age U.S. engineer, applied scientific techniques to the study of output and productive efficiency, and made a science out of management. At the same time, he demonstrated how machines could replace humans, further undercutting the power of human capital to extract higher wages. While wages did rise, they did not rise at the same rate as the incomes of owners of financial capital did. This widening income gap heightened the tension that income disparities create. Such gaps in the incomes of human capital owners versus financial capital owners are a familiar phenomenon in times of dramatic economic growth.

In economics, each of these inputs is treated mathematically like a commodity. Each can substitute for the other. A little less human capital is compensated by a few more machines. A broken machine can be easily replaced by a new machine or by a few more workers. In this model of commodified labor, the characteristics of individuals are lost in the shuffle. If their education is left to others, their health and safety is also ignored.

Corporations did try, nonetheless, to engender worker loyalty in the Gilded Age. The concept of career tracks was an innovation that allowed employers to invest in their employees' human capital. By starting the corporation's workers at low salaries with the implicit promise of "moving up the ladder," some of the problems of investing in mobile labor could be alleviated. However, most job categories would not lend themselves to such career ladders.

Finally, large monolithic corporations may dominate certain sectors of the labor market just as they can monopolize sectors of the product markets. By doing so, they can artificially hold down wages or depress working conditions.

Countervailing power

Between 1776 and 1866, there were major wars in almost every generation. A nation had been created from birth to offer a framework for a dynamic economy, at least once domestic peace prevailed.

However, in the subsequent era of big business and small government, it would have been impossible to anticipate the market failings of increased monopolization or have the political will or insight to stay ahead of a looming problem.

Labor unions, having recognized that changes from corporate or government leaders were not forthcoming, instead created a grass-roots movement to rebalance an increasingly skewed economy. Failing other alternative solutions, their role was almost inevitable.

While there are certainly differences between labor markets and product markets, some similarities allow us to better understand the role the early union movement had in mind.

We described earlier why economists label a monopoly a market failure. In essence, when compared to a competitive market, a monopoly will reduce output in an effort to drive up prices. What a monopoly may sacrifice in quantity of sales by raising its prices, it more than makes up by the increased price of its product. Consequently, revenue rises and costs fall, because of the reduced output. Profits rise from these dual effects.

One might observe that consumers were worse off in the process of monopolization, while the producers were better off. Without imposing a value judgment on whether producers or consumers deserve a greater share of new wealth generated, we might superficially conclude that there was no net effect of such a transfer of wealth and income from one segment of society to another. However, while producers may have deferred the profit on some sales foregone to realize a bigger profit on the remaining sales, consumers were unambiguously worse off. Not only did they pay a higher price for products, but also some consumers who could have once afforded the product were subsequently cut out of the market altogether.

Economists conclude that the losses from sales foregone and from consumers cut out of the market equal the money left on the table. These losses are labeled "deadweight losses," and represent an economic inefficiency, or a market failure.

Market failure

Economists abhor market failures and seek to remedy them at every opportunity. In the case of a monopoly, policy makers might foster market competition by allowing, or even encouraging or subsidizing, new competitors to the market.

Even a market with a number of firms may be prone to this monopolization if they all act in concert, as they would in a monopoly. In such cases, policy makers may try to regulate the prices charged or the level of services provided by the corporations to rebalance the marketplace and correct the market failure.

Sometimes, consumer groups can try to redress the imbalance. For instance, if a monopoly began to exploit a market, consumers could simply refuse to pay the higher prices and go without the product. They could employ boycotts, mount public relations campaigns, or buy less ideal products in an effort to induce the monopoly to reverse its strategy. In this model, the power of a monolithic corporation is balanced by the power of monolithic consumers, in a countervailing influence approach. Alternatively, they could demand government impose regulations that would have a similar effect.

Unions can be viewed in this light of consumer reaction to a monopolist. If a large corporation develops a strategy to exploit its workers, a union can organize the workers and withdraw their labor; much like what consumers can do with a boycott of a product.

However, there is one fundamental difference in the challenge of unions to market failure, as a series of diagrams will show.

While a consumer boycott will force a corporation to lower prices and raise output, and through this reduce the deadweight loss, the countervailing power of a union forces corporations to offer higher wages and prices and, consequently, reduce output still further, thereby increasing the deadweight loss. This form of countervailing power may be necessary, but it reduces competitiveness rather than enhances it.

To see this, let us analyze the market for a product and the labor used to create it. I begin by describing the demand curve that represents final demand for a product.

A demand curve is simply an aggregate representation of the willingness to pay of all those who demand a product. For instance, for any product, some would be willing to pay a higher price than others do, or purchase more units of a product at a given price, perhaps because they are wealthier or because they value the product more highly. If we sum their quantities desired from the highest valuations to the lowest, we can determine a market demand curve.

For any factor, good, or service if the price is too high, no demander would purchase any. We call this the choke price p_c. It can be represented as the highest price on the demand curve, when the demand is zero.

Alternately, there is a perhaps large demand for the product even if we were to give it away. This quantity demanded at a zero price is not infinite, though, because no person has the capacity to absorb an infinite amount of anything. We call this point at which people have had enough, even at a zero price as the market satiation quantity q_s.

Between these two extremes, we can draw a line that shows the quantity demanded of a service, a final good, an intermediate good necessary to produce final goods, or a factor of production. For any price, we can determine the total amount of the product desired.

We also know that a lower price will make the product more desirable or more affordable by a greater number of individuals. This implies that the demand for any good or service would slope downward as price drops result in an increase in the quantity demanded.

This relationship between the quantity demanded and the price per unit of a good or service is represented by the "demand curve" in Figure 2.

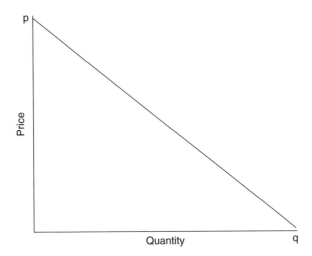

Figure 2 The demand curve

While demand curves will not typically be straight lines, and may, in some unusual cases, be upward sloping, this simplified representation suits our purposes.

We can put any currency denomination, per unit of our good or service, on the vertical axis of the graph of the market demand curve, and place any range of quantities, be they units, pounds, tons, number of workers or machines, etc., on the horizontal axis. For all of these goods or services, the demand curve works the same.

Companies are obviously interested in the level of demand for their products. A company that operates in a very competitive market for commodity recognizes that it has little control over the actual price, and must instead take the going price as given. On the other hand, a monopoly that has total control of the market recognizes it can choose to operate at whatever point on the demand curve that will yield highest profits.

Profits are made up of two components – revenue, or the product of price and quantity, less its costs of production. Let us ignore costs for now and see how a monopoly will make a pricing decision to maximize its revenue.

Revenue is simply the income a company receives, equivalent to the price it charges for its product multiplied by the quantity it sells. Given this definition of revenue, a firm would not operate by setting a price equal to its choke price, or sell so much of its good that it reaches the satiation quantity. The first of these points yields zero quantity sold, and the second point yields a zero price. Either point on the market demand curve would generate zero revenue.

Somewhere between a zero price and a zero quantity is a combination of positive prices and quantities that yield positive revenue. While a competitive firm simply takes the price as given, the monopolist can choose a quantity in between zero and the satiation quantity q_s that offers it the best combination of quantity and price to maximize revenue. It can vary the quantity it offers to the market to receive the best price, or, more accurately, the best product of its price and quantity.

It seems intuitive that this best quantity that maximizes revenue should lie about halfway between a quantity of zero and the satiation quantity q_s. Actually, we find that the revenue maximizing point is indeed exactly halfway between these two points if demand is linear as shown. At that halfway point, revenue peaks out. A slight reduction in the quantity offered forces up prices by a smaller percentage than the quantity reduction, resulting in decreased revenue. Alternately, a small percentage increase in quantity requires a larger percentage decrease in price, again resulting in a decline in revenue.

It is this interplay between small changes in the quantity offered and its effect on revenue that drives the monopolist's decision. Economists label this change in revenue for a small change in quantity as "marginal revenue". We know that the marginal revenue is about equal to the choke price if the monopolist chooses to sell just one unit of the product to the sole highest bidder. We also know that, at least in the case of linear demand, this marginal revenue is zero at some intermediate quantity between zero output and the satiation quantity q_s. This is because at the intermediate quantity, a small change in quantity offered is offset by a corresponding change in price. It turns out that if demand is linear, so is marginal revenue.

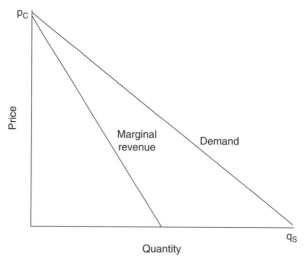

Figure 3   Relationship between demand and marginal revenue

Because marginal revenue equals the choke price p_c at a zero quantity, and equals zero at the intermediate quantity halfway between zero and the satiation quantity q_s, the marginal revenue curve must be twice as steep, as shown in Figure 3.

If changing costs were not a consideration, monopolists would indeed choose to operate halfway down the demand curve at a point where marginal revenue equals zero. However, if costs rise as production rises, the monopolist will perform a slightly different balancing act. Instead, they are doing the best they can do to maximize profits if they produce up to the point where their marginal revenue earned by selling another unit is balanced by the marginal cost incurred by making that last unit.

Marginal cost is defined as the cost a producer incurs to make an extra unit of production. It represents the additional costs of all their factors of production necessary to produce that last unit, but none of the costs incurred for the previous units produced, including overhead costs. Marginal cost cannot be less than zero because an efficient operation cannot produce more with less. These marginal costs can fall with increased production as greater production allows greater efficiencies.

We have called this increased efficiency "economies of scale." Alternately, marginal costs can rise as a production process becomes inefficient. These "diseconomies of scale" arise if a company becomes so large that labor begins to shirk or work less hard beyond a certain point. For instance, diseconomies prevail if the left hand no longer knows what the right hand is doing, if the price of their factors of production start rising as a consequence of greater output, or if management simply becomes sloppy and inefficient.

Every enterprise will eventually enter into this region of diseconomies of scale and increasing per unit costs for an additional unit of production. To see this, let us assume for the moment that a company can always grow through greater economies of scale. If there were always economies of scale and decreasing costs for that last unit of production, then a larger company will always have an advantage over smaller companies.

On a more macro scale, one might erroneously conclude that a larger empire will always be more efficient than a smaller empire, or an ever-larger dinosaur would be mightier than smaller dinosaurs. In fact, every natural activity reaches some point in which it cannot support greater scale and remain nimble, efficient, and effective. Monopolies are no different.

When it is maximizing its profits, the monopolist will balance its marginal revenue (MR) with its typically increasing marginal costs (MC). Indeed, this relationship of MR = MC is the golden rule of profit maximization. In one form or another, it defines equilibrium for almost all economic relationships. It certainly defines to the monopolist the point at which it will maximize profits because, if MR < MC, it is losing money on the last unit produced. Alternatively, if MR > MC, its profits will rise by producing more instead (Figure 4).

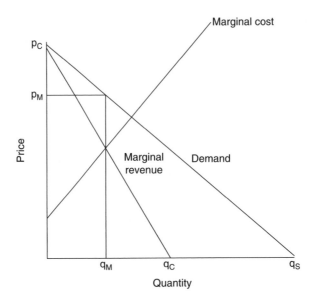

Figure 4   Relationship between market demand, marginal revenue, and marginal cost

By setting marginal revenue to marginal cost, the monopolist explicitly recognizes its ability to set prices by controlling quantity. The monopolist chooses
the output q_M and then moves up from that quantity to determine the price p_M
to extract for its good or service. The product of the price p_M and the quantity
q_M then yields the monopolist's revenue.

What if the monopolist was less strategic and instead kept producing up to
the point in which the marginal cost has risen to the price received for the
product? This is what a competitive firm would do. If so, output would be
expanded from q_M that the monopolist chooses to a higher value q_c that results
when firms are not so strategic. In other words, the monopolist strategically
reduces output to raise prices.

We discovered earlier that this strategy is good for the monopolist but not
good for the consumers who buy the monopolist's products. Obviously, by moving up the demand curve through restricted output, the monopolist is raising
prices on all consumers. Some consumers still get a bargain. Those consumers
high up on the demand curve, because they are willing to pay more for the
product, still receive a surplus, defined as the difference between what they were
willing to pay and the price they actually had to pay. We call this a "consumer's
surplus," and mark it at that area above the price but below the demand curve.

Producers also receive a surplus. It is the difference between the price they
receive and the amount it costs them to produce their first unit, their second
unit, and so on. If their marginal cost curve is simply these incremental costs

for each unit produced, the difference between the price at which the monopolist sells its wares and the marginal cost curve is a measure of their surpluses for each unit produced. We call this the "produce's surplus."

We can see these surpluses represented in the Figure 5 as CS_M and PS_M respectively.

Let us compare the surpluses that consumers and producers enjoy under monopoly with the surpluses they would have enjoyed had the monopolist

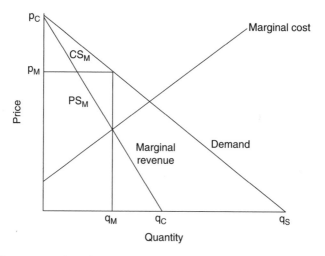

Figure 5 The consumer's and producer's surpluses under monopoly

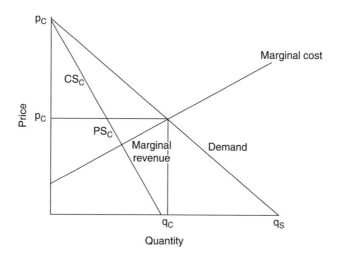

Figure 6 The consumer's and producer's surpluses under competition

not reduced output to increase prices. These larger surpluses to consumers are compared to smaller surpluses to producers.

By comparing Figures 5 and 6, we see that a monopolist sacrifices some of its own producer's surplus in an effort to capture a greater share of consumer's surplus. In doing so, a surplus that both the consumer and the producer would have enjoyed under competition is lost to all. We referred earlier to this as dead-weight loss. It is this reason that monopolies are not in the public interest.

What if a single entity tried to monopolize the purchases of a good or service rather than the provision of a good or service? For instance, we described earlier the actions of the British East India Tea Company and others in the colonial history of Britain. This company had a franchise to be the sole buyer of tea in some regions, even as it had the right to be the sole seller of tea in others. Similarly, laborers under indentured servitude could not sell their services to the highest bidder. Rather, they wear forced to sell their services only to one buyer.

Another type of monopoly

When one buyer can set the terms of a market, it is labeled a monopsony rather than a monopoly.

A monopsonist commits to a similar strategy as does the monopolist. If it knows sellers of their goods or services must deal with the monopsonist or no one at all, it will lowball the price it offers for their goods, services, or factors of production. In doing so, it realizes that some of the sellers of factors of production will choose not to sell at all, even if they would have sold their services had the monopsonist not undercut the wage offered. Because the monopsonist, too, leaves some mutually advantageous potential trades untraded, there is, again, a deadweight loss. This time, rather than the price of the service being too high, the price of the service is set artificially low. The same effect of a deadweight loss nonetheless results.

On the other hand, a competitive industry offers fair and competitive wages and sets competitive prices. In comparison, a monopolist will reduce output and reduce their demand for factors such as labor. While they may be a monopolist in the market for their product, it is possible that they will still be forced to offer a competitive wage in the market for the factors they produce. However, if either a competitive or a monopolistic corporation has some monopsony power in their ability to set wages, they will reduce wages accordingly, or cut corners in worker safety or working conditions.

These big employers were able to flex their monopsony muscle and depress wages that eventually gave rise to labor unions. A union in essence produces a monopoly for labor services to balance the monopsony power of a corporation. However, a union can also flex monopoly power over industries that are operating competitively in both the factor and the product markets.

From innovation creation to rent seeking

Either way, unions raise wages by restricting the provision of labor services. Just as the monopolist creates deadweight losses in product markets when it does the equivalent, labor unions create deadweight losses in the human capital market under similar circumstance. It is willing to create these deadweight losses as it tries to capture some of the surpluses previously enjoyed by the corporation.

It is only human that the only human factor of production would seek its share of the spoils of free enterprise. Labor is the most human of factors of production. We all are endowed with the capacity to work, and most of us survive by selling our time and effort to others. It is only natural for us to attempt to extract the largest reward for our labor. It is also natural for those who command our services to offer us the least we would accept. History is replete with such struggles of caste, class, and segments of society. However, as inequitable as such struggles may be in the eyes of the beholder of injustice, economies thrive on the pursuit of efficiency rather than equity. The realm of politics must instead be used to redress the inequities that result from a myopic quest for efficiency.

When times are good and the economic pie is expanding dramatically, such rent seeking to redress imbalances between sectors of society is often unnecessary. A rising tide will lift all boats, and a rapidly rising tide leaves none behind. It is only when the imbalances become too pronounced or the increases in surpluses become more scarce that an empire's collective efforts are reoriented away from surplus creating and toward rent seeking.

The later part of the Gilded Age resulted in just that shift toward rent seeking. Without economic theory sufficiently well developed to explain what was happening, or a political machine sufficiently insightful or potent to gather the rising storm, a social revolution was on the horizon.

Ultimately, the Gilded Age was battered with a number of financial calamities beginning with the Panic of 1893, its ensuing depression, and further panics in 1907 and 1929, as we shall discuss in depth later. While many commentators mark the end of the Gilded Age as the major political battle, change of government, and the beginning of the Progressive Era in 1896, reform continued on for another two generations.

This period of rapid economic and social upheaval during the Gilded Age, and the Progressive Age that followed, expanded the meaning of democracy. By extending suffrage beyond just the owners of property and to all races and both genders, society heralded in a new era of party politics and class warfare. This gave rise to new government institutions at the behest of whichever political philosophy was in power.

From free enterprise to class warfare

A new era was actually emerging well before a renewal of the power of class warfare. The world's first billion dollar company, United States Steel, resulted from innovations in steel making. The railroads doubled their mileage every few decades, and huge trusts dominated those sectors that fueled the economic expansion. This vibrancy and inventiveness was perhaps best epitomized by the creativity of Thomas Alva Edison. He amassed 1,093 patents in his lifetime, and created General Electric, a company that competed with Nicholas Tesla to electrify the world. Electrification and communications, through the creation of American Telephone and Telegraph Company that brought communications over long distances to the masses, were the envy of the world. At the same time, the efforts of Standard Oil, in both monopolizing a very compact and efficient energy source and in spurring transportation and heating based on oil and gasoline, created the spark from which Henry Ford and others could revolutionize manufacturing and bring consumer goods to the newly created consumer.

These innovations also created the world's first consumer class, a vast group of households that could provide a ready market for the mass produced goods these same households created in factories across an ever-expanding country.

Let us document a growing dissatisfaction with the emerging status quo that had been awakened by growing income disparities and heightened by recurring recessions and depressions.

Unions and the disaffected

There has always been an American folklore that this first economic empire was built upon hard work, and was a meritocracy in a broader world of aristocracies. The American Dream offered a chance to reach for the sky if only one could work harder or produce a better mousetrap. After a generation or two of dreams that rarely came to fruition for the vast majority, this American Dream began to lose its luster. In its place grew a labor movement that would demand a bigger piece of the economic pie if it could not secure a fair share of the growth of the pie.

Labor first flexed its muscles in a significant way in the Great Railroad Strike of 1877. That first broad-based labor disruption ended after a month and a half only when then president Rutherford B. Hayes ordered in federal troops to force rail workers back to work. The grievances continued to smolder, however, and another railroad strike and riots occurred within a decade of the quashed worker rebellion.

By the Great Panic of 1893, still more disaffected workers striked, beginning in the company town of Pullman, Illinois, spilling over as a national rail strike, and ending in the lap of the Supreme Court that ruled such organized withdrawals of labor was tantamount to the very collusion and monopolization that gave rise to the Sherman Antitrust Act.

It would take almost four decades for unions to secure the political support that would permit them to form the coalitions prohibited by the Supreme Court. Meanwhile, politics as usual was taking a turn for the worse.

Major cities such as Boston, Philadelphia, Chicago, and most notoriously, Boss Tweed's Tammany Hall of New York City, raised government corruption and fraud to new levels, and, in turn, raised voters' cynicism. Following the Civil War, parties and new coalitions formed in search of platforms that would ring true with an increasingly disenchanted populace. Some advocated liberalized trade, while others commended protectionism and higher wages. Some labor-oriented groups decried the monopolies, while all decried a corruption that popularly observed government allied with the biggest of business.

The one constancy between both parties was a demand for reform, with the message differing primarily in which direction that reform would take.

Meanwhile, workers the world over still viewed this new and dominating economic empire as a land of, albeit imperfect, opportunity. The Irish fled their land following the years of the Irish Potato Famine and continued to travel to America for generations so they might reunite with their successful American family members. The population of the country swelled, mostly in Eastern Seaboard cities that were the hub of manufacturing and ocean-going commerce.

The immigrants also came from China to build the railroads and work in the mines of a nation ever thirsty for natural resources and the means to bring them to the major manufacturing hubs. While the class struggle was growing with increased economic disaffection, this American economic empire grew more new classes in society than the world had ever seen before.

Actually, rather than embracing these newfound disadvantaged immigrant classes, organized labor shunned them. In the model of monopolization of the supply of labor, unions needed to accomplish two goals.

The first goal was to limit the number of workers eligible for union jobs in their effort to drive up wages. Second was the need to ensure that employers could not draw upon an alternative source of available workers outside of the unions. These second-class citizens were relegated to their own communities, with such ethnically homogenous areas forming in all major cities.

A primordial stew of social change

This economic empire was rapidly growing into a large number of discreet peoples, each with their special interests and peculiar problems and perspectives.

The Irish had their community and interests, as did the Italians, African-Americans, and Chinese, among others.

Women were still looking for the vote, and unions had the goal of controlling the supply of labor just as the robber barons controlled the supply of goods needed for economic prosperity. Groups organized around their interests rather than their country, and each group asserted it had been unfairly excluded from the growth of the economic pie.

In a reactionary response, a movement grew that advocated social Darwinism. This belief extended Darwin's notion of the survival of the fittest in the animal world to the human world and the world of commerce. Many saw advantage in associating themselves with a movement that advocated self-reliance. The theory argued that coddling the poor only creates more poor people in the long run.

None other than Darwin's own second cousin Francis Galton (1822–1911) was a founder of a new social theory called eugenics. Its proponents advocated for selective breeding of humans in order to bring out what were perceived as superior human properties. This theory would also be employed to argue that some races or cultures were simply more adapted to modern economic success. After all, they reasoned, the wealth of the privileged must be some indicator of an innate ability they must have in all matters commercial.

At the same time, groups who had been successful in their own version of commerce were accused of only trading with each other. Resentments over the success of the Chinese, despite the hardships they endured, or of the Jewish, or even the Mennonite, were excuses fueled by frustrations of those who could not get ahead, despite what they perceived as their own best efforts.

With every hardship came greater resentment and disaffection. Elsewhere, in the mid-twentieth century, these resentments eventually resulted in the rise of great powers: Hitler in Germany and Mussolini in Italy. Democracy, combined with disaffection, turned out to be a potent mix that would out-swamp those focusing solely on prosperity.

Even the poor were able to define themselves not from the characteristics they had in common, for they were a most diverse group, but rather for a common enemy – the advocates of Social Darwinism. While Karl Marx had so eloquently observed and labeled a division of classes between the proletariat and the bourgeois, his repositioning of workers over capitalists was downright simplistic when compared to the multitude of divisions emerging in this growing empire. An era of special interests had begun.

Fruit of the rise becomes the seed of decline

The Gilded Age was fueled by an unprecedented Second Industrial Revolution that even eclipsed the brilliance of the First Industrial Revolution secured in England just a century earlier.

Britain was an empire long divided by the aristocracy and the working poor. Philosophers like John Stuart Mill recognized the need to provide a buffer between these two classes through the creation of an educated middle class. English tradition and the rule of law were helpful, though, in preventing the types of isolation and disaffection that could fester into social revolt.

An empire fostered on democracy in politics and in commerce, and a meritocracy that does not confine one to a station in life, has both a new set of opportunities and challenges.

Such opportunities abounded in the United States. Protection of property and the creation of free markets uncork creativity and enterprise never before seen. A country rallied around a growing economic pie, and increasingly began to focus on how the pie was sliced. The democratization of opportunity led all to believe that any individual could be the next millionaire. When millionaires were being created and displayed almost constantly, it was easy to subscribe to an American Dream that was likely more fiction than reality for the vast majority.

There can only be so much economic creativity and explosive growth, however. Growth requires markets and that growth can outstrip the ability of markets to absorb the newfound bounty. Likewise, if it becomes impossible for people to work any harder to purchase the goods of others, growth begins to stagnate.

However, it is dangerous to take material growth away from a culture and an economy that has come to expect it. An economy grown accustomed to double-digit economic growth is downright despondent if growth falls to a still strong but much more sustainable 2% or 3% rate.

The United States was poised for similar growth in the early part of the nineteenth century, not unlike India and China today on the cusp of dramatic economic empowerment. Both countries regularly experience double-digit economic growth, not solely from the entrepreneurial spirit of its people, but also from its great capacity to grow.

If real growth begins to falter, a few weaknesses of this model become much more apparent. In an effort to maintain growth and prosperity in an economic downturn, it is enticing to focus on paper wealth rather than real wealth. Real production is then replaced by financial production and illusion, as we will see in the next chapter. The stock of real wealth production is instead leveraged by attempts to make it flow more rapidly.

Big financial capitalists and big human capitalists, alike, increasingly try to expand what is theirs by coveting what is another's share of the pie. Financial capitalists can expand their surpluses by securing more consumers' surplus or by depressing wages of workers. They do so by reducing output to raise prices or by reducing their demand for, and hence the wage offered to workers. In turn, workers demand a greater share by limiting producers' access to labor and by advocating "closed shops" in an effort to drive up wages.

Meanwhile, government prone to laissez-faire economics finds it impossible to stay ahead of economic evolution.

Finally, while everyone is a hero in good times, every group clamors to find scapegoats to blame in more challenging times. A plethora of special interests form, with each group arguing that another is to blame, and each group demanding, through whatever political channels it can tap into, a greater share of a slowly growing, stagnating, or declining economic pie.

Indeed, this division into special interests can become downright destructive. The focus eventually shifted away from production and into redistribution of wealth from a group out of favor to a group in favor. Political coalitions form that are adept at peeling off just enough of the disaffected to win an election. This skews the balance into its constituency's favor, at least until another coalition can form.

9
Private Solutions to Public Problems

He who fears he shall suffer already suffers what he fears.
(Michel Eyquem de Montaigne, 1533–1592)[39]

The Gilded Age was one of the most rapid periods of economic expansion and innovation ever seen. It was enabled by a new form of government by the people and for the people, and on the premise of private property, personal responsibility, and limited government. It thrived in the first nation to adopt "laissez-faire" as a prevailing economic principle, with a government that had an inherent bias to stand out of the way of commerce.

Government, especially one in its infancy, certainly could not anticipate every possible form that commerce would take. A new American government wanted to encourage the expansion of its economy based on hard work and production, and not through rent seeking and attempts to circumvent or transform laws for personal benefit. The government, and the economic empire the government engendered, was very much an experiment in progress.

The inability of a government to stay ahead of, or at least not too far behind, commerce is illustrated by a series of economic missteps, made all the worse by a government that failed to respond in time. In other times, government responded in the most unfortunate of ways. We will delve into some of these missteps to demonstrate the groping process that is undertaken to rein in entrepreneurial exuberance over time.

Insufficient banking

Within a generation of ratification of its constitution, a young United States was facing its first economy-wide panic. Saddled with debt from its defense against Britain in the War of 1812 and the westward rural expansion, and without a reliable and sufficient base for tax revenue, the government had borrowed heavily. Meanwhile, banks had been expanding rapidly, but without the oversight of a public agency.

This overexpansion culminated in the necessity to curtail lending and call in loans. As we have repeatedly seen, most recently in the global Credit Crisis of 2007, a banking industry unable or unwilling to lend is a drag on the economy. As a consequence, in 1819, an infant nation experienced its first economic panic.

A federal government in its infancy and founded on laissez-faire principles was reluctant to intervene in the private banking industry. This reluctance was despite the facilitating role banks had in providing the government with access to funds that helped support the war.

When President Monroe did act, it was inadequate. He first imposed a moratorium to prevent the conversion of soft money like notes into hard gold or silver. This moratorium helped trigger a panic as depositors demanded their cash. However, with banks increasingly failing, the industry could not meet the needs of these demanders. Without sufficient currency, the oil that lubricated the economic machinery was disappearing. Hoarding of cash and an insufficient supply of money caused prices to fall.

On first blush, price deflation sounds like a good thing. Consumers appreciate falling prices. However, producers do not. They are too often tied to long-term obligations in loans and factor markets, but unable to cover their costs when product prices are falling. In addition, lenders will not loan money if they believe the value of the loan may soon be larger than the value of the asset that collateralizes the loan. Without lenders and producers, the economic machinery comes to a grinding halt.

Just as in the more recent Credit Crisis of 2007, there was a clamor to forgive borrowers of their underwater loans. There was also an effort to reflate the money supply by printing more cash. Neither policy was sound as both imposed the inevitable costs on one economic group or another. And, neither policy should be advocated in the absence of a politically independent monetary authority. Solutions that appeal to the populous are often unsound upon closer scrutiny. The economic leaders would not understand the crucial mechanics of monetary policy until more than a century later. While the panic eventually abated, the lessons unlearned would come back to haunt the nation within a generation.

Britain's more advanced monetary system

A few years later, in 1825, Britain, too, was experiencing an economic breakdown driven by its monetary system. While Britain's monetary system was more sophisticated, it, too, was insufficient to meet all needs pressed through Britain's borrowing for the War of 1812 and the Napoleonic Wars. Britain was expanding rapidly, which also challenged its market for borrowing and loanable funds.

Exacerbating this growing credit crunch was a London Stock Market that was experiencing a speculative bubble. The bubble-induced increase in wealth and the spending fueled by debt was sufficiently inflationary that the monetary authorities discerned the need to sop up market liquidity. By selling some of its stockpile of government bonds, the Bank of England absorbed excess cash and reduced market liquidity.

This monetary tightening caused a contraction of credit, too, and induced a run on its banks and increased defaults from business borrowers.

An economic empire creates an unfortunate aspect. An economic virus in the homeland quickly spreads to the hinterland. The panic quickly spread to Europe and to British colonies in Latin America and elsewhere. While the central bank's effort to curb the speculative bubble worked, the unintended global consequences demonstrated the danger of pursuing a national economic policy in a global environment.

It is unnerving that a monetary crisis in 1825 could so easily be replicated in a much more global and affluent economy 183 years later. A growing body of experience and a better understanding of monetary theory and the role of banks could not avert a credit crisis and a global financial meltdown, even in 2008.

Panics give way to depressions

Neither the U.S. nor the British panics caused the more severe collapse of an economy that we might call a depression. However, the U.S. panic of 1837 could not be so contained.

This failure to control the 1837 panic illustrated the weakness of a government one step behind the private sector. It also pointed out that policy is most dangerous when it adheres to ideology in times of crisis.

In 1837, a new President Van Buren steadfastly refused to intervene with sufficient engagement to prevent a market panic from descending into a depression that rivaled the Great Depression a century later. Indeed, it would not be until the panic of 1907 that the United States would generate the will to place monetary policy in the hands of an independent monetary authority. Not until the failure of President Hoover to avert the Great Depression would there be broad acceptance for the role of fiscal spending by government in times when every other sector refuses to spend would not occur.

The government's free market idolatry in the wake of the economic crisis in 1837 gave rise to rioting in the streets of New York City, followed by a depression that would last for the next few years. The roots of the panic should by now be familiar. A huge run-up of paper profits in financial markets, a growing income disparity between the haves and the have-nots, and the untoward relations between a government and some of the nation's largest banks.

As we see time and time again, intervention was too slow in 1837. Consequently, almost half of the country's banks failed. The scale of bank failures was as mammoth as the failures in the Great Depression, and pointed out first, but not for all time, the important role of banking as a backbone of the economy. The ensuing deflation and depression held the nation back for five years.

Crashes go global

While we often think of global economics as a recent phenomenon, the Panic of 1857 proved that history repeats itself. In what has become a common theme, a dramatic bank failure created a panic that could not be contained within an economic empire.

In 1857, an act of embezzlement at the Ohio Life Insurance and Trust Company created a crisis of confidence within the insurance and banking industry. Investors then repatriated funds away from U.S. markets. In this case, the U.S. Treasury simply did not have the resources to stem the tide and maintain market liquidity. This loss of currency resulted in the now familiar deflation that exacerbated a growing credit crisis. Just as in other crises in a nation in its infancy, inadequate economic leadership induced the economic system to worsen significantly before it could mend itself.

The global economy proved, though, that growing trade fueled by one rapidly growing economy can also fall victim to inadequate economic leadership in that economy. Just as do our leaders today, the common response to economic hardship was to repeal to mercantilism and curtailed international trade. This inward looking reaction also fueled the growing voices of division in the United States, which soon culminated into its Civil War.

Importation of financial crises

The implication of the export of domestic economic crisis can work both ways. In 1873, excessive debt, malfeasance, and expansion in Germany precipitated the failure of the Vienna Stock Exchange and a number of European banks. At the same time, a major railroad expansion in the United States, led by American financier Jay Cooke, went into bankruptcy.

With the collapse of one of Europe's major stock exchanges, and with the movement of the U.S. Treasury away from a dual gold/silver standard to a gold standard, commodity and asset prices collapsed in the United States as well. For the first time, monetary issues and currency/precious-metal standards were the subject of presidential campaigns. An awareness of the important role of the Treasury and economic leaders was beginning to coalesce.

In the height of the panic in 1873, the New York Stock Exchange was forced to close for ten days in the wake of the failure of a quarter of the nation's railroads.

Unemployment escalated to double-digit levels, and labor strife gave wind to the sails of the U.S. labor movement. This depression would go on to last six more years.

Lessons not quite learned

The money supply, a vulnerable banking industry, and precarious finances in rapidly expanding railroads seemed to be prevailing themes in all previous panics. One would imagine that these repeated patterns would eventually be better recognized. However, the problem is not in recognition. Rather, it pointed to inadequate tools free markets employ on occasion to curb the excesses.

In 1893, the United States celebrated the 400th anniversary of the arrival of Christopher Columbus. In tribute, the Chicago World's Fair celebrated America's Gilded Age and rapid technological and industrial transformation. Moving pictures, fluorescent lighting, power generation, and modern consumer novelties such as hamburgers, Cracker Jack, the Hershey Bar, Juicy Fruit gum, and the Ferris Wheel fascinated a new and burgeoning middle-class America.

This exuberance spilled out into financial markets in the form of a speculative bubble. Just as we saw a global dot.com bust in the 1990s following a wave of high priced and high profile acquisitions, we saw an equally spectacular crash of the railroad mergers of the 1870s, that were fueled by unprecedented levels of debt and speculation.

Early in 1893, the Philadelphia and Reading Railroad was bankrupted, and the same notorious Northern Pacific Railroad that precipitated the 1873 panic also went under, followed by the Union Pacific Railroad and others. Banks who lent these railroads money soon failed and European capital that had been flowing into a rapidly growing U.S. economy just as quickly flowed back out.

This panic especially hit the ports and mill towns of the Eastern United States that were the engines of U.S. industrialization. The resulting high unemployment induced millions to migrate west, in search of gold and growing western infrastructures. In some sense, the calamity of 1893 created an opportunity for another wave of growth.

Financial chicanery

Certainly, bank inadequacies and the overextension of credit, crises of faith in the financial system, and inadequate monetary policy fueled by economic idolatry help explain most panics. The panic of 1901 came from a more nefarious source. Again, railroads were at center stage.

This time, a battle of the financial titans created a panic that remained confined primarily to financial markets. On one side was William Rockefeller, through his First National City Bank and Standard Oil, and James Stillman, New York financier. On the other side were J.P. Morgan and Jacob Schiff, with the Union Pacific Railroad. This battle of titans was over an attempt to monopolize all railroad traffic in and out of Chicago, America's gateway to the midwest and the west.

This attempt at monopolization brought down the entire railroad sector as panicky stockholders unloaded their railroad stock. With railroads the premier sector on the market, the Dow Jones Industrial Average gave back the run-up it had enjoyed in the previous three years. In the end, a railroad empire did manage to monopolize the Chicago market, only to find itself broken up by application of the Sherman Antitrust Act designed to prevent just the formation of trusts, or holding companies, that monopolize markets.

This financial failure ran its course, without the economic disruptions seen in previous crashes. It also induced a wave of regulations with the Interstate Commerce Commission given the power in 1906 to regulate railroad rates. And, it also set the stage for perhaps the final stand of the private sector to regulate itself.

The panic of panics

This last stand of private failure and benign public neglect came in perhaps the greatest panic to that date. In 1907, financier Otto Heinze, his brother, the Montana copper magnate F. Augustus Heinze, and an investor named Charles Moore were implicated in a scheme to manipulate the price of the stock of F. Augustus' copper company. In the end, the ploy failed, forcing Otto to sell quickly the copper stock he had hoped to manipulate. In the end, the price of United Copper toppled, as did the Knickerbocker Trust Company that bankrolled this scheme.

Once the market got wind of the scheme, there was a run on Knickerbocker Trust and of the large New York bank that F. Augustus, as a member of its board, had convinced to invest in United Copper. As these failures winded down, other major banks refused to lend. This tightening of capital caused a series of bank failures that went well beyond New York City finances.

J.P. Morgan was the king of the New York banking and finance network at that time. In a pique of private-sector proaction, he called an emergency meeting of the Wall Street financial kingpins. Those attending reported that he assembled the group in his library, had the door locked from the outside, and insisted that no one would leave the room until they had come up with a solution.

The ploy worked, and the bankers pledged sufficient funds to keep vulnerable banks afloat. Morgan also assembled two committees – one to convince the newspaper press that order had been maintained, and the other to have clergy tell their flocks on Sunday to have faith in the prevailing financial system. Morgan maintained a firm grip on the tiller to the private-sector economy in the meantime, and even convinced then President Theodore Roosevelt to suspend regulation of one particular merger that Morgan felt was essential.

These efforts in total were partially successful. While the stock market lost almost half its value, and bankruptcies and unemployment doubled over the next year, perhaps potentially the most dangerous collapse to that date was averted. However, the calamity also induced President Woodrow Wilson to sign legislation in 1913 creating the U.S. Federal Reserve System to regulate banks and financial institutions. While the system was not sufficiently sophisticated to avert the Great Depression, it did emerge as the world's most powerful economic institution over the next half century.

The end of private solutions

By the 1920s, it seemed like almost everyone had forgotten past panics. As with the run-up to previous panics, almost everybody with some surplus cash were fully invested in yet another rapidly rising financial market. The Gilded Age had become co-opted by the middle class, who had since discovered consumerism, high finance, and borrowing on margins to speculate in a rapidly growing financial market.

This was a golden age for an economic empire that was barely a century old and had just recently eclipsed Great Britain as the world's largest economy. Anything seemed possible, driven by a rapidly growing private sector. The theory of Social Darwinism was taking hold in the United States and Europe, and affluence was thought to soon breed even more affluence. F. Scott Fitzgerald wrote about excesses and affluence in a manner that piqued the interest of the entire world.

In this wave, Calvin Coolidge was elected to the U.S. presidency, followed by Herbert Hoover. Hoover's landslide election, in particular, was a testament to a wave of confidence in free markets and the private sector. Again, economic idealism translated into political ideology and idolatry. Taxes on the wealth were cut back as many developed a faith in trickle-down economics, and many more felt that they too would be wealthy some day. The Dow Jones Industrial Average rose more than 500% in eight years, while inflation remained subdued.

Hoover won his election in 1928 with a landslide victory, despite the fact that he had never stood for public office before. He had been a Republican cabinet secretary based on his success as a manager in the private sector and received acclaim for his handling of a disastrous flood in Louisiana while a secretary. He had an almost blinding faith in free markets, which did not allow him to recognize the looming economic tragedy that would follow in the aftermath of the Great Crash of the U.S. stock market in 1929.

The Great Crash, following the 500% run-up of the stock market over eight years, was no longer confined to wealthy financiers. Millions of small "investors" were highly leveraged, too, having borrowed substantially to buy more stock, with past stock run ups acting as the collateral. When a market correction occurred in October of 1929, many of these investors were forced to sell to cover their margin loans. These forced sales converted a market correction into a major crash.

However, it would be simplistic to conclude that a stock market crash plunged the economic empire and much of the developed world into the Great Depression. Indeed, a year later, the market had recovered 90% of its 1929 value.

Instead, it was a wave of bank failures, once again, that precipitated the crash. From 30,000 banks in the 1920s to 15,000 banks in the midst of the Great Depression, millions of families lost their life savings. A fear-gripped economy caused both consumers and producers to stop spending.

A common impulse in any crisis is to shut the gates to the fort. Actually, a year before the Crash, Congress had passed the Smoot Hawley Tariff Act in an effort to sustain domestic growth for an economy increasingly transfixed by financial production over the production of real goods and services. The Act of neo-mercantilism in a country, which had not yet entirely shaken off its mercantilist tendencies, was designed to discourage imports and, hence, stimulate domestic demand. However, like every effort at mercantilism, it instead resulted in retaliation from other countries. Ultimately, like most beggar-thy-neighbor policies, all lost out, with world trade declining by two-thirds in just five years.

Meanwhile, president Hoover was reluctant to commit the federal government to intervention in the private economy. To his credit, he finally allocated funds to the states to prevent layoffs and initiated some large-scale federal projects, most notably the Hoover Dam. However, his efforts were too little and too late.

A self-fulfilling prophecy

In the tailing years of the Hoover Administration, industrial production in the United States fell by almost one half. Ten million people joined the ranks of the unemployed. Like other panics, this one was fuelled by gloom and fright. Understandably, nervous producers laid off workers until they could sell off their inventories. In addition, consumer purchases dropped off, as people feared for their jobs, which further extended the inventory selloff. Reduced demand and layoffs created subsequent waves of reduced demand and layoffs as producers and consumers alike kept tightening their belts. The downward spiral was the consequence of a self-fulfilling prophecy that the depression-era economist John Maynard Keynes would label "the paradox of thrift." Meanwhile, bankers were caught in the middle.

This economic crisis is now the most studied economic event of all time. However, at that time, there was no theory that would explain the economics and the human tragedies that were slowly unfolding.

Economists of that day had subscribed to a classical economic principle called Say's Law. Named after Jean-Baptiste Say, a nineteenth century political economist, this law argued that the supply of goods and services creates its own demand. Borrowing from the microeconomic concept of equilibrium, it was believed that the production of goods created the income for workers that would subsequently create the demand for the goods produced. If the macro economy could be viewed as a collection of microeconomic markets, and if supply creates its own demand in microeconomics on average, the macro economy could not underperform for long.

Consequently, the prevailing theory was that not only could government do nothing to combat economic downturns, but also there was nothing that government should do to get an ailing economy back on track.

At that time, Keynes had not fully described the Keynesian theory that would repeal Say's Law. Keynes understood that human psychology had been left out of the economic models. While he agreed that income creates spending, and that income must equal the sum of all spending in equilibrium, he acknowledged that consumers and investors, government and international traders, also played a role.

Keynes also recognized that, with the richest 1% of all households owning 40% of all wealth, changes in the spending pattern of some could have a dramatic effect on the rest. He realized that, with this concentration of wealth, a broad but shaken middle class could not mount the spending necessary to drag a nation, and indeed a world, out of the greatest global depression in history.

The lack of understanding that reduced demand from anxious consumers and producers contributed to a self-fulfilling prophecy was further reinforced by a lack of appreciation of monetary policy. While the United States had created a central banking system two decades earlier, the Federal Reserve did not yet have a coherent policy based on an extensive understanding of the macro economy. The Great Depression calamity would create both an activist government, through fiscal policy in times of economic crises, and an activist Federal Reserve charged with keeping inflation at manageable levels in normal times and unemployment at manageable levels in hard times.

In addition to the repeal of Say's Law in the Great Depression, the U.S. economic empire also repealed a form of laissez-faire economics it had originally helped forge.

Fruit of the rise becomes the seed of decline

Just as the social upheaval following the Gilded Age demonstrated, it is exceedingly difficult for government to anticipate and control every misguided attempt of free enterprise to innovate in less than economically healthy ways. An economic empire eventually recognizes the symptoms that give rise to the problems that bring down an economy. However, almost as quickly as an unhealthy economic innovation is kindled and put out, another new scheme is hatched.

A young nation that grew very quickly and was thrust into the role of the world's largest economy also demonstrated painful vulnerabilities. Rapidly evolving capitalism vastly outstripped the ability of government and regulation to keep up. While free enterprise prefers to self-regulate, even mighty attempts at self-regulation fails when an economy becomes sufficiently complex.

What government is slow to remember each time is the need to recognize the problems when it means taking away the punchbowl during a fantastic party. The very nature of free market ideology gets in the way time and time again. However, this free market nature is also what leads economies to new heights.

Part III
The New Mercantilists

The original economic empire grew based on its free market principles. However, its period of ascendancy was also based on the convenient theory of mercantilism. This theory that maximized exports, but discouraged imports not in the form of gold or raw materials, took further hold in the 1920s and helped fuel the Great Depression.

This new mercantilism can take many disguises, as we will see.

10
The Consumer as King

> Therefore, to be possess'd with double pomp,
> To guard a title that was rich before,
> To gild refined gold, to paint the lily,
> To throw a perfume on the violet,
> To smooth the ice, or add another hue
> Unto the rainbow, or with taper-light
> To seek the beauteous eye of heaven to garnish,
> Is wasteful and ridiculous excess.
>
> (William Shakespeare, *King John*, 1595)

Power and status were once the privilege of the aristocracy. Indeed, France's Louis XIV (1638–1735) made ostentatious display of wealth, power, and status an essential element of his leadership. The opulence of wealth by the aristocracy served the dual purposes of displaying the relative position of royalty and its lords in the king's court, while at the same time bleeding lesser elites dry of financial resources that might be used in rivalry to the royalty and others.

Louis XIV developed elaborate systems that indicated the relative position of the elite in his court.[40] These systems allowed the king to rule from 1643 to 1715, an unprecedented 72 years, as the aristocracy was forced to devote resources to "keep up with the Jones'" rather than vie for power by challenging the king.[41]

The tradition of excesses was followed by Louis XVI, whose rein began in 1774 and ended quite abruptly in 1792. This tradition of conspicuous consumption as an indication of social status ultimately fomented revolution in France and caused Louis XVI to lose his head, quite literally.

These same forces also induce affluent economic empires today to shift toward consumption rather than production.

Conspicuous consumption

Inevitably, those accumulating or earning surpluses will consume in a way that, almost unavoidably, is observed by others who are less fortunate. The rapid and ostentatious shift in this conspicuous consumption can be destabilizing; Louis XIV's concern about up-and-comers and their destabilizing effect on elaborately constructed and balanced hierarchies induced him to develop rules for social and economic advancement.

Although Shakespeare (1564–1616) died 22 years before Louis XIV was born, his line "to gild refined gold to paint a lily...is wasteful and ridiculous" could have as easily been a comment on the Louis XIV's court. Its conspicuous consumption shifted the emphasis of an economy from production to a striving for the fruits displayed by others. We should not be surprised that such conspicuous consumption in America's Gilded Age would shift a nation's eyes from efficiency toward equity or envy, just as this call for greater equity motivated the French Revolution a century earlier.

The prevailing neo-classical model of economics assumes that households derive happiness, satisfaction, or utility by their consumption of goods and services. It is intuitively interpreted that this consumption from contemporaneous income, or in the future through savings, is derived from the ability of goods or services to satisfy our needs. However, economic theory does not preclude a less utilitarian interpretation. It might be the case that individuals purchase goods and services simply to signal to others their status in society.

While such conspicuous consumption might appear to serve no utilitarian function, it nonetheless represents a form of spending not inconsistent with economic theory. The noted nineteenth-century economist Thorstein Veblen was the first to model such consumption in his book *The Theory of the Leisure Class*.[42] His theory will become a central part of our later description of the contemporary form of conspicuous consumption.

Hierarchy of wants and needs

There is nothing in economic theory that would require consumers to prefer more substantive, socially useful, and utilitarian consumption over other forms of consumption. Sociologists and psychologists recognize a tiered level of activities that can satisfy human wants. In the 1943, Abraham Maslow, an American psychologist, argued in his paper "A Theory of Human Motivation" that there is actually a hierarchy or pyramid of human needs.[43] The lower, more basic, needs are physiological deficiencies and include the need to breath, to eat, to satisfy the sexual instinct, and to seek basic physical comfort. Anxiety is created if these needs are not met.

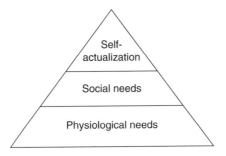

Figure 7   Simplified Maslow's Hierarchy of Wants and Needs

With the satisfaction of basic physiological needs, the individual turns her attention to the need for health and safety, and for personal and financial security. These longer-term needs are in recognition that present survival is provided for, inducing a shift of emphasis toward future survival. Failure to provide for these longer-term needs creates worry and anxiety for an individual.

Next are social needs that satisfy the wants of human emotion. Humans strive for belonging, to family and to community. These communities could be organized around a common religion or spirituality, a common love of sports, or even a common participation in larger phenomena like a simultaneously viewed television show or movie. Those who fail to meet this need have a sense of loneliness or depression.

A modern economy allows participants to meet present physical needs and save for the future to give participants confidence that future physical needs will also be met. Society also provides a culture within which all participants operate. This culture and sense of shared heritage and destiny provide individuals with a sense of belonging.

Once an economy and a society can comfortably meet these basic needs through production and through institutions, individuals increasingly want to know that their position in society is respected and valued. This pride and respect of one's self, derived from a sense of personal value and contribution to social institutions, is satisfied with increasing sophistication in a more diverse and complete society that is able to satisfy the various lower needs for the vast majority of its citizens. Without this satisfaction, a society's citizens feel inferior or depressed.

This need for esteem may be further divided into lower needs of respect, recognition, or prestige. These needs require external validation and are dependent on how others regard the individual. Those who can move beyond these more primitive needs depend more on internally derived self-respect or self-esteem. These inner competencies, according to Maslow, are more productive and less dangerous than the wants that must be satisfied through external validation.

Finally, the last want in the hierarchy is for self-actualization. This highest level in the Hierarchy of Wants and Needs is realized if an individual can recognize she has reached her potential in life and hence has satisfied an inner calling. While these callings are different for each individual and may keep changing for an individual over time, the realization of self-actualization gives one the sense of belonging in a greater scheme of life. With this level of contentment comes acceptance and greater comfort with life, with all its glories and failings.

Inevitability of special interests

Likewise, a growing economy moves through this pyramid of wants and needs. Moving from a nomadic culture without firm roots to an agrarian economy, households found it easier to meet their basic needs for food and shelter. Specialization of labor further enabled households to acquire surpluses and plan for the future. The agrarian economy also allowed society to more easily create community and to grow in size.

Security in the basic needs and the ability to build community led households to focus on higher-level wants. As the population grew, an economy produced a greater diversity of goods to best meet household needs. It also created allegiances to smaller clubs and communities. These sub-communities not only reduced allegiances to the greater community. A plethora of clubs allow almost every citizen to meet their needs on more individual bases.

This disassociation from a larger community and allegiance to a special interest is almost inevitable as the larger community becomes more dilute and impersonal. Community can be rebuilt by such constructs as patriotic zeal that can, occasionally, bring an economic nation together and give all a sense of belonging.

When nationalistic fervor unites an economic empire, as when a war-torn Britain is united by its "blood, toil, sweat, and tears" in the words of Winston Churchill, an economy can put special interests aside in the interest of a greater principle. However, without such a tie that binds a growing community, economies eventually evolved into a collection of special interests rather than an aggregation around a national interest.

A baser yardstick

A thriving economy does not obviate the need for its participants to somehow measure themselves against each other. While it is simple to communicate social worth and esteem to a close-knit group that can easily discern one's accomplishments, it is more difficult to convey this esteem in a larger community.

With innovations in transportation and communications, it is much more likely that the community with which one most closely associates is not the community in one's neighborhood. As an economy grows, the associations we make are less geographically based. One will have an allegiance to one's town, and perhaps even an association to one's street, without knowing most, or even many, people in the town or on the street.

This disassociation from one's neighborhood does not change humans' need for esteem from others. However, if it is difficult to signal to others living near us the degree of our individual successes, how does one demonstrate that she has arrived?

This measurement of success must be correlated with spiritual, cultural, or economic success, and must be easily signaled to others. Households may construct shrines to their spirituality to signal to others their commitment and accomplishment in spiritual enlightenment. Others can demonstrate taste and sophistication in evidence of their cultural enlightenment. However, not all observers understand more sophisticated spiritual or cultural signals, especially if these signals are not ones universally recognized.

The measure denoting one has arrived economically is a signal most all understand. Because all households participate in the marketplace, all understand the cost and significance of consumer icons. A nice house, nice cars, a nice yard or pool, and children who attend exclusive schools are all indicators that a family unit has succeeded economically. These forms of conspicuous consumption are statements in the absence of other more substantial and less frivolous activities.

Trappings

These trappings of success, purchased not only for personal enjoyment but also to generate envy and esteem from others, are not new. Opulence has always been an activity practiced by the wealthiest and the aristocracy.

The unusual phenomenon that occurs when an economic empire comes of age is that these trappings become more affordable and more important to the middle class who are more easily able to satisfy their lesser needs. These trappings of the middle class become conspicuous consumption for an economy as a whole.

In the process, an economy transcends from one that emphasizes production to one that emphasized consumption. And that makes all the difference.

Such a transformation is an almost inevitable consequence of growth. Economic growth is rarely distributed evenly. Instead, there are winners and losers, or at least big winners and those who are less successful. The differential growth naturally causes humans to compare their lot to others more or less successful. This dynamic nature of a growing economy is disruptive for economic empires, just as Louis XIV found up-and-coming aristocrats disruptive of the balance he strived to establish in his court.

Some cultures have prevented movement between the classes. For instance, the caste system of India defined one's place in society from birth. Even critics of such a system acknowledge its roots in creating contentment for one's station in life and in preventing the destabilizing effort to transcend the classes. Such a system is liberating at least from the perspective that it attenuates otherwise natural comparisons between individuals and certainly between classes.

Nouveau riche

When Veblen began to write about the excesses of the nouveau riche in the throes of the Second Industrial Revolution and the Gilded Age, he was describing the mansions of the Vanderbilts or the grand yachts and parties of what others were labeling the robber barons. In 1899, he could not have anticipated the masses of an emerging middle class that would soon emerge.

Of course, the excesses the wealthiest could and would afford were more gold plated than the conspicuous consumption afforded by a middle-class worker who had "arrived." However, the tens of millions of people in the middle class of an economic empire aggregated to greater total excess than the top percentage of wealth earners who could afford the most excessive trappings of success.

In our modern times, these trappings of the middle class may go beyond nice homes. Fads allow those on modest means to signal to others that they, too, have arrived. An individual may not be able to afford a nice home. However, that individual can still dress fashionably, eat at expensive restaurants, drive nice cars, and give indications to others that they have arrived. Only those who live down their street or in their apartment building would know otherwise.

Authors Stanley and Danko, in *The Millionaire Next Door* argue that the wealthy may not feel the need to display the trappings of wealth. These individuals can transcend the need for esteem from others and can recognize from their self-esteem that they have succeeded in their chosen callings.[44]

These individuals of higher wealth are found to be more careful with their money, invest their wealth carefully for long-term profit rather than short-term signaling, and often live modest lives. Meanwhile, their neighbors of more meager means often are in debt and fail to provide for their retirement, but drive large Sport Utility Vehicles (SUVs) and live in much larger homes with each generation.

Indeed, John Stuart Mill, the economic philosopher who commented on an emerging middle class in the sunrise of the Second Industrial Revolution wrote on the need to tax luxuries to avoid the caustic and unproductive effect of conspicuous consumerism. Writing in 1848, in his book *Principles of Political Economy with some of their Applications to Social Philosophy*, he commented on the need to levy taxes impartially on consumption but with prejudice toward those luxury goods that we may now label as vehicles for conspicuous consumption:

There are some forms of indirect taxation that must be peremptorily excluded. Taxes on commodities, for revenue purposes, must not operate as protecting duties, but must be levied impartially on every mode in which the articles can be obtained, whether produced in the country itself or imported. An exclusion must also be put upon all taxes on the necessaries of life, or on the materials or instruments employed in producing those necessaries. Such taxes are always liable to encroach on what should be left untaxed, the incomes barely sufficient for healthful existence; and on the most favorable supposition, namely, that wages rise to compensate the labourers for the tax, it operates as a peculiar tax on profits, which is at once unjust, and detrimental to national wealth. What remain are taxes on luxuries. And these have some properties that strongly recommend them. In the first place, they can never, by any possibility, touch those whose whole income is expended on necessaries; while they do reach those by whom what is required for necessaries is expended on indulgences. In the next place, they operate in some cases as an useful, and the only useful, kind of sumptuary law. I disclaim all asceticism, and by no means wish to see discouraged, either by law or opinion, any indulgence (consistent with the means and obligations of the person using it) that is sought from a genuine inclination for, and enjoyment of, the thing itself; but a great portion of the expenses of the higher and middle classes in most countries, and the greatest in this, is *not incurred for the sake of the pleasure afforded by the things on which the money is spent, but from regard to opinion, and an idea that certain expenses are expected from them, as an appendage of station; and I cannot but think that expenditure of this sort is a most desirable subject of taxation.* If taxation discourages it, some good is done, and if not, no harm; for in so far as taxes are levied on things that are desired and possessed from motives of this description, nobody is the worse for them. When a thing is bought not for its use but for its value, cheapness is no recommendation. As Sismondi remarks, the consequence of cheapening articles of vanity is not that less is expended on such things, but that the buyers substitute for the cheapened article some other which is more costly, or a more elaborate quality of the same thing, and as the inferior quality answered the purpose of vanity equally well when it was equally expensive, a tax on the article is really paid by nobody: it is a creation of public revenue by which nobody loses. (my emphasis added).[45]

Veblen's treatise entitled *The Theory of the Leisure Class* supports this theme broached by Mill and others. While he meant his treatise as an essay of social commentary, his analysis on the institutions of our society that cater to conspicuous consumption transformed his social essay into a textbook of modern commerce. For instance, he observed that professional sports were at once an activity that formed community and an opportunity for spectators to signal they were sufficiently affluent to afford such leisure. He also wryly contemplated that silver spoons cost more, and perform their function perhaps less effectively than less expensive alternatives.

Veblen's argument that manners and etiquette are useless and inefficient frivolities induced some to view his work as a social satire rather than economics. His argument that merchants serve no function but to extract income from true producers and consumers by injecting themselves into the middle appealed to the common sentiment of those always searching for a bargain.

In fact, his commentary has been embraced more by sociologists than by economists. However, his reasoning is familiar to many economists. He questioned those institutions that do not contribute directly to consumption and to the satisfaction of basic human needs. At the time of his writing, he did not have the benefit of Maslow's study of a hierarchy of human wants and needs.

Perhaps a better parallel can be offered in the example that began this chapter. Louis XIV created a race for opulence among his aristocracy in an effort to distract them from more damaging pursuits. In a conspicuous consumption analogy, an expensive race in which everyone ultimately keeps up serves no differentiating power to discriminate between who has truly arrived. Instead, the effort can be viewed as a distraction and an unfortunate waste of effort.

Other similarly costly races to the bottom could be the arms race, the drive toward bigger and consequently less fuel-efficient cars in the interest of safety, but resulting only in bigger cars for everyone and thus no additional safety, or the competition among states in a union to attract industry from other states. Each of these activities appears necessary in isolation but provides no gains, and considerable costs, in the long run as everyboby adopts the same strategy.

Such races to the bottom should be differentiated by competitions that improve economic welfare or productivity or human excellence. A race to innovate and reap the rewards of patent protection, or a sporting race that creates better athletes, each has redeeming economic or human value.

A rationale for taxation

Mill also observed the caustic economic effects of conspicuous consumption. He recommended that the unproductive, and even destructive, aspects of conspicuous consumption warranted economic discouragement in the form of luxury taxes.

Economists argue two purposes for taxation. One purpose for taxes is to raise the revenue necessary to provide the goods and services that only government can efficiently provide, or provide in any event. Such taxes should be non-distorting, designed not to distort the pattern of consumption that would otherwise occur.

The second justification for taxation is to remedy market failings. Sometimes the market produces or consumes too little of something of value. This under-production or under consumption may warrant subsidies. However, at other times, an economy produces or consumes something that provides unfortunate consequences. Cigarettes, alcohol, and other vices that impose costs on others or on society as a whole are prime candidates for taxes to offset their negative "externalities" and remedy their consequences.

Mill was arguing for luxury taxes on such conspicuous consumption as if it, too, was a vice. In doing so, he recognized that a race toward opulence solely for its purpose of signaling station should be discouraged, even penalized. This notion of using taxes to remedy the excesses of the rich is one argument put forward for a progressive income tax system. If greater wealth is correlated with greater opulence, such a tax on the wealthy makes sense.

This tax may be somewhat misplaced, though. The tax more correctly belongs on those aspects of consumption that could be deemed most frivolous. More correctly, we see such taxes imposed on goods deemed luxuries, like expensive cars and yachts.

Fruit of the rise becomes the seed of decline

An economy that is growing in prosperity is often also growing in population and diversity. In turn, participants increasingly associate themselves with special interests or smaller communities and, hence, become detached from the greater community. While such prosperity allows the vast majority to meet their more basic needs, the increasing fragmentation makes it more difficult for them to realize their communal needs of respect and esteem.

Some overcome this frustration through self-actualization. However, many others look for icons that can communicate to the greater community that they have "arrived." Some yardsticks in this race for esteem are unnecessary accumulations of wealth, home size, or vehicle luxuries.

Ultimately, conspicuous consumption and the accumulation of wealth rather than the pursuit of happiness are treated as unproductive activities. A shift from production to consumerism is a great leveler that redirects economic growth. In the short run, the impetus to consume in such a manner can sustain an economy. However, consumption for consumption's sake does not create the efficiencies and innovations that are associated with emerging economic power.

The affluent economic empire falls into the trap of conspicuous consumption. Rather than concentrating resources to maximize production, the affluent economic empire diverts production to conspicuous consumption. Growth suffers, as does the quality of life, ultimately.

11
A New Colonialism

> In seed time learn, in harvest teach, in winter enjoy.
> (William Blake, *The Marriage of Heaven and Hell*, 1793)[46]

Economic dominance gave rise to a new colonialism. No longer was the colonial model maintained solely through military might. Economic power, backed up with military power when necessary, became the tool for expansion and global influence.

However, we shall see that this economic power may be as fleeting as the financial capital that flows so easily across borders made permeable by globalization. Aspiring nations quickly learn the lessons that allow them, too, to take best advantage of their capacities.

Sustainable underdevelopment

Economists have long recognized that the rate of economic growth varies depending on the level of infrastructure and sophistication of markets in a given country. Until there is a rule of law that will protect property rights and enforce contracts, there can be no markets to provide an efficient outlet for surpluses.

We see this phenomenon happen still today. Haiti, a land once known as an exotic getaway, plunged into chaos and poverty as corrupting dictatorships distorted their economy to the point that it failed. Financial capital dried up, and, few would divert capital for investment in Haiti when they could invest in potentially more successful emerging markets. The lack of the rule of law and new economic infrastructure becomes a self-fulfilling prophecy that causes markets to decay and economic activity to decline.

Undeveloped nations remain undeveloped because of their failure to provide the economic infrastructure necessary for growth. However, once people begin to market their surpluses, production would grow dramatically. This would in turn result in surpluses to sellers of goods and services and surpluses to the providers of the factors of production – the entrepreneurs, the resource owners, and human capitalists.

The virtuous cycle

These surpluses arising from markets create income and wealth. In an economy that is expected to grow rapidly, these surpluses are plowed back into the economy with the expectation of producing even greater surpluses later.

Ultimately, growth follows expectations and the capacity to grow. Both undeveloped and emerging economies share the same economic asset. There is typically an unemployed or underemployed workforce. Often this untapped resource is vast, as in the homegrown population in India and China in the late twentieth century. This resource may also be imported, as in the United States in the late nineteenth and early twentieth century, as immigrants around the world traveled to that land of opportunity to be a part of the American Dream.

The other factors of production may be equally vast. Countries, such as Canada and Russia, Brazil and Australia, with populations that are relatively small compared to their vast land and natural resources, are also ripe for sustained economic growth as their resources are channeled into factor markets.

Still other nations are able to harness a spirit of entrepreneurship. Britain, a tiny island with a relatively large population, had entrepreneurs who could bring the innovations of the First Industrial Revolution to market, and had, in its colonies, the ready markets and the supply chains that were equally essential for its emergence as an economic empire.

Finally, some nations are endowed with tremendous financial capital. For instance, the Organization of Petroleum Exporting Countries (OPEC), by fueling the Western world's thirst for oil in the 1970s and after, amassed huge pools of investment capital.

However, natural resources are bound to a land's geography. Likewise, entrepreneurs and human capital are discouraged from flowing freely from country to country. But, financial capital can flow across borders with relative ease, in an effort to seek the greatest returns.

If there is the rule of law, market infrastructure, and untapped capacity, financial investments will flow to provide additional infrastructure to bring resources to market. Investment in roads, supply chains, mines and wells, agriculture lands and forests will add value and transform natural resources to marketable products. Education will add value to human capital so it too can benefit the marketplace. Entrepreneurs also can be trained and given the opportunity to invent the better mousetrap and bring innovations to the market.

Countries able to harness these resources and plow the resulting surpluses into even greater investment and production create a virtuous cycle that acts as a positive feedback loop.

The triumph of positive feedback

As we shall see, feedback loops are central to an economy for both its success and failure. The term "positive feedback loop" is an expression borrowed from physics. It describes a phenomenon that produces a byproduct that further stimulates the phenomenon. If this "positive feedback loop" is sufficiently reinforcing to overcome any moderating or dampening tendencies, the phenomenon is amplified.

For instance, global warming has been associated with the burning of hydrocarbons that increased rapidly with the onset of the Second Industrial Revolution. The burning of hydrocarbons with oxygen necessarily and unavoidably generates carbon dioxide. Increases in the concentration of carbon dioxide, from such economy-induced activities or from natural tendencies, acts as a thermal blanket around the earth by allowing the full spectrum of energy from the sun to impinge on the earth but reflecting back downward the lower frequency infrared light that would otherwise be radiated back into space as excess heat.

The net effect is a rising global average temperature. However, this increasing temperature induces another effect. The rising temperature melts the snow and ice cover in the polar regions of the earth that would otherwise help reflect the sun's energy back into space.

This positive feedback loop causes global warming which in turn melts ice-caps still further and causes further warming. This is not arrested until the ice and snowcaps stop melting or until some other moderating influence can out-swamp this feedback loop.

Rapidly developing economies too follow positive feedback loops, at least until those factors energizing the feedback loop are attenuated, moderated by other forces, or decay by themselves.

The positive feedback mechanism for rapidly developing economies cannot function effectively unless there is sufficient excess capacity to work symbiotically with the mechanism. However, if there is potential for growth, the surpluses created by production can, and typically will, be directed back into the creation of additional economic infrastructure. In this way, growth begets more growth, and the economic growth compounds rapidly.

Indeed, this positive feedback loop can be sufficiently strong to weather economic storms. The global financial meltdown that began in late 2008 plunged most developed countries into what has been called the Great Recession. The economic decline in the developed nations was in stark contrast to the slightly reduced but still spectacular growth in China. By continuing to build their infrastructure even when other nations were hunkering down, China was able to continue to generate employment and sow the seeds for greater economic potential once prosperity returns. While other countries committed to almost unprecedented public investment simply to moderate and arrest the economic decline, the surpluses of production and the willingness of an economic authority in China to continue to invest placed its future on a much firmer foundation.

Mobilization of capital

One of the best indicators of surplus reinvestment is the national savings rate. Savings are an indication that income generation exceeds basic consumption needs. These surpluses of production over necessary consumption make their way from savings into loanable funds markets. If these loanable funds are redirected into investment, into the means of production, or into the infrastructure that can facilitate further production, the economy's productive capacity will expand.

Of course, those who save need not be the same as those who actually invest in the physical machines, infrastructure, innovations, and economic foundations that spur future growth. Markets for savings and investment, such as stock markets, venture capital funds, or even bank savings accounts, facilitate the match between consumers willing to invest and investors willing to produce. These consumer-investors and investor-producers are vital partners in a rapidly growing market.

Interestingly, in these days of global capital movements, consumer-investors need not reside in the same country as the investor-producers that sow the seeds of future prosperity. While consumers can reap benefits of their investments from afar, the economy receiving the investment in production and infrastructure garners the greatest long-term benefits.

The promise of growth and strong subsequent consumption must be sufficient to overcome the natural tendency of mortal consumers to focus on the now rather than the future. Economists are beginning to recognize that market psychology is also an important factor.

For instance, there is little that differentiates an economy the day before and the day after a major stock market shock, except for the sudden fear and pessimism that grips a market. Clearly, a market is economic; but it is also partially psychological. These psychological forces of unwarranted optimism and exuberance in a speculative bubble and unwarranted pessimism and depression in a market crash are important determinants of the strength and sustainability of economic growth. There is nothing like the confidence-building effect of sustained and real economic growth on the backs of true economic production improvements to provide the confidence to fuel sustained investment and further economic growth.

Positive feedback in reverse

Sometimes, consumer-investors remain pessimistic even if there is a great deal of excess capacity and economic opportunity. For instance, in the midst of a severe recession or depression, there is a vast pool of unemployed and under-employed human and productive resources that lay as economic waste. Despite the opportunity to harness these unemployed resources, consumer-investors remain wary of investing in a declining economy.

This tendency, too, is a positive feedback loop. Economic decline breeds pessimism and a flight of capital to cash rather than to productive capacity. This pessimism and capital flight toward healthier economies result in further economic contraction, and even greater pessimism. Positive feedback can work in both directions.

In such an environment, an investor of last resort can force a turnaround in investment and production. The Keynesian school of economics has taught us that government spending can be employed to turn around a contracting economy.

Part of such a turnaround can occur if an economic entity can simply provide the unemployed with income to spend. This ability to spur greater consumption will induce producers to restock their shelves and hence reemploy more workers. A positive feedback loop can be employed to turn around the contraction that was brought about when another positive feedback loop led to its decline.

Such attempts to induce a helpful positive feedback loop require the employment of public resources to correct a market failure. These public resources will have to be repaid at some time in the future, through higher taxes perhaps. However, if the strategy works, an improved economy will have the greater surpluses and tax revenue to replenish the coffers.

In effect, government can be viewed as a long-lived institution that can overcome or reverse the short-term and shortsighted decisions of mortal investors. By taking the long view, an institution can create the foundations for investment and economic growth and overcome a bias toward consumption and the status quo.

A moderating influence

This positive feedback mechanism can be disrupted in a number of different ways.

First, if there is not sufficient excess capacity to offer investors the "low hanging fruit" that all but ensures good returns, there may not be a sufficiently attractive perceived economic return to act as an incentive to save and reinvest.

Second, consumer-investors also abhor taking disproportionate risk on their investments. A risky investment environment, perhaps based on external economic threats, investor pessimism, regulatory uncertainty, or emerging global forces, can lower the perceived return on investment and reduce investment.

Third, an individual who makes savings is sacrificing today's consumption in trade in the hopes of a even greater consumption tomorrow. And, he must be compensated by the promise of a positive return if he has to make this sacrifice.

If investment returns are not sufficiently high or are perceived to be risky, consumers may prefer to focus on consumption rather than investment today. This lack of reinvestment may generate strong demand for consumption goods, but at tremendous long-term costs that will impinge on future economic growth. Consumer-investors must decide to what degree their present consumption governs their decisions and to what degree future consumption is preferred, through present investment.

This tradeoff between the present and the future is commonly demonstrated in our individual savings and investment behavior. Financial managers recommend that we invest more conservatively as we age. This decision to accept lower reward by taking on lower risk is a natural response to a shorter time horizon. The lower return also signals reduced future consumption for any consumption sacrificed today to save more for tomorrow. As an economic empire becomes more secure, wealthier, more short-term oriented, and perhaps more fearful of future uncertainties, it makes more conservative investment decisions, saves less, and consumes more.

A starving economy that has little to lose and much to gain; is willing to roll the dice and invest heavily in the future. Once an economy becomes more affluent, it becomes more consumption oriented, consumption dependent, and consumer-driven. The dynamism and excitement of an emerging economy, stretching to reach the apex of the innovation wave is sacrificed in favor of consumerism and maintenance of the status quo.

Fourth, as surpluses grow and an economy transitions from a production orientation to consumption orientation, government, too, becomes less a promoter of new economic activity and more a major participant in the maintenance of the status quo. Government revenue and spending creep up until many economies are characterized by a government sector that is the largest sector in the economy. If consumer-investors begin to practice a consumerism that forces them to purchase unnecessary goods and services, government too becomes consumer-oriented and fails to invest in the infrastructure necessary for growth.

If government spends beyond its means, it necessarily competes for a growing share of a dwindling supply of loanable funds. As consumers save less and invest more conservatively, government treasuries can dominate borrowing by

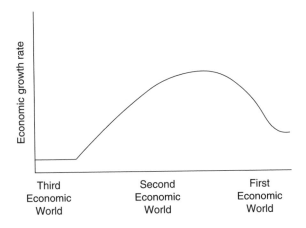

Figure 8 Growth rates at various stages of development

offering low risk and returns that need not be paid through profits but through their ability to tax future generations. A government that falls into the trap of imitating consumers who spend beyond their means and that focuses on short-term goals will likewise forgo dynamic investment and an innovative economy and will find it difficult to raise funds and create economic growth.

Taken together, we observe a development cycle in which the least developed nations cannot sustain economic growth; the aspiring market nations grow rapidly once the positive feedback loops work to enhance infrastructure and investment; and the developed nations in the First Economic World attain a long-term, steady-state, but unspectacular rate of growth as it shifts from a production orientation to consumerism. A graph of this phenomenon of sustained zero growth for the least developed nations, double-digit growth of 10% to 20% for the most dynamic emerging economies in the Second Economic World, and 2% to 3% growth for developed and consumer-oriented economies is as shown in Figure 8.

Equity over efficiency

At the same time, economists have observed a shift in economic inequities as economies transition.

On one hand, an economy languishing in seemingly perpetual poverty has relatively little inequality. There may be riches for those that profit by keeping the economy down, but the vast majority of the society is subsisting in poverty. Overall, these inequalities are comparably small. Almost everybody is equally miserable, in an economic sense.

On the other hand, an economy growing rapidly will not likely grow evenly. The First Industrial Revolution in England created the nouveau riche. This opulence and excess in the Second Industrial Revolution in the United States coined the term the "Gilded Age." As a nation develops still further and adopts the taste for luxuries like democracy and income distribution it could not previously afford, income inequalities narrow once more.

Simon Kuznets, a Nobel Memorial Prize winning economist, observed this phenomenon in his seminal paper, "Economic Growth and Income Inequality." According to him, the transition from an agricultural, subsistence-oriented economy to an industrial economy would differentially reward those most dynamic entrepreneurs first out of the block. This increasing growth is at the expense of increasing income inequality.[47]

However, as growth is established and workers are drawn out of the low productivity agricultural sector and into the higher productivity sector, they have a greater incentive to invest in and enhance their human capital. As they do so, through education and further modernization, workers who are more skilled earn greater surpluses, and income inequalities reduce.

The ultimate leveler

As an economy transitions into a wealthier, more steady-state, and ongoing concern, the narrowed income inequality creates a vast middle class that shares many characteristics. Education attainment is more evenly distributed and of a higher level of accomplishment and a growing government begins to cater to the needs of a broad middle class that demands democracy. Thus former luxuries such as regard for income equality, health, and the environment become luxuries they can afford.

With the democratization of society around a dominant middle class, and with an increasing emphasis on the consumer wants of the middle class rather than the rapid growth goals of the entrepreneurial class, economic growth of 2% to 4% tracks population growth and productivity improvements. This phenomenon is simply a corollary to the Law of Diminishing Returns. Growth levels off when an economy matures and when there are few untapped economic opportunities.

The great non-debate

The crux of a description of long-term growth is the subject of a great debate that remains unresolved because participants share different assumptions.

In one corner, scientists and citizens accurately note that a fair amount of production is based on the use of fixed factors. These resources include land, minerals, hydrocarbons, and water, all of which are in fixed supply and are being steadily depleted with growing population and economic activity.

There is no denying the reality of their observation on the limits of scarce resources. However, it also overestimates the depleting effect. If economic growth is 3%, this does not imply that all resources are being depleted with equal acceleration. The other school of thought claims technology will be our economic salvation.

To illustrate this point, let us look at crop yields. The U.S. Department of Agriculture estimates that corn yields will increase from about 40 bushels per acre in 1950 to more than 200 bushels per acre by 2030.[48] It is possible to increase production without increasing inputs of our most scarce resources.

Similarly, the U.S. Department of Agriculture reported that, while 41% of the U.S. workforce was employed in agriculture to feed a nation of 76 million people in 1900, 1.9% of the employed workforce fed a nation of 291 million in 2000.[49]

The increased productivity of agriculture, this most important product of the land, demonstrated another important principle. The economy shifted its emphasis on the production of manufactured and agricultural goods, as a share of the gross domestic product, to one that is predominantly services oriented. Edward Lazear, formerly the chair of the United States Council of Economic Advisors, reported in 2007 that the share of output in the service sector has risen to 77% of private output from less than 5% in 1840.[50] These services sectors are labor-intensive and require few of the fixed factors of production used so intensively in manufacturing. However, their greater income levels still allow urban workers to consume great amounts of fixed factors of production through their purchases of manufactured goods and greater demand for energy.

Economist Joseph Schumpeter once made an empirical argument that innovations regularly occur over time. This reoccurring cycle allows the economy to continue to expand accordingly.

A modern Schumpeterist, Paul Romer recently quit his tenured position at Stanford University, one of the most prestigious universities in the United States, to prove Schumpeter's point.

Romer's vision is to engage in the creation of model cities and regions in undeveloped countries. By creating institutions that will mobilize production, he expects to show that production can increase over time by doing things better rather than doing things more. He has a faith in a wellspring of new ideas that will continue to propel his communities forward, especially those economies that have floundered for lack of effective institutions to channel production.

The dismal argument that the depletion of earth's resources will eventually constrain economies neglects a somewhat ameliorating factor of increased productivity. More accurately, commentators could note that such increases in productivity must eventually demonstrate diminishing returns, unless there emerges an almost unlimited source of power, such as the fusion that fuels the sun. Absent unlimited resources, we cannot deny the dismal economic prophecy, and must heed the clarion call for greater economic stewardship. The discussion ought to be when and how severe, rather than if.

While the capriciousness of this empirical observation may not satisfy those stewards most concerned about the depletion of the earth's resources, the pattern of steady global progress has shown itself to be amazingly robust. However, while we as a society may want to invest in research on the innovations that would allow this pattern to continue, few would want to bet their future on steadily and spectacularly growing production fueled by increasingly efficient resource consumption.

Fruit of the rise becomes the seed of decline

The development cycle is a natural consequence of institution formation, increasing returns to scale followed by diminishing returns and decreasing returns to scale, a democratization of production and institutions, and an increase in consumerism. It would be folly to imagine that spectacular growth, of a kind demonstrated in emerging economies, can continue unabated and indefinitely. Such growth arises from positive economic feedback loops that can vaunt its economy forward, but not indefinitely.

The positive feedback loops arise because greater production gives rise to greater surpluses. If the recipients of the surpluses are sufficiently confident of the continuation of growth, the surpluses will be reinvested into future economic capacity, thereby fueling still further growth.

This positive feedback loop depends crucially on the willingness of the recipients of surpluses to reinvest their share of production. When the surpluses were once concentrated in the hands of a few who likely had almost every one of their needs met, it would be surprising to imagine that these entrepreneurs would do anything but reinvest their surpluses into greater future productive capacity.

However, once the surpluses are distributed across a vast middle class, every individual will attempt to raise their level of consumption.

Eventually, the positive feedback loop can reverse itself. More affluence results in decreased savings and investment and a government of growing size that also emphasizes equity over efficiency and short-term goals at the expense of long-term debt. The resulting decline in savings and drain on loanable funds leads financial capital to flee elsewhere.

Fortunately, for aspiring nations, financial capital is mobile and can easily cross borders to nations that have a production emphasis and strong work ethic, and are willing to protect property and investment capital. Unfortunately, for an economic empire, the positive feedback loop that allowed for spectacular growth and the attainment of an apex of economic power is often reversed in a way that acts as a great economic leveler.

12
Dependency Economics

I venture to allude to the impression which seemed generally to prevail among their brethren across the seas, that the Old Country must wake up if she intends to maintain her old position of pre-eminence in her colonial trade against foreign competitors.

(King George V, 1865–1936)[51]

As an economic empire reaches its apex and transcends from a production emphasis to a consumption emphasis, further growth must rely on the combination of productivity improvements and population increases.

There was a time when population rose with economic growth. Before an economic empire matured and provided a social welfare net for all, an extended family was necessary for economic security. A growing population also served a resource-thirsty industrial sector.

However, with affluence came a shift in consumption patterns. The lower needs for shelter and food that Maslow identified are easily attained, and population increases are no longer viewed as a pathway to prosperity. In addition, an aspiring empire recognizes that population growth accelerates its economic ascendancy.

An economic empire that has arrived, instead, seeks to protect its bounty. Immigration becomes more difficult. Increasingly urbanized residents begin to favor smaller families that can better concentrate and conserve their bountiful resources, rather than larger families that support the rural economy and contribute to greater national production.

At that point, an economic empire must look beyond its borders for ready markets that will purchase its goods. This new, or neo-, colonialism has the daunting and, perhaps, inconsistent goal of creating and controlling markets abroad without opening borders to potential migrants.

The colonial model so successfully employed in the First Industrial Revolution was projected and protected through military might. Global supply chains that spanned borders and continents rendered obsolete colonialism through militarism. These increasingly liberated supply chains, in combination with internationalizing treaties, removed the advantages economic empires previously enjoyed.

Neocolonialism and empire building

Some still argue that vestiges of neocolonialism remain, in part, in some empires. Certainly, the United States, France, Great Britain, and the former Soviet empire have been accused of using colonialism, backed by military power, as a tool for empire building.

However, it is unlikely that governments view militarism as an avenue for economic expansion any longer. More likely is the tendency of companies to pressurize government to support their industrial policies through the apparatus of the State. The roots of neocolonialism as practiced today must then be in the global strategies of multinational corporations.

For instance, a country like Haiti remains the poorest country in the Western Hemisphere, despite its proximity to the United States and its status in the past as a tourist haven. Sharing an island with the Dominican Republic, the CIA Factbook reported its 2008 per capita income of just 15.9% that of its wealthier neighbor on the island.[52]

Compared to the Dominican Republic, Haiti lacks public and commercial infrastructure and a strong and robust political and legal system. It also receives benign neglect from its neighboring economic empire, not necessarily because of a state-sponsored system of economic imperialism, but rather in an effort to protect corporate interests.

Haiti is but one example in which an economy pursues the interests of its corporations rather than the direct interests of the State. In an era of free enterprise that is embraced by nations as a means for economic growth, this shift from direct State intervention to the representation of corporate interests is a natural conclusion. *The New York Times* reported on the political demise of Jean-Bertrand Aristide, a populist reformer who tried to reverse the corruption of the long-ruling Duvalier family in Haiti:

> *"(Aristide) was espousing change in Haiti, fundamental populist change," said Robert Maguire, a Haiti scholar who has criticized American policy as insufficiently concerned with Haiti's poor. "Right away, he was viewed as a threat by very powerful forces in Haiti."*[53]

Aristide had proposed to impose business taxes, raise the minimum wage, and challenged U.S. influence in Haitian affairs. The *Times* reported the comments of then Senator Christopher Dodd, who was commenting on policies of President George W. Bush and the administrative policy of his father, George

H.W. Bush: *"We had interests and ties with some of the very strong financial interests in the country, and Aristide was threatening them."*

Attempts by an economic empire to make, break, make again, and break again the leaders of sovereign countries is no longer an effort to secure military dominance. Rather, greater ideological and economic principles are articulated as reasons for such meddling in the affairs of sovereign nations. Rarely do empires exercise military and geographical dominance any more. Instead, economic empires may support the corporate strategies of domestic industries with multinational interests.

A market failure

Global empire-building generates more economic inefficiencies than might otherwise be the case for representative democracies determined to expand their sovereign reach.

To illustrate this, let us compare expansion through economic union with expansion through economic dominance.

The European Economic Union is constructed primarily as an economic commonwealth, even as it now pursues social as well as economic harmonization. All members of the union are represented in the deliberations that determine their collective economic policies. These policies are designed to advance the interests of all member countries, even if any policy will benefit some more than the others.

In a system of participatory economic union, any member can withdraw if it believes the advantages of membership are outweighed by the disadvantages. All members have similar policy-making potency, and the goal of the economic union is to squeeze maximum economic efficiency out of the system.

Contrast such a system with a loose affiliation, voluntary or not, between an economic power and an allied economy. Let us assume that the powers of the State are designed only to promote the interests of a domestic company operating in the allied country. In the spirit of Senator Dodd's comments, let us explore how these economic interests are exercised.

The company extending its reach to the allied economy is obviously interested in creating a potential market for its goods. However, the primary advantage of locating productive capacity in the allied nation is to provide for lower cost of production that will ultimately serve the economy of the empire. If the country were as affluent as that of the economic empire, wages would be too high, and market power likely too low, to produce efficiencies that could be realized more easily at home. Instead, companies looking solely to expand markets in countries of similar economic influence would locate productive capacity in these nations only if there were some transportation or domestic production advantage to do so.

Rather, the advantage of offshore production in an allied nation is derived from lower factor costs, most often labor costs, and in the advantages of economic imbalance.

Shifting balances

The cost advantage of offshore production cannot help but be mitigated over time. Indeed, this is how markets work. By creating new economic activity in the allied economy, income is created, purchasing power is expanded, and jobs in related sectors are created in turn. Economists speak of a multiplier effect that amplifies the initial benefits.

For instance, if a company locates in another country, it generates direct jobs. It will also generate demand for other necessary factors of production that are best supplied locally. A textiles plant employs workers and creates jobs in related industries that weave or dye cloth, grow cotton, or make boxes for shipping the final product. These induced jobs can sometimes be as plentiful as the direct jobs the new industry generates.

In addition, the incomes from those direct and induced jobs created allow tertiary economic activities such as baking, teaching, home building, and all the various other goods and services producers an expanding economy demands.

Of course, this is precisely how any economy grows and diversifies. As long as there is sufficient excess capacity in the local economy, and as long as the new jobs created are of higher quality than the old jobs obviated, there is constant economic growth.

Single crop agriculture puts sugar in our tea

Such growth may, with some technology transfer and best practices, eventually create a viable local market for the product. In such a case, expansion abroad is no different from domestic expansion. The gains are hard-won, and the profit margins are competitive and slim.

However, greater profits can be had if a company can maintain its monopsony power. To do so, it must actually depress economic growth in the hinterland economy. Greatest profits are earned by the motherland when wages and other factor costs can be kept low, and volume low, preferably by encouraging competition with another similarly positioned hinterland nation or corporation.

We are familiar with this monopsonist model discussed in an earlier chapter. To keep factor prices low, a company must limit the economic power of the owners of factors. Modern companies can do this by employing a number of strategies. They can keep profits high by keeping wages low. This strategy will also have the effect of decreasing subsequent induced jobs and of reducing economic diversity in the hinterland economy.

A privately optimal corporate strategy will also allow a company to reduce the induced jobs by providing as many of the other factors of production as possible from other economies, including the home country. For instance, Coca Cola can insist that all syrup be sourced in the United States. A textile company can ensure that the cotton used comes from yet another country. Alternatively, an electronic assembly plant can assemble parts made in different countries. In doing so, the company can keep its hinterland economy plant as dependent as possible and, hence, as profitable as possible, for the home company.

Of course, a corporation can embark on similar strategies in each of the countries that takes one small slice of the overall manufacturing operation. By fostering two offshore plants in two hinterland economies for one part of the production process, the home company can even induce a competition between the two jurisdictions in an effort to keep costs low.

Such strategies are commonly employed in the home economy. It is not unusual for various states in a nation to compete with each other in their bids for a new plant that would employ a number of its state residents. A state or local jurisdiction can offer tax concessions, cheap serviced land, infrastructure subsidies, training, or even legislation to prevent the unionization of labor, all in an effort to attract industry to its state.

Companies have been known to search elsewhere once these state-sponsored concessions expire. The size of the plant in a small town that is desperate for work creates the same dependencies as can the movement of productive capacity offshore to less developing economies.

The franchise profits that flow back to the home company also prevent the wealth accumulation in the hinterland economy that would eventually rebalance the economic relationship.

Notice that such strategies are ineffective in well-developed and diversified economies. These strategies are not conspiratorial, but are rather efforts to profit from asymmetries in economic power, wealth, diversification, and sophistication. These policies are simply the result of an economic theory. To the extent that economic empires may promote, or at least not discourage, such economic policies, there may be some state conspiracies. However, the state does the same on occasion within its own border.

Deadweight losses

These strategies of monopolization keep economy-wide demand for labor from rising, and allow the monopsony employer to keep wages low. However, these monopolistic and monopolistic policies are contrary to good public policy because of the deadweight losses they create.

Public policy-motivated threats to the profitability of monopolists include efforts in the hinterland economy to diversify, to raise wages, and to impose business taxes. Each of these tools will lower the profitability of monopoly behavior and curb some of its excesses.

Only counterbalancing power or extensive regulation can equalize such monopolistic tendencies. An individual company or empire has every incentive to maintain the power imbalance in their domestic interest. This is not an ethical question – it is merely a corporate strategy designed to maximize shareholder wealth.

These imbalances, when they emerge within an economic power, are often countered with regulation. Antitrust regulations, sunsets on patent protection, and other policies are designed to enhance competition and reduce deadweight losses within a nation. However, such laws do not extend to offshore subsidiaries of the home company. Instead, the domestic laws of the hinterland nation must evolve over time.

This interest in monopolization of the hinterland may implore an economic or political response. Such rent seeking, designed to maintain power imbalances to enhance profits, nonetheless produce the same sort of deadweight losses we described at length earlier. The community of nations is poorer for such policies, even if a subset of the community of nations benefits.

This economic evolution can be a slow process.

The hinterland nation is often desperate for jobs, even jobs as carefully contained, consistent with the home company's corporate strategy. These jobs must be, at least at first, better than prevailing jobs. If not, the company cannot succeed in establishing itself.

However, unless a hinterland nation can parlay the increased wealth into an economic infrastructure that can promote rapid growth and diversification, it is difficult to redefine its role in the corporate strategy. This is especially true of companies that reinvest some of its profits into efforts that co-opt local political leaders.

Even trade treaties can sustain such imbalances. By favoring bilateral trade between two related nations, trade between the hinterland and other nations is discouraged, on a relative basis.

On the contrary, free and fair trade treaties that may protect working conditions and child labor, international contract law, protocols that prevent environmental degradation, and even rules that require nations to respect intellectual property can create an environment for economic growth. At times, though, these same policies may protect the very profits that flow back to economic empires.

Fruit of the rise becomes the seed of decline

Economic theory has long recognized the profits that can flow to those with greater economic power. It should come as no surprise that well organized and sophisticated companies can employ a variety of corporate strategies that maintain, and even enhance, their power over partners in intra-company trade. While national policies may, at times, try to thwart the domestic exploitation of economic power imbalances in the interest of sound domestic public policy, there is no such bar to companies that are determined to exploit such imbalances across borders.

There are a number of tools that can be employed by a company that is a member of an economic empire. Efforts to avoid jurisdictions with minimum wage laws or organized labor, the requirement that foreign plants use domestically produced factors or factors from yet other offshore subsidiaries, and the repatriation of profits abroad back to the home company can all be employed to permit economic power to reside within the economic empire.

To some extent, a state can be complicit in maintaining these relationships. It rarely can do so through military power, but it can still help maintain economic power for its home companies through other more subtle means.

Only a most insightful foreign political regime can thwart such natural attempts at economic rent seeking. Even these efforts must overcome the natural tendencies of multinationals to lobby friendly regimes to create a friendly business climate as well. Only a most determined political regime can take the best of economic development, disregard the rest, and parlay the new economic activity into greater diversification and increased independence.

However, as more and more nations reach the level of development that require them to look elsewhere for fuel continued growth, developing nations may find themselves with more suitors. Just as the developed nations learned of the great leveling power of a well-educated middle-class nation, so too can developing nations.

There is little difference in the struggles of aspiring nations to join the club of affluent nations and their past struggles. It is compelling for an economic empire to attempt to impose standards, sometimes which they themselves find difficult to meet, upon aspiring nations.

The major difference is that, while a country can create the legislative environment necessary to foster an uniform and sustainable economic growth, international conventions that establish these same principles are difficult for aspiring empires to accept, given their stage of economic development. The very differences in these stages of development commend differing values and solutions that cannot easily be bridged by international convention.

An economic empire is torn between two forces. Companies within the empire grow by fostering and maintaining monopoly or monopsony power in their cross-border strategies. These strategies are good for the economic empire.

However, an empire does not thrive in isolation. These same policies can at first enhance and subsequently slow down economic development elsewhere. Membership of an economic empire in a community of nations implores it to pursue international partnerships rather than international paternalism. Good international citizenship clashes with the very forces that give rise to economic empires.

Part IV
Aspiring Nations

By the 1960s, the U.S. economic empire was nearing its neo-mercantilist apex. It had conquered space and was the center of global commerce. However, the 1970s challenged its economic relevancy, both domestically and abroad. This was the decade of the OPEC oil crisis and the Eurodollar, with huge amounts of wealth diverted oversees, first because of rising oil prices, and then as a consequence of the manufacturing ascendency of Japan.

At the same time, other nations were reluctant to buy U.S. products that failed to keep pace with innovations emanating from Japan. The United States was reaching the limit of mercantilism. In a flash of economic pragmatism, an unpopular president nonetheless reoriented a nation's trade policies toward free trade and opened up relations with China, a nation that would soon emerge as the next economic empire. The shift from the undisputed hub of global technology to a purchaser of technology from elsewhere was remarkably rapid. We next document how the innovations of an economic empire cannot be contained for long in a globally oriented world.

13
Transfer of Technology

Give a man a fish and you feed him for a day. Teach a man to fish and you feed him for a lifetime.

(Chinese Proverb)

Sell a man a fish, and he can eat for a day, teach a man to fish, and you lose a great business opportunity.

(attributed to Karl Marx)[54]

Before the printing press and its democratization of the written word, information was a power closely held by the elite. A common language, the ability to read and write, and a medium that could move ideas as quickly as it could move people and products meant that ideas and inventions could no longer be closely held. This democratization of information made all the difference.

We have noted the strategies employed by the agents of an economic empire to retain their economic power through the same tools always employed by monopolies and monopsonies. It turns out that the inevitability of technology transfer is a great leveler that equalizes power between an economic empire and the aspiring nations. While there is little novelty in the efforts of monopolies and monopsonies to hold on to economic power, technological innovations have given rise to technology transfer that is at once inevitable and rapid.

This rapid and historically unprecedented transfer of technology may mean that economic superiority will be increasingly short-lived.

Best practices

Technology itself can be a tool for the preservation of economic power.

The term "technology" portends to one of the tools companies may use to preserve economic power. However, economists use the term to describe the system in which inputs, called "factors of production," are efficiently combined in a particular way to produce maximum outputs. Some of these "technologies" may refer to the unique system a company employs in their production processes. The technology may involve its proprietary supply chain that moves goods and services around the world so all the items of the production process are in the right place at the right time.

The technology may also employ proprietary machines used to produce goods, or secret formulas a company such as Kentucky Fried Chicken or Coca Cola uses to make food and beverages.

Indeed, these technologies and systems may define a company more than the product market within which it competes. For instance, Wal-Mart was listed as the world's largest company in 2008.[55] With more than $400 billion in revenue by 2009, Wal-Mart has revenue larger than the gross domestic product of all but the world's top 25 nations. However, while most consider Wal-Mart to be a retail company, some argue that it is a logistics company with an incredibly sophisticated supply chain system. This ensures that goods arrive in its stores so efficiently that it confers upon Wal-Mart an almost insurmountable competitive advantage.

Others note that the superior market power conferred upon Wal-Mart because of these efficiencies allows Wal-Mart to extract monopsony concessions from its suppliers that no other competitor can enjoy. The Wal-Mart system purchases goods and services in the most competitive markets around the globe, and delivers them to a consumer-oriented nation with such efficiency that it has become the most profitable company in the world.

Some of the Wal-Mart advantage is from supply chain systems that other sophisticated logistics providers should be able to replicate. Other buyers have also established sophisticated purchasing relationships in the same emerging countries that have so profited Wal-Mart. Certainly, there are also others able to retail their products with equal efficiency. However, no other company does so with the incredible scale that allows Wal-Mart to behave as a natural monopsony in wholesale markets and have natural monopoly power in the retail marketplace.

As a consequence, one can replicate the Wal-Mart system. However, without also replicating its size and hence its market influence, no company has successfully rivaled Wal-Mart's profits.

A natural monopoly

Economists label a natural monopoly as a company that can maintain a monopoly position and extract monopoly profits without exercising a strategy that artificially maintains power. In some sense, Wal-Mart's system and scale is its mousetrap, fairly invented and maintained to sustain Wal-Mart profits.

If Wal-Mart maintains a proprietary supply chain technology, other companies may maintain market power through innovative invention, ownership of a unique factor of production, or even on the strength of a unique promotion.

For instance, the United States once maintained the National Helium Reserve that created, in essence, a global monopoly on helium. Apple maintains its monopoly by inventing such products as the IPhone, the IPod, and the IPad. Companies such as Calvin Klein, or even Apple, led by the iconic Steve Jobs, have some monopoly power on the strength of a personality that leads the company.

Each of these is an example of a natural monopoly that confers rents on some very scarce and highly valued factor of production. Other monopolies are maintained by less noble means. Such artificial monopolies could maintain their monopoly power either by buying out competitors, colluding with competitors to act as a monopoly in the aggregate, by buying up and then burying patents that might erode their monopoly power, or by preventing their employees from competing with them upon separation, as a condition of their original employment contract.

Each of these artificial strategies takes advantage of non-competitive strategies rather than from the invention of techniques to make the better mousetrap. Natural monopolies need not employ these artificial strategies to confer upon them any monopoly profits.

Something to protect

Such natural monopolies, through inventions and innovations, represent an important source of monopoly profits and economic power. However, such systems, while increasingly sophisticated, are also becoming easier to replicate and imitate. It is the very march of technology that undermines the monopoly profits that technology once conferred.

One way this happens is through a process called "reverse engineering." If a complex production system is called a black box, meaning inputs are opaquely transformed into outputs, this transformation can be "reverse engineered" by observing what comes out of the black box. A reverse engineer can then imitate the process, perhaps in the same way as the original designers did, but possibly in a novel way that is even more efficient than the original design.

The ability to imitate or reverse engineer complex processes improves with the sophistication of production engineers and the tools and software they may employ. Reverse engineering is made more difficult with greater process complexity.

Such reinvention is becoming more commonplace precisely because affluent empires necessarily depend on the intellectual capacity of citizens of aspiring nations.

When Einstein formulated the special theory of relativity in 1905, only a few physicists in the world understood his innovation. Einstein lived in an era in which the surface area of the sphere of human understanding was quite small. Few were on the frontier of knowledge Einstein explored, and, therefore, only those initially understood his innovation.

Now, the sphere of human knowledge is of a much larger radius, with many more scientists and engineers pursuing the research on its frontier. There are few, if any, working in isolation. Indeed, advances in knowledge often require large teams, large budgets, and large institutions. Scientific secrets among the humans who make their livelihood on invention and innovation are rare. A highly secretive industrial research and development laboratory may be able to secure an advantage over competitors that gives it an advantage that may last only months, or years, at best.

Even an innovation that can successfully obtain a patent is able to claim its monopoly right only for 20 years, typically. This protection, under the doctrine of equivalence, also applies to similar processes that perform substantially the same function in the same way to yield the same results. However, patent protection also requires the publication of a full description of the insight, and offers competitors an opportunity to formulate insights of their own that are distinct from, even if functionally equivalent to, the patented innovation.

This mechanism of patent protection balances the incentives to invent with the need for a growing economy to enjoy the fruits of the innovation, first by the inventor, and then by everyone gaining utility from the innovation. The very publication of a patent sows the seeds of obsolescence of its fleeting monopoly power.

Edison and Einstein

Economic civilization is now far too complex to be advanced by the innovations of an Einstein or Edison scribbling or inventing alone in a shadowy room. In that simpler time more than a century ago, Einstein was reputed to be skeptical of what he would learn in his university classes. Edison, renowned as the most prolific inventor of all time, with 1,093 patents to his name over the Gilded Age from 1869 to 1933, did not even attend formal school.

Now, most significant innovations are owned by corporations, laboratories, or universities, and are the product of increasingly specialized research and education. Sophisticated systems and devices require increasingly sophisticated research and development facilities.

While the complexity might suggest greater proprietary research, this increased sophistication is a natural leveler.

Today, the scientists and engineers who develop our new breakthrough products are products themselves of a highly advanced education network. This network of very high quality science and technology programs at major research universities has become the hallmark of many, if not most, innovators.

A divergence of innovation philosophies leads to this great leveling. Universities are in the enterprise of formulating and disseminating knowledge and innovation. To do so it must attract the best and the brightest scholars from worldwide. The most successful universities are global resources. The country that can best foster this basic research and translate it into successful products will stand a good chance of becoming an economic empire. While the basic research and skills development can be tapped to help improve empire status, it cannot be contained.

Only by both attracting and retaining the world's best minds can an empire secure a steady flow of innovations. However, it cannot prevent other nations from also developing top quality universities, research laboratories, and production facilities. Nor can it prevent those scholars originally drawn to an economic empire from returning home, with all the intellectual property in his or her head.

Increasingly, the First Economic World is educating the citizens of the Second Economic World. These aspiring nations greatly value higher education as an acknowledged path to modernization and membership in the First Economic World. The export of First Economic World education to the Second Economic World is a rapidly accelerating convergence. Even those international students who travel to the First Economic World are increasingly returning to their homeland upon graduation as they are afforded opportunities that arise because of their homeland's rapid economic growth.

The Internet

Dramatically accelerating this democratization of knowledge is the Internet. Now, information is at the fingertips of interested scholars and innovators almost immediately and everywhere. This ability to spread knowledge at almost zero cost and in an instant could be contemplated by just a few dreamers a generation ago. Now, a generation has been created that assumes little is proprietary and nothing is secret. With so much known so easily, there are few process secrets a company can keep.

The Internet also allows a company to communicate more effectively internally, and communicate to shareholders and stakeholders outside the company almost immediately. It allows journalists to access instantly the reporting of other journalists, and it allows anybody with an Internet connection to blog ideas to anyone else.

This democratization of ideas and knowledge is the revolution that may just prevent any single entity from retaining a knowledge or proprietary edge for very long. It also allows any companies to market any product from just about any location. No longer must a company invest in developing market strategies. Moreover, no longer do existing companies with access to established markets have the same advantage they once maintained.

For instance, in 1999, in Hangzhou, China-based innovator Ma Yun created Alibaba, an Internet-based network of business-to-business international marketing and e-business, online retail, online payment, and Internet-based data and software storage. He also created a Chinese language portal that is now called "Yahoo! China." In ten short years, this system of marketing and markets has amassed almost 50 million registered users worldwide.

Perhaps more than any other nation, China is plugged into the virtual global supply chain. The ability of China to access world markets has been instrumental to its phenomenal growth. China reported economic growth of more than 9% in 2009, which translates into a gross domestic product of approximately $4.6 trillion. Meanwhile, Japan's GDP of $4.9 trillion in 2008 was estimated by the World Bank to have contracted by 6.6% in 2009 to $4.58 trillion.[56]

To put this growth in perspective, in 1999, China's GDP was $1,083 trillion, at seventh place among nations. The United States' GDP was first among nations at $9,216 trillion.[57] In one decade, China moved from seventh to second, at $4.6 trillion, while the United States remained first among nations with a GDP of $14.261 trillion.[58]

The average, nominal (non-inflation adjusted) growth over the past decade was 14.5% in China versus 4.4% in the United States. If each nation maintains these rates of growth, China will have overtaken the United States as the world's largest economy by the end of the year 2021. China may have moved from just outside the world's ten largest economies in 1991 to the world's largest economy in merely 30 years.[59] Much of this dramatic growth occurred during the same 30-year period that saw the dramatic expansion of the Internet, and with it, electronic, or e-commerce.

Back offices

One of the complaints of residents of an economic empire that is passing its apex is that the fruits of the empire go to benefit those elsewhere. The necessity to trim costs and increase global competitiveness and profits at one instance through outsourcing becomes a diabolical plot to take jobs away from the empire.

At the same time, those countries that allow the empire to bring down its costs become the repository for the very technologies that built the economic empire. India and Ireland, both English speaking countries with strong education infrastructures, started off serving the telephone service, transcribing, software documenting, and medical imaging reading needs of the United States in the 1990s. A decade later, these back office companies such as Infosys and Tata Consultancy in India became world leaders in such enterprises as software writing, accounting, and medical diagnoses. The technological transfer was almost inevitable. Consequently, the rate at which aspiring nations could profit from these new technologies was astounding.[60]

Fruit of the rise becomes the seed of decline

An economic empire has proprietary secrets to protect. However, as an economy and empire grows, population grows, processes must necessarily involve more people, and ideas that once gave rise to monopoly profits become increasingly difficult to protect.

Further accelerating the great leveling power of transfer of knowledge and the dissemination of information is the Internet. Indeed, it may be the case that the Internet is the greatest leveler of modern history. For instance, from 100,000 host sites used primarily by university researchers 1989,[61] the Internet grew to a tool that has surpassed 1.73 billion users in 2009.[62]

This exponential growth in Internet usage occurred in an era in which we saw China move from outside of the ten largest nations in the world to the world's second largest economy. At the rate of growth demonstrated in China over the decade 1999 to 2009, it is extrapolated that the growth rate of China will surpass that of the United States by the end of the year 2021. Such dramatic growth could not have occurred without technology transfers and the democratization of information.

However, if England dominated global economics for two centuries and the United States dominated commerce for a little more than a century, if our study of recent and more distant history is any indication, China's expected ascendency might be short-lived. Economic empires find it increasingly difficult to maintain superiority through monopoly and secrecy in this era of instant communications and global competition.

14
Economic Imitation Is the Sincerest Form of Flattery

> By three methods we may learn wisdom: First, by reflection, which is noblest; Second, by imitation, which is easiest; and third by experience, which is the bitterest.[63]
>
> (Confucius, China's most famous teacher, philosopher, and political theorist, 551–479 BCE)

Just as a nation cannot forever contain invention and innovation, it also cannot prevent its imitators from replicating its innovations elsewhere. Corporations cannot patent an economic or business system, although some have tried. Just as humans are free to pursue happiness, so they are free to pursue any innovation that makes their lives easier or puts more food on their table.

Likewise, the spread of free markets was inevitable. With this broad global diffusion of a more efficient and motivating economic system, those advantages secured by its early adopters are eroded.

An evolution of economic schools of thought

Economic schools of thought have paralleled the prevailing systems of economic empires. Of course, success breeds imitation and induces the adoption of effective economic systems. In the modern economic era, the first such system to gain a strong following was the mercantilist economic philosophy that previously took hold in the First Industrial Revolution.

Mercantilism grew out of the initial success of the capitalist model. This model emerged in the First Industrial Revolution, as great surpluses and wealth were concentrated in the hands of comparatively few owners of capital. These vast fortunes were often fed back into other ventures, and gave rise to the belief that it was the supply of capital, not the access to international trade, that was the essential ingredient of economic success.

In an age of military projection, these fortunes could also be used to fund their navies. This theory of amassing capital as a measure of economic strength also gave rise to an emphasis by the State on their balance of trade. The mercantilist balance of trade theory required a surplus of exports over imports so that financial assets, mostly in the form of gold and silver, could be concentrated in the hands of the empire.

This economic philosophy of hording hard assets as a measure of economic strength also gave rise to some of the least fortunate aspects of trade early in the First Industrial Revolution. The encouragement of exports abroad, including to the colonies, with the simultaneous discouragement of high valued imports, concentrated wealth and capital in the homeland. This capital employed to afford a strong navy and the ability to fund wars also sowed the seed for resentment abroad.

The mercantilist theory guided European expansion during the Renaissance. The expansion of trade routes and the wealth derived from trade funded navies and wars. This model was little different from that adopted by the Romans and Greeks in their empire-building days. Hoarding of the spoils in the homeland was hardly a new concept, even if it may have been taking advantage of a new push for trade between homelands and new hinterlands.

If mercantilism appeared to be something new, it may have been because the First Industrial Revolution's emphasis on capital formation and wealth concentration gave renewed zeal to both counting surpluses and scientifically creating surpluses. Empire building by the Spanish and English in the seventeenth and eighteenth centuries required the enumeration of new resources, the creation of new markets that would not make great demands on the concentration of wealth on the homelands, and new banking and financial institutions that could facilitate the needs of empire building.

This role of the state in advancing economic empire-building remained strong in France, England, Germany, Spain, and the United States, well into the nineteenth century. Indeed, Alexander Hamilton, a signer to the U.S. Constitution and the nation's first prominent Secretary of the Treasury, advocated such an economic policy based on three reports he submitted to Congress in 1790 and 1791.

His First Report for the infant nation dealt with the creation and assumption of the colony's public debt by the federal government. His Second Report defined the terms for a national bank meant to facilitate the finances of government and, later, of the entire banking system. And, in his Third Report, Hamilton advocated for a strong role for government to create the infrastructure necessary for broad economic success.

Hamilton was trying to tailor for a new nation an economic theory that was common elsewhere. Mercantilism, with its emphasis on positive trade imbalances and unfavorable terms of trade, and the translation of these surpluses into domestic investment and production, was the raison d'être for the type of colonialism exercised by England, Spain, France, Italy, and the Netherlands. It was a system eventually replaced by capitalism and the American School, although the transition that began in the Gilded Age took a century to complete.

During the transition, the former Soviet Union adopted its own marriage of communism and mercantilism, while the nations of China and Japan have exercised mercantilism within their sphere of influence in Asia, and more recently in Africa. While modern mercantilism no longer attempts to concentrate bullion in the homeland, the new model of development economics still practiced by some is built upon a positive balance of trade arising from the importation of lower value resource extraction from the hinterland and the exportation of high-value goods production from the homeland.

Roots of mercantilism

One of the founding fathers of mercantilism and of early economic empire-building is the Austrian writer Philipp Wilhelm von Hornick. In his 1684 book *Austria Over All, If She Only Will*, von Hornick advocated a nine-point plan that would pave way for an economic empire. He required[64]

1. A nation's land should be extensively devoted to agriculture, mining, and manufacturing.
2. A nation's natural resources should flow into value-added domestic production to concentrate wealth.
3. The population should join the workforce to the maximum possible extent.
4. Gold and silver should be hoarded in national coffers, with paper money adopted as the national currency.
5. The importation of foreign finished goods should be discouraged.
6. If imports are necessary, they should be obtained in trade for domestic goods, not in gold or silver.
7. Imports should be concentrated only in raw materials so the empire can enjoy the surpluses flowing from value added domestic production of finished goods.
8. No imports should be permitted if similar goods can be supplied through domestic production.
9. Moreover, the empire should seek opportunities to sell its finished goods exports to other countries, in exchange for gold and silver.

This economic philosophy sought to seek surpluses and rents at every opportunity, especially at the expense of other nations. It viewed trade as a constant sum game, under the principle that an economic empire can advance best at the expense of others. The problem escaping early writers of such a policy was that it cannot work if every empire exercises the same approach.

Indeed, an economic empire at its pinnacle is unafraid of competition and views the world as a positive sum game in which it can progress as others, too, succeed. An empire falls into a constant sum, or even negative sum game, when it is threatened economically and responds to the urge to retreat into protectionism and isolationism.

A Smithian view

The isolationist and asymmetric principles of mercantilism had its critics. Certainly, Adam Smith objected to such asymmetry on a philosophical and moral basis. He was also concerned that markets function best if the invisible hand is unfettered by regulations promulgated to satisfy nationalistic agendas. He recognized that, just as water finds its own level, controls and quotas imposed by regulation would only encourage black markets.

Still others questioned the motives of the mercantilists themselves to extract rents from others. Opposed to Smith's explicit belief in the positive-sum-game nature of trade, mercantilism subscribed to a decidedly constant sum worldview.

This anti-mercantilist movement had other critics as well. English philosophers David Hume and John Locke also favored markets that were free to realize the relative values buyers and sellers placed on goods. Later, economist David Ricardo offered more concrete arguments for gains from mutually advantageous trade, especially in the international context. He noted that voluntary trade made both trading sides better off. This conclusion demonstrated the fallacy of trade as a constant sum, rent-seeking game. Instead, trade should be viewed as a positive sum game that takes advantage of both traders' comparative advantage.

In the end, Smith's logic from *The Wealth of Nations* eventually won out. His laissez-faire philosophy of trade promotion and positive sum games induced a movement to deregulate trade that began in the mid-nineteenth century, and continues to this day.

The American system

Out of the Gilded Age and the Second Industrial Revolution flowed a new school of economic thought that followed in the Smith tradition. However, the new approach to free markets also had to repeal the American School as advocated by Alexander Hamilton in the United States in the early part of the nineteenth century. This new mercantilism was based on an argument that some industries must be protected through selective high tariffs on imports of certain goods. Some infant industries may also warrant economic encouragement through government subsidies. Such subsidies, most notably put in place as a response to the Great Depression, took decades to dismantle.

Government also invested in economic infrastructure by providing efficient publicly funded transportation modes. Albert Gallatin, one of the nation's first treasury secretaries (1801–1813), envisioned a broad network of railroads and canals that would open up commerce across a fledgling nation and permit natural resources to flow east from an expanding western frontier.

Earlier, as the country's first treasury secretary, from 1789 to 1795, Alexander Hamilton had also called for a national bank that could raise the capital for such infrastructure investments. These various forays into providing economic infrastructure to the free market system were seen as necessary steps to promote a prosperous new nation.

The willingness of government to foster and subsidize economic infrastructure, in combination with a vibrant Second Industrial Revolution capitalist system gave rise to a mixed economy that was expected to combine the best of the mercantilist and the laissez-faire systems. Indeed, this system allowed the relatively new country of the United States to surpass the economy of Great Britain in size and influence by the early part of the twentieth century.

Henry Carey, economist and author of the treatise *The Harmony of Interests: Agricultural, Manufacturing, and Commercial,* advocated in 1868 that economic prosperity can best be promoted through the creation of a harmonious, classless society. In ways that are similar to those advocated by John Stuart Mill, Carey's proof rested on the relative strength of the American system over the British System.[65] He noted:

> Two systems are before the world; ... One looks to increasing the necessity of commerce; the other to increasing the power to maintain it. One looks to underworking the Hindoo, and sinking the rest of the world to his level; the other to raising the standard of man throughout the world to our level. One looks to pauperism, ignorance, depopulation, and barbarism; the other to increasing wealth, comfort, intelligence, combination of action, and civilization. One looks towards universal war; the other towards universal peace. One is the English system; the other we may be proud to call the American system, for it is the only one ever devised the tendency of which was that of elevating while equalizing the condition of man throughout the world.

Carey influenced the thinking of the then president Abraham Lincoln sufficiently to induce Lincoln to increase tariffs dramatically, subsidize the construction of portions of the transcontinental railroad, and move from a gold or silver backed currency to fiat money.

While this evolving neo-mercantilist approach was couched in terms of the enhancement of economic infrastructure and the protection of infant industries, its goals and methods were no different from those asserted by every empire in the Industrial Revolution era. The system was based on a beggar-thy-neighbor philosophy that could not act as a logically consistent basis for a global economy.

Nonetheless, advocacy of a mixed system with heavy government sponsorship in infrastructure and in tariffs, and occasionally in direct subsidies to manufacturing continued through the New Deal programs of President Franklin Roosevelt. This neo-mercantilist approach prevailed for more than a century and a half after Hamilton's American School reports.

The New American System

Richard Nixon, President of the United States from 1969 to 1974, finally verged away from mercantilism by slashing U.S. tariffs and moving boldly into a regime of free markets. His implementation of the conclusions of the "Kennedy Round," a multi-year series of talks on freer trade under the auspices of the General Agreement on Tariffs and Trade (GATT), well fit the evolving needs of the U.S. economy in the latter half of the twentieth century.

Once it abandoned protective tariffs and adopted free market principles relatively unhindered by government regulation, the American System embraced the principles promoted by Adam Smith 200 years earlier.

The New American System stood in contrast to the European model designed to protect labor or to shield the smaller economies from the free market American juggernaut. The European System held for greater regulation, in stark contrast to the broad perception of lower levels of intervention by their American counterparts. The European model supported greater protection for workers and for labor groups. Meanwhile, many American states declared themselves "right to work" states, a move that undermined the closed union shops of the American Rust Belt.

If the new American System celebrated Henry Carey's philosophy of elevating the common man so he may attain the American Dream, it also seized on one goal upon which all agreed. The emphasis was on the profitable corporation, under the premise that profits will reward management and labor alike. An emphasis on profits will also ensure that companies strive to increase revenue through innovation and decrease costs through a constant drive for economic efficiency. Either way, competitiveness is improved, and this too will ultimately favor those who produce goods.

One tremendous advantage of such a system that emphasized profits, efficiency, and competitiveness is that it was simple. An ideology based on the premise that a rising tide lifts all boats has since become the prevailing model for globalization. Indeed, globalization, with its myriad of national agendas, would be confounded in its ability to coalesce around any other system. Global cultures are simply too diverse, and global supply chains simply too ruthlessly efficient, to thrive in any more subtle or complex model.

Leveled on this New American System are accusations that the one-dimensional pursuit of profits tramples over human and worker rights, national sovereignty, and quality of life considerations. There is merit in these concerns, as we will address later.

The role of national cultural norms

Nations must inevitably layer their own cultural and social requirements on their participation in the emerging global economic system. Nations must also deal with consumerism emphases that are an outgrowth of the global economic model in an age of affluence. However, unlike colonialism and imperialism, it would be inaccurate to claim that the new global system is a conspiracy of economic empires. Rather, its greatest advocates are often the emerging economies that were formerly exploited by colonialism and imperialism.

Instead, the new global economic system has evolved as a way to deal with the clash of cultures that globalization has exposed. Institutions have learned to trade profitably with each other by maintaining a common focus on profits. However, there is less universal acceptance of other premises that affect terms of trade. The General Agreement on Tariffs and Trade, United Nations resolutions, bilateral and regional treaties, and the laws of sovereign nations must all combine to define a new globalization. This globalization must also respect other national and human goals. It seems beyond reach to imagine a global economy united around principles loftier than the principle of profit. We shall see in a later chapter that the tension of competing ideals across nations has yet to be resolved.

In the meantime, the American business model, long versed in maximizing shareholder value, has become the predominant business model globally. The necessity to raise large amounts of capital, often through American stock markets or stock markets modeled after American market principles, has forced large publicly traded companies to operate very much like American firms. It is the great necessity to raise financial capital to fuel global expansion that has caused the American model to spread.

The network externality

Part of this dispersion of the American model is no doubt due to the very success of the economic empire. America's empire status meant that its financial market conventions, tailored to the American corporate model, became the de facto standard for global imitators. Part of the dispersion is that success breeds success. One pathway for this success is through a network externality.

An analysis of network effects is borrowed from systems engineering. In the language of economists, these advantages of networking create a positive externality, defined as a benefit conferred on others without any cost to them or required action from them. Other labels and analogies describe these network externalities that arise when entities function better by working together. They include symbiosis, critical mass, positive sum games, or growing pies.

Many of the economic advantages conferred by the construction and growth of networks are seen in the Internet innovations Facebook and the professional networking group LinkedIn. Similar networks for online exchange of information include blogs, resumé exchange sites like Monster.com, and the like.

These modern versions of markets for intellectual and professional exchange are merely recent examples of exchanges that have long been the backbone of twentieth and twenty-first century commerce. For instance, exchanges for stocks, bonds, commodities, and future contracts have been long used to best match buyers and sellers of securities. These networks that began with the telegraph, telephone, and ticker tape, now perform tasks that are even more complex over the Internet with almost instantaneous speed.

The advantages of large and liquid markets also had the effect of encouraging broad, arms-length markets. At the same time, the impersonal nature of modern networking has created democratization and a standardization of information.

While the exchange of stocks has become much more liquid and predictable, it also forced certain conventions on the packaging and exchange of these stocks. The creation of much broader markets with a substantially increased diversity of participants also forced these networks to adopt simplified and unifying goals. Broader corporate goals may be more appropriate for a closely or more narrowly owned publicly traded corporation. However, once a corporation is listed on a broad exchange, such subtleties are lost. Instead, the necessary emphasis is on the piece of information that can most easily be communicated across the network.

This artifact of the network effect is a positive externality in increased liquidity and better share prices, but may also have a negative externality in the increased emphasis on short-term profits as a unifying and easily communicated corporate objective.

Other examples of the network effect include electronic business, or e-business, and e-commerce. These networks allow for much more extensive and geographically diverse markets for wholesale products and for factors of supply. They also force a certain standardization or commoditization of products. This standardization is necessary because such markets must cater to the subset of needs and specifications for a much larger set of potential market participants.

Such a democratization of markets may also mean that the market for non-standardized and idiosyncratic goods becomes much smaller. This dilution of potential quality or subtlety of commerce may, in fact, be the most significant negative externality of the network effect.

Fruit of the rise becomes the seed of decline

It is often the case that the winner gets to set the rules on how the game will be played. This tenet is partly by design but also partly because success breeds imitation. The initial success of the U.S. economic system allowed it to grow in both prominence and stature. While it began by taking the best of Adam Smith's free market principles and Henry Carey's mercantilism modified to fit an era striving toward economic classlessness, this mixed economy approach proved successful when other nations stood firmly in mercantilism.

With globalization, the mixed economic system gave way to a more universally accepted emphasis on profits and shareholder value. However, in doing so, the global system had implicitly accepted a new model of empiricism. Success, in profits and gross domestic product, became the yardstick to compare companies and countries, respectively. We will see that such simplistic yardsticks are not without serious limitations.

15

Heckscher, Ohlin, and Two Billion

> America was indebted to immigration for her settlement and prosperity. That part of America which had encouraged them most had advanced most rapidly in population, agriculture and the arts.
>
> (Attributed to President James Madison,
> Founding Father of the U.S. Constitution)

While a prevailing global economic model began to emerge following the Kennedy Round of the General Agreement on Tariffs and Trade (GATT) talks in the 1960s, not all countries have been equally able or willing to adopt it. Indeed, most economies still remain unable to capitalize on an ideology based on free flows of factors of production, goods and services, and capital across borders.

The primary reasons that not all countries subscribe equally to a unified global economic model are that each country differs in culture, population, factor endowments, wealth, capital assets, and even legal systems. These differences create opportunities for nations to take advantage of the global economic model in different ways. Economic systems allow each participant to make best use of its comparative advantage by using its assets and endowments to best effect. This principle dictates the specializations a particular economy may employ, and predicts the advantages that could bring some up-and-coming nations to the apex of global economic dominance.

Once considered a liability for countries like China and India, population is now seen as the new prime resource. Unlike other scarce resources in fixed supply, with population, a nation can always make more.

Nations have learned to leverage a rich population endowment that may have in other times been considered a liability. This significant excess capacity of labor offers much headroom for growth. The art is in endowing this large quantity of human capital with equally substantial quality. Meanwhile, an affluent empire may try to lever its assets by negotiating terms of trade that favor these same assets. Indeed, all nations simultaneously try to negotiate global agreements in ways most beneficial to them. To do otherwise would belie human nature.

Comparative advantage

Economist David Ricardo was one of the principal challengers of mercantilism in the early nineteenth century. He observed that nations would produce those goods that offer it the best cost advantage. This advantage may not make a country the lowest cost producer worldwide. It may simply yield the best cost advantage compared to other goods it could produce.

For instance, Ricardo uses the example of cloth and wine produced in England and Portugal. Portugal may have an absolute cost advantage in producing both, given its climate for grapes and for cotton. However, Portugal also has a large advantage in producing grapes, and a lesser absolute advantage in producing cloth. Therefore, it makes sense for Portugal to devote its resources to producing wine, and for England in cotton and cloth, and have the two trade their surpluses for the good they do not produce.

Another example of comparative advantage may be a lawyer and a law clerk. The lawyer could be excellent at both courtroom work and legal research. If the clerk were also a competent researcher but inexperienced in court, it would not make good economic sense for the lawyer to do both. Instead, the lawyer has the greatest advantage, relative to the clerk, in courtroom work, and should devote her time to the courtroom. The clerk, only a little less skilled at research than the lawyer, will devote his time to legal research. In other words, while the lawyer may have an absolute advantage in both activities, the advantage is comparatively larger in the courtroom. A lawyer skilled in both courtroom work and legal research in effect trades on courtroom work to purchase legal research.

The reason the lawyer exercises a comparative advantage in this way is partly because courtroom skills and expertise is scarcer and more highly valued. Similarly, countries typically have a comparative advantage in the goods that it can produce because of its rich endowment of a scarce and valuable factor of production the good needs. If the factor were difficult to transport across borders, it would make sense for a country to utilize its highly prized resource to make an equally highly prized product.

Alternately, a country may have an abundance of a resource, at low cost, that other countries do not have. In this case, the country may parlay its abundant resource in producing a good that uses this resource intensively. Therefore, the country can leverage its low cost asset to make a product at lower cost than it could be produced elsewhere.

Two such factors might be intellectual capital and labor. A country with a large, well-educated labor force ought to devote its labor force to intellectual capital industries such as education, software engineering, legal and financial analysis, writing, and other intellectual pursuits. The country's labor force might also enjoy working in agriculture, and may even be quite skilled at it. However, another country with a large, less educated workforce and equally high quality land would be better off devoting their labor force to agricultural production.

Heckscher-Ohlin and two billion

The Swedish economist Eli Heckscher and his student Bertil Ohlin elaborated on Ricardo's gains from trade theory by observing that a capital-rich nation will tend to make and export goods that require a relatively large amount of capital to produce, while a labor-rich nation will produce and export labor-intensive goods. In the absence of free trade, the surplus of production of capital-rich goods will drive its price down, while labor-intensive goods in the other country will command a low price there. Once trade between the two countries is permitted, it is profitable for both countries to trade to the other the good that each finds relatively cheap to produce.

The mercantilist instinct of imposing tariffs on imports frustrates these gains from trade. If the tariff is sufficiently high, a capital-intensive nation may find it unprofitable to import the otherwise less expensive products of labor-intensive nations. Therefore, there will be an incentive to produce labor-intensive goods domestically that would otherwise be purchased more efficiently abroad. A nation would be forced to divert part of the labor force from the more productive, capital-intensive sector into labor-intensive sectors.

While isolationism may appear to be a good job creation strategy, and this strategy of protectionism is certainly appealing in recessionary times, the result is a drawing away of resources from the capital-intensive and profitable sector. The result is a rise in the price of the goods the capital-intensive nation will produce. In turn, the export sector is also harmed as tariffs discourage imports.

Extensions of Heckscher-Ohlin

Most significantly, if a nation reduces production in the capital-intensive sector of its economy as it diverts jobs to the labor-intensive sector, the reduced output in the capital-intensive sector will cause its physical capital to be directed elsewhere. In an environment with import tariffs but no control over the flow of capital globally, there will be a flight of capital away from protectionist domestic production and toward production elsewhere. With capital mobility, free trade nations will benefit while protectionist nations will suffer.

Capital appropriately flows to seek the greatest return. In the twenty-first century global economy, financial capital can flow almost instantaneously to almost any corner of the world. However, if financial capital is mobile, and produced goods can cross borders with relative ease, but humans are restricted by borders, capital will flow to opportunities with lower labor or production costs, all else being equal. In capital-rich countries that also have high labor costs because of restricted labor movement across borders, there will be a flow of jobs and production out of the capital-rich countries and into those labor-rich countries that can produce equally efficiently.

We see this global tendency toward outsourcing to low labor cost countries as a consequence. However, this process, too, has its limits. As jobs flow abroad, both the demand for and value of labor increase, giving rise to higher wages and higher incomes in the aspiring nations. With higher wages comes a reduced incentive to outsource. In addition, with higher incomes comes increased capital formation in the aspiring nation. Over time, a transfer of production and technologies to the aspiring nation will equalize wages and the return to capital, and the outflow of capital and outsourcing of jobs from the relatively affluent nation to the aspiring nation will cease.

Postponing the inevitable

In other words, free trade acts as a leveler of economic wealth, decreasing the prominence of an economic empire while increasing the stature of an aspiring nation. An economic empire can do little to avoid this inevitability short of a protectionist policy toward mobility of capital and the import of goods and service that will damage the empire's economy even more.

This principle of comparative advantage and factor price equalization cannot be avoided, but can be frustrated. An economic empire is so because it exercises its more advanced infrastructure and access to technology. In the 2002 book *Kicking Away the Ladder – Development Strategy in Historical Perspective*, Cambridge economist Ha-Joong Chang argues that economic empires sometimes show a paternalistic and flawed understanding of the necessary ingredients of economic development at best, or subtly frustrate economic development at worst.[66]

Chang's basic premise is that an economic empire, with its vastly superior access to capital, its capital-intensive industries, and its workers who are able to use extensive technologies in their production, has a level of affluence and capital formation that perpetuates its advantage.

Meanwhile, the low level of wages in the labor-intensive developing countries prevents these countries from moving far beyond subsistence. This polarization of wealth is sustained by protectionist and interventionist policies by the economic empires.

Chang argues that free trade has actually been an obstacle to the development of poorer countries. He also observes that aspiring nations may even imitate these protectionist policies as they too vie to become economic empires.

Benign maliciousness?

Economic empires have a certain moral responsibility to their trading partners, present and future, to foster their development, to a point. While encouraging development in other nations may seem counter to the goals of the empire, such development assistance also creates ready markets for the empire's products.

An empire can encourage development from a position it knows best – its own. By encouraging economic practices that work well for the empire, it naturally assumes that a similar path for the developing nation will be equally successful.

For instance, competing economic empires have recently been debating the issues of the protection of intellectual capital and protection of the environment.

One of the essential ingredients for a dynamic economy is the protection of the inventiveness of entrepreneurs. Without these protections, entrepreneurs would spend too much energy obscuring and protecting their innovations and not enough energy inventing subsequent innovations. Consequently, patent protection is seen as an essential element in the protection of property, in this case intellectual property.

The export of values

We spoke earlier of entrepreneurial zeal that often outstrips the ability of an empire to develop sufficient legal or economic infrastructure capacity. For instance, an empire can establish protections for intellectual property, but can only over time, perhaps even decades, establish the jurisprudence and enforcement mechanisms sufficient to punish transgressors.

Once these legal and regulatory systems are established and are well understood and followed, it is compelling to export these conventions and expectations to less developed nations. After all, the empire had been able to take full advantage of the intellectual property infrastructure to develop an economy well adapted to such conventions.

Similarly, an affluent empire will also evolve environmental regulations suited to its wants and needs at each stage of its development. An affluent nation has superior health care to protect and prolong the productivity of its labor force. The empire also has a set of residents that can easily satisfy the basic needs of Maslow's Hierarchy of Wants and Needs, and begin to devote greater attention to higher wants. One such higher desire is for a healthier and cleaner environment that can afford residents a high quality of life over an extended longevity.

This noble value of environmental concern is what economists call a luxury good. As an economy becomes more affluent, its residents demand much more environmental stewardship than they may have desired in a less developed era. This is not necessarily to say that the affluent appreciate clean air or clean water more than their less developed ancestors do. Rather, it is simply a reflection that they can better afford the luxury of a pristine environment.

Unfortunately, affluent nations may not quite understand how a poor nation hears the affluent empire's pronouncements that the poorer nation should adopt stricter environmental standards. These pronouncements can be likened to the response of the French Queen, Marie Antoinette, on being told about the peasants who were starving for lack of bread. She was purported to have responded, "Let them eat cake."

Of course, a developing country would choose to adopt an economic empire's paternalistic insistence that they too have high environmental standards – if only they could afford it. Unfortunately, for the economic empires, it is always too easy to look into its past and find the same environmental transgressions that they now rally against in emerging countries. Then the retort must be "Do as I say, not as I did."

Finally, empires go through stages of mercantilist protection of domestic markets and hording of foreign capital as they then grow rapidly through export-oriented development. The implicit and explicit protection of infant industries, and the import substitution policies designed to encourage full domestic employment, are typically employed early in their development.

The evolution of economic empires

Britain went through its era of asymmetric trade policies designed to further the interests of the empire at the expense of the colonies. These practices were a primary motivation for the American Revolution. Likewise, the mercantilist policies of Alexander Hamilton, followed by the more refined and egalitarian, but still protectionist, policies of President Abraham Lincoln, flourished until free trade began to take hold following the Kennedy Round of the GATT talks in the 1960s.

The evolution of economic empires seem to follow steps that naturally, and perhaps even conveniently, evolve toward systems of free trade, environmental stewardship, and the protection of property. With stronger expectations of global trading partners, the evolution of future economic empires may be much more rapid. However, empires do not evolve instantaneously. Past economic empires that thrived precisely because they were afforded the time to move through these requisite development cycles. There can be no rushing the great cost of economic empire infrastructure building until nations have the capacity for such investments.

In order to create a level playing field, economic empires often try to export their evolved systems to aspiring empires. However, at best, from the perspective of the aspiring nation, the economic empire is simply trying to lock in a system that works best for it. At worst, an aspiring nation may accuse an affluent nation from imposing standards on it that the other nation knows it cannot afford. Just as the opulence of Louis XIV's royal court was designed to drain wealth, onerous standards can be viewed the same way by aspiring nations. The resistance, or even militancy, of aspiring empires is understandable.

To be fair, economic empires should confront this past and should be willing to enter into the great debate with aspiring nations to address squarely the elephant in the room. Such a straightforward approach of non-denial would be most healthy to navigate a path that works for economic empires and aspiring nations alike.

Such an accommodation may require some financial concessions. After all, environmental degradation knows no borders. If an established economic empire is legitimately concerned about the environmental policies of aspiring nations, then empires ought to be prepared to help pay for improvements. There is a solution somewhere between insistence that economic empires pay for the environmental improvements of aspiring nations and the requirement that these aspiring nations pay the costs of raising their standards to those of the economic empires.

There are cultural hurdles that must be overcome as well. This is the subject of another chapter. These cultural differences, toward the protection of intellectual capital, of human rights, of democracy, and of appropriate economic practices, will take time, and perhaps wealth, to overcome. Recognition of these hurdles will likely speed the process of accommodation and hasten the success of aspiring nations – at least if that is truly what economic empires seek.

Fruit of the rise becomes the seed of decline

The empires that came of age with the onset of the First or Second Industrial Revolution, each went through similar stages of economic development. They all advocated the creation of a domestic economic infrastructure to further production in the private sector. They also practiced increasingly sophisticated forms of beggar-thy-neighbor neo-mercantilism that emphasizes exports while discouraging imports and thereby protecting domestic industries.

While there was an increasing awareness by the 1960s of the logical inconsistencies of mercantilism, the road to free trade is long indeed. It is also strewn with the obstacles that naturally occur when cultural differences or differential stages of development are glossed over in GATT talks or other international trade negotiations. The complications of multi-lateral talks force economic empires and aspiring empires alike to focus primarily on free trade, just as their domestic economies may have focused on the universal goal of profits.

Lost in the mix are the subtleties that represent different cultures, different stages of development, different factor endowments, and even different legal and political systems. We see that the path of development, for both economic empires and aspiring nations, is one of nuance. Principles that work for one nation at a given time may be entirely inappropriate for another at a different stage of development.

It may even be the case that the understandable, if not misguided, attempts of economic empires to set global trade standards that best suit their needs may be unproductive for all concerned. In the process, economic empires may marginalize aspiring nations, and vice-versa.

16
Hungry and Willing to Work for Change

An empire, as we remarked, seldom outlives three generations. The first maintains its nomadic character, its rude and savage ways of life; inured to hardships, brave, fierce, and sharing renown with each other, the tribesmen preserve their solidarity in full vigor: their swords are kept sharp, their attack is feared, and their neighbors vanquished.

With the second generation comes a change. Possessing dominion and affluence, they turn from nomadic to settled life, and from hardship to ease and plenty.

In the third generation the wandering life and rough manners of the desert are forgotten, as though they had never been. At this stage men no longer take delight in glory and patriotism, since all have learned to bow under the might of a sovereign and are so addicted to luxurious pleasures that they have become a burden on the state.

> (Fourteenth-century Arabic historian and
> economist Ibu Khaldun, from *Prolegomena*)[67]

Within any nation are haves and have-nots, despite their best efforts to create equal opportunity, if not equality. However, between nations, there are inevitable differences in average incomes, and differences in incentive to work.

A country that is homogeneous in terms of wealth, race, skills, cultures, religion, and politics would be easier to rule. The division of a nation into special interests, often divided along the lines of the haves and have-nots, frustrates wealthy nations in the First Economic World in advancing still further. Differences in wealth between the First and the Second Economic Worlds also challenge the effort of the SEW to vie for membership in the most prosperous club of the FEW.

The desire to attain affluence is a powerful motivator for the SEW countries that aspire for membership of the FEW. Affluence also explains why it is so difficult for an economic empire to maintain its vaunted position indefinitely.

Haves, have-nots, and different factor endowments

The Ricardian and the Heckscher-Ohlin models explain why populous aspiring nations have a low wage rate and export goods that are more labor-intensive, and why nations that are more affluent export capital-intensive goods. We now delve deeper into the forces that give rise to differences in the income distribution in emerging countries and economic empires.

In any economy, the four factors of production – human capital, entrepreneurial capital, physical capital, and resource capital – are combined to produce goods and services. Presumably, these goods and services are sold for more than their cost of production. The difference, labeled profits, goes to the entrepreneur – the capitalists who employ the other three factors of production.

Typically, the capitalist also owns or rents the physical capital, those machines, factories, technologies, and processes that must be purchased to produce goods. These entrepreneurial capitalists must also rent human capital, and either rent or purchase the resource capital that is necessary to purchase goods and services.

How much the entrepreneur purchases of these various forms of capital depends on the relative prices. For instance, if human capital is very expensive, the entrepreneur may economize on its rental by purchasing more machines or more resources. In other words, in the black box of technologies economists label as the production function, the entrepreneur can substitute one factor of production for another, and will do so depending on their relative costs.

This approach implies that the prudent entrepreneur will buy or rent less of the most expensive factors of production and instead employ the more abundant and lower priced factors.

The income that accrues to a nation's factors of production can be measured in a number of ways. An affluent economy is measured by its high level of per capita income. This average income is measured by adding up the value of all goods and services produced in a year and dividing the total by the number of residents in the nation. An alternative and equivalent measure is to sum all the various forms of income earned by entrepreneurs in the form of profits, employees in wages and salary, rents to the owners of machines, and payments to natural resources, and divide by the number of residents.

Either method will yield a measure of the average income earned, per person, in an economy. However, no person earns exactly this average. Most typically earn less than the average and many earn more than the average.

We can predict which sectors command greater rewards and income and which earn less. The relative earnings of entrepreneurs, employees, machine owners, and resource owners depend on the supply and demand for each of these factors of production.

The price of scarcity

While the demand is complex, and depends on the price of a factor, the relative price of other factors, the overall demand for a nation's product, and the ability to buy and import similar factors of production from elsewhere, the supply of each factor is more basic.

The supply of factors is ultimately related to their scarcity. If there is a resource in good demand but in scarce supply, its price will be bid up accordingly. In addition, if a factor is in good demand but can easily be created, its price will be close to the cost of creating more of the factor.

While all factors can be in short supply in the short run if demand rises quickly, some factors can be more easily created in the long run.

For instance, physical capital, the machines, factories, equipment, and high technologies used to produce goods and services, can often be created relatively quickly and easily. Machine production can be expanded with relative ease and a shortage of a machine or piece of equipment domestically can, perhaps, be purchased abroad and imported. Consequently, the price of this form of capital converges relatively quickly to its long-run value.

On the other hand, if an economy expects strong and increasing demand for skilled labor over time, it can create additional skilled labor by training the unskilled labor force. The cost of such skilled labor will be the cost of unskilled labor plus the cost of their training.

Alternately, if there is a shortage of unskilled labor, a nation may encourage procreation or may permit and encourage immigration, as was done during the Gilded Age and the Second Industrial Revolution in the United States.

As these forces have time to play out, the cost of labor converges toward a level of income an economy considers sufficient to choose work over leisure. A wealthier nation with a citizenry better able to take care of its basic needs may require a higher wage to induce its citizens to become workers.

In order to secure profits, entrepreneurs borrow money, labeled financial capital, to buy machines and technologies, rent labor, and secure resources. Usually, these entrepreneurs are rewarded just sufficiently to induce them to perform their roles, commensurate with the risks they must take.

In a less developed economy, a much scarcer subset of the population have the entrepreneurial skill, the superior access to borrowed financial capital, and the networks necessary to coordinate production. Consequently, it is not unusual for entrepreneurs in developing nations to earn more substantial rewards. The aspirations of the have-nots who see these well-to-do entrepreneurs induce them to invest in education and to save so that they, too, can become successful entrepreneurs.

A unique form of capital

Natural resource capital is different from the rest. A nation can make more machines with relative ease, and can even create more laborers and entrepreneurs, through procreation, education, and a supply of financial capital. However, it cannot create more resources. Natural resources, such as land, minerals, oil, and water, are in fixed supply. They can be recycled but cannot be created. For this reason, they can command a premium.

In a growing economy, the rewards to these factors are directly related to the extent that they can be expanded over time. Given the relative scarcity of these factors, a developed economy will reward machine producers and the providers of labor less than it will reward those most scarce factors such as the brilliant inventor, the highly skilled and rare sports star, or the land, minerals, oil, and water that become increasingly scarce as our needs for them expand.

For these reasons, economic theory predicts that the value of land, minerals, and other factors in fixed supply can rise dramatically as production grows over time. However, the earnings of laborers will rise more slowly and more in proportion to the average value of production economy-wide.

For instance, as population grows and the economy replicates, the total value of production increases approximately proportionally. However, the good land close to the population centers becomes increasingly scarce, meaning that its share of the income from production rises more dramatically. Economies that begin to feel a constraint in available land resource will see dramatically rising land prices as a nation develops, leading to the conclusion among many that land close to the centers of production is the best investment for a growing economy.

In effect, it is these most scarce factors of production that usurp the bulk of the surpluses generated by a growing economy. Moreover, it is the owners of these natural resources such as land and minerals who earn the greatest rewards and income over time. As population grows, we see that the disparity between the income of laborers and the income of resource owners grows over time.

I can offer a concrete example of this wealth redistribution effect. In the most developed countries toward the end of the Second Industrial Revolution in the 1950s, it was typical that a single income earner in a family could support the financial needs of an entire family. A third social and industrial revolution began in the 1960s that moved many more women into the workforce. However, while a family might be able to produce more income, their quality of life did not rise substantially. Instead, homes that once cost perhaps two or three year's income for one breadwinner quickly rose to three or four year's income for two breadwinners. Meanwhile, single income earning families found it almost impossible to buy homes.

This example demonstrates how the additional surpluses generated by an economy rapidly expanding because of an increase in labor participation may absorb the gains by making one sector, the resource owners, much better off. Meanwhile, the larger sector of wage earners find it increasingly difficult to make ends meet.

In other words, such a growing economy typically does not grow evenly. Instead, entrepreneurs, resource owners, and those who own the financial capital desperately in need in a quickly growing economy may profit proportionally more with expansion. Others' income may rise as well, but their purchasing power can fall if prices rise more quickly. Meanwhile, income disparities between the haves and the have-nots may widen over time.

This natural tendency for income disparities to widen over time as the supply of scarce resources is stressed can be partially ameliorated through progressive taxes designed to shift income from the rich to the poor. Such progressive taxes are couched in terms of the "fairness" they create.

A 100% tax?

Such redistribution of wealth can be obtained in other ways. For instance, the nineteenth-century economist Henry George recommended a large, indeed 100% tax on the value of land.[68] His rationale was that land increased in value not because of any effort from the landowner, but rather as a natural consequence of a growing economy.

George noted that an economy grows because of the infrastructure a society invests in its own economic future. Therefore, a 100% land tax would compensate government for its investment in the economic infrastructure that gave rise to growth. He also observed that such a land tax would obviate the unproductive speculation of land and would make land more affordable, if not more profitable.

However, George did not propose to tax the capital improvements on land. He proposed a tax on the physical land to pay for the cost of government in an era in which the size of government was substantially smaller. Then, government did not engage in significant transfer payments between various classes of taxpayer. Consequently, it would have been possible to have taxes on the land pay for the government-provided economic infrastructure that gave rise to land values in the first place.

Such a tax would also narrow the income gap that arise in a growing economy. Gaps would remain in the incomes of those who invent and create and those who labor. However, by reducing the burden of economic infrastructure on all and concentrating it primarily on the owners of fixed factors of production, the average income of laborers would rise. So would their ability to purchase land that no longer rose in value for speculative purposes.

A necessary gap?

Humans aspire to ascend through Maslow's Hierarchy of Wants and Needs. As their average income rises, they more easily meet the basic needs of food and shelter. Then, they seek to satisfy higher needs – for financial security, and for basic needs in the future. Finally, they look toward education, fulfillment, and other needs such as self-actualization and esteem that is more difficult to buy.

After a point, humans aspire for such increased wealth not to meet their basic needs, but rather because humans naturally compare themselves to each other. A wide gap in wealth between the haves, who own property and other fixed factors, and the have-nots provides an incentive to invent, create, and produce. Income is important not merely in an absolute sense. Relative income between others in their social class is an important, if transient and ethereal, human motivation.

Of course, the motivation to advance economically can be doubly powerful when one is striving to satisfy basic human needs and when one is conscious of the brass ring of social attainment. Those who have no wealth to protect may put in great effort and take large risks to secure an economic future. Hunger and room to grow are big incentives to change and to work.

On the other hand, when most members of the economy have sufficient wealth, they increasingly become more conservative in their major economic decisions and motivations. Their wealth causes them to maintain the status quo that induces complacency and economic stagnation, and look to preserve a past that worked well for them.

Motivation, too, suffers from the Law of Diminishing Marginal Returns. If workers have a pressing need to meet their most basic wants, then a low level of prevailing income combined with a realistic optimism for economic growth can produce a strong work ethic and effort. This effort to meet basic needs is followed by further effort to attain what is possible. However, just as a developing economy will grow rapidly initially and then grow much more moderately, individuals also have a diminishing opportunity to attain even greater wealth as they move up the income ladder.

If we combine this reduced motivation to get ahead as income rises with the tendency to protect wealth as income rises, we may conclude that motivation to succeed declines with greater income. In other words, a nation most hungry for economic advancement will be able to support greater growth than a nation at the apex of economic power.

Fruit of the rise becomes the seed of decline

A large and populous nation, or a nation able to attract a hardworking and motivated workforce, has great opportunity for growth. Such a nation would afford a competitive wage rate and produce labor-intensive goods and services comparatively cheaply. This production puts income in the hands of the owners of human capital, creates a strong and sustainable middle class, and helps fuel rapid economic growth.

This success narrows the gap between what income is and what it could be. Rising income reduces the comparative advantage and reduces the motivation and the capacity for further growth. At the apex of economic power and size, further spectacular growth becomes more difficult.

The capacity of an economy to grow still further is mitigated as production based on human capital shifts toward production based on physical and financial capital. However, goods and services, and physical and financial capital can easily cross borders. They will flow to countries that have the basic economic infrastructure, a lower cost and motivated labor force, and the capacity to grow rapidly.

Consequently, an affluent and mature economic empire may be able to sustain a modest growth rate of 2% or 3%, fueled by technological improvements and population increases. In the meantime, an aspiring nation can sustain dramatic growth of 8%–10% for years and decades, based on the motivation of its citizens and the unrealized capacity of underemployed laborers.

It is the motivation of workers, the unrealized capacity for economic growth, and the natural development cycle that creates a great opportunity for growth in aspiring nations. Likewise, these motivations are a great leveler of growth in economic empires that have long since fully utilized their once-untapped potential. This leveling effect is unavoidable, and is simply a consequence of success, combined with the law of diminishing marginal returns.

Part V
Growing Pains

In the latter half of the twentieth century, an economic empire was bursting at its seams. The economy of the United States had become unwieldy. Production had become exceedingly complicated and difficult to coordinate, especially as the empire assumed a role as the world's only superpower and beacon of free marketeering. Chaos theory shows us that exponential growth can also cause exponential growth in divergences from an optimal economic trajectory. At the same time, institutions grow too big to fail. Once an empire reaches this point, it begins to suffer from a winner's curse.

17
Complex Economic Systems

But by an equality, that now at this time your abundance may be a supply for their want, that their abundance also may be a supply for your want: that there may be equality.

(2 Corinthians 8:14)

The great strength of laissez-faire economics can also be its greatest weakness. The uncoordinated efforts of millions of economic participants, channeled through markets and priced through the invisible hand of the marketplace, produces incentives and innovations that can fuel dramatic economic growth. This same melee of human activity also gives rise to colossal coordination failures.

The greatest failure of any modern economic system occurred during the Great Depression. Interestingly, the Soviet Union, the bastion of central economic planning at that time, did not suffer the same decline experienced in free market economies and countries. What is it about free markets that make them so vulnerable to economic shocks, and what can be done to ameliorate such economic crises?

The veil of laissez-faire

One of the great innovations of the modern economy is the use of money and markets to decentralize economic activity. Free market participants no longer had to find traders who happened to want what they produced in exchange for what they wanted. Such a "double coincidence of wants" was obviated by money as a medium of exchange, which both sides valued, and by markets that offer a forum for the wants and needs of all demanders and the goods and services produced by all suppliers.

In a simpler economic system, laborers and producers were told what to make and when, and the laborers, as consumers, were given a share of the production. The importance and role of money and markets are minimal in such a simple, centrally planned economic system.

In a more complex free market economy, it is more difficult to tabulate precisely what production leads to what consumption. In contrast, a centrally planned economy ensures that the number of rolls of toilet paper produced is matched with the number of toilet paper rolls distributed to consumers. The very mechanism of distribution, outside of free markets, ensures that supply and demand is matched.

However, with free markets and money, we only know that supply translates into demand because we have faith in the efficiency of the invisible hand of markets to determine the correct price that will equate supply and demand. This faith is attributed to Jean-Baptiste Say, a French economist and businessman who weighed into the great mercantilist debate that was raging through the nineteenth century. In his book *A Treatise on Political Economy – Or, The Production, Distribution and Consumption of Wealth*, Say remarked

> Having once arrived at the clear conviction, that the general demand for products is brisk in proportion to the activity of production, we need not trouble ourselves much to inquire towards what channel of industry production may be most advantageously directed.
>
> The products created give rise to various degrees of demand, according to the wants, the manners, the comparative capital, industry, and natural resources of each country; the article most in request, owing to the competition of buyers, yields the best interest of money to the capitalist, the largest profits to the adventurer, and the best wages to the laborer; and the agency of their respective services is naturally attracted by these advantages towards those particular channels.[69]

Say was arguing that, in general, production is followed by consumption. He was writing to rebut those protectionists who would isolate an economic system in a futile attempt to maximize the wealth for an economic empire. He used this argument to explain why purchases of products from other countries resulted in a like demand for domestic production, and for consumption in both countries. He was also arguing that, while money may facilitate these transactions, it should not obscure the aggregate effects of such mutually advantageous exchanges, on both sides of the transactions.

This theory is often restated as "supply creates its own demand." However, proponents of this theory time and again fail to take notice of Say's caveat a few paragraphs previous:

> ... the encouragement of mere consumption is no benefit to commerce; for the difficulty lies in supplying the means, not in stimulating the desire of

consumption; and we have seen that production alone, furnishes those means. Thus, it is the aim of good government to stimulate production, of bad government to encourage consumption. (pp. 139)

Say was rebutting the corollary most often attributed to him, that demand creates its own supply.

John Maynard Keynes, perhaps the most influential economist of the modern economic era, took on Say's Law in a revolutionary approach to the macro economy, popularized at the height of the Great Depression.

A Keynesian faith

Keynes' abandonment of Say's Law, in favor of a theory that left room for the spending psychology of consumers and producers, government, and international traders, forced us to recognize that the modern economy can suffer bad equilibria even if it is more typically at rest in a good equilibrium. The role of what he labeled "animal spirits" changed our view of macroeconomics and, ultimately, in our belief of the need for activist government intervention in the economy.

Keynes recognized that the way the government manages the money supply might affect the investment decisions of households and producers alike. In normal times, money acts as a lubricant, ensuring that there is sufficient currency flow in the economy to support the purchases of production by consumers. In other times, the supply of money becomes ineffective, as households choose to hoard their cash rather than reinject it into the circular flow of income between households and firms.

Keynes saw an avenue for central economic coordination in an otherwise decentralized economic system. He observed that, if households were unwilling to consume, a greater supply of money in the economy could allow these households to continue to hoard some cash, but spend the rest. An increase in the money supply could coax households to inject any excess cash into the banking system, which presumably would lend these new savings out to producers wanting to expand.

While this pathway for effective monetary control to stimulate investment and production may work most of the time, it fails at the times when we most need government to direct an economy spinning out of control. Before we describe such coordination failures, let us first describe why government coordination need not fill any gap between what is produced and what should be produced.

Let us assume that the economy is producing and consuming less than the optimal number of jobs and amount of production. If an economic authority can create a new job, the income earned from this job will be spent to create new consumption, and hence demand for new labor somewhere else in the economy. The income from this original job ripples and reverberates around the economy.

Keynes demonstrated that one new job created would ultimately generate many more new jobs. While the precise number of jobs created depends on many economic factors, it is fair to say that the ultimate job growth factor is more than one and less than ten in total.

The multiplier effect

This ability of one job to spawn other indirect and induced jobs allows government to augment gaps in employment rather than fill the gaps entirely. In typical times, this ability of the government to steer the economy through the occasional stimulus or tightening is practiced with great regularity. This same ability is challenged in the most difficult times, too.

This ability to induce the formation of additional jobs through the creation of a single job allows government spending, through fiscal policy, and stimulation from the central bank, through monetary policy, to fine-tune the economy. Indeed, central banks do this fine-tuning on an almost daily basis. By encouraging banks to hold more cash, a central bank can discourage banks to lend to businesses that wish to expand production.

Alternately, by encouraging banks to lend their cash to the businesses that produce jobs, a central bank can encourage production and employment. Whatever employment a central bank can encourage or discourage through their monetary policy translates into a multiplied effect in the overall labor market.

The ability of central banks to adjust employment, through its manipulation of interest rates and bank cash reserves, is a best-case scenario. Banks have to cooperate by extending loans. If they refuse to do so, a monetary authority loses its potency. When that happens, there is little recourse but to engage in direct fiscal policy by having government create jobs more directly.

A failure to coordinate an economic empire

There are a variety of reasons why monetary coordination may fail.

First, central banks force banks to shift the balance of cash and short-term interest bearing assets in their financial portfolio by manipulation of the interest rate. If a central bank offered to lend cash to commercial banks at a low interest rate, banks may be encouraged to lend to their customers. This lending results in new deposits somewhere in the banking system which, in turn, creates new cash for other banks to lend still further. In other words, banks have their own deposit expansion multiplier that allows them to take some cash offered by their central bank and create deposits and loans that may be upwards of ten times larger than the original cash injection from the central bank.

However, while we can lead a horse to water, we cannot make it drink. If a wary commercial banking sector refuses to lend under any circumstance, the central bank can become ineffective.

If there are differential investment opportunities for commercial bank, they may even take the stimulus and invest instead in other, more promising, economies. Even if the commercial banks choose to lend to domestic industries, there are leakages in the form of purchases of capital equipment from other countries that may reduce the ultimate effectiveness of domestic monetary policy in generating domestic jobs.

Even if the monetary policy is effective in generating domestic jobs in the first round, subsequent rounds of job creation through the multiplier effect require consumers to spend. These wary consumers may, nonetheless, suffer from the paradox of thrift. In effect these consumers hoard their cash under their pillow rather than cooperating with the economic authorities by spending any newfound income thereby creating additional jobs.

Finally, when government spends directly to counteract these failings, they inevitably either drive up taxes or the debt. If taxes rise, consumers have less income to spend. In addition, if the federal debt is increased, the economic authority must offer higher interest rates to secure these additional funds. The higher interest rates may raise the prevailing rate on business loans, too, thereby "crowding out" private investment as public investment is increased.

On net, either of these tendencies reduces the effectiveness of job creation policies by an empire's economic leaders.

Automatic economic stabilizers

An economic authority can also put into place certain policies that serve to stabilize economic activity without any activist interventions. For instance, such social welfare nets like unemployment insurance ensure that consumers can continue to spend even if unemployment rises. Likewise, a fall in income results in a decline in taxes paid, which leaves more income for consumers to spend.

These interventions can reduce the severity of a downturn. Similarly, an economy in an upturn will see moderated growth as taxes rise with higher income generated. These stabilizers can even out the peaks and valleys of the business cycle and allow an economy to realize growth with less uncertainty and cyclic movements.

However, these same safety net benefits introduce their own set of challenges. By indemnifying workers from the effects of unemployment, an unemployed worker is less motivated to seek work. Offering these built-in stabilizers creates what economists call a moral hazard problem. When an economic empire takes on the risk of the private sector, individuals in a private sector make decisions without contemplation of the risk they impose on the larger economy. Instead, policies designed to put the unemployed back to work can be more effective than those that permit an individual to remain unemployed.

A matter of time

Despite our understanding of the occasional role for activist policies on the part of our leaders to prevent economic downturns, policymakers remain divided into two camps. All agree that there is an important psychological dimension to the macro economy. In addition, all agree that the economic authority can command certain types of economic activity in our modern systems that have become a mix of free market and command economies.

However, some conclude that a mixed public/private economy reduces the reward to the private sector. Mixed economies also evolve toward a greater portion of public enterprise.

Almost all economists also believe that an economy will heal itself, if given sufficient time. However, economists do not universally agree on the speed or efficiency of an economy's self-correcting ability.

If it takes a long time for a free market economy to grope toward equilibrium, proponents of activism advocate a greater government role. Opponents of activism, however, have greater faith in the laissez-faire approach, or remain skeptical of the ability of the government sector to improve the economy. Indeed, some argue that a greater share of the command economy will invariably cause the private sector to suffer. Consequently, they may conclude that they can withstand temporary displacements in economic activity until the economy can return to equilibrium without intervention. Even in the height of a prolonged Great Depression, some remained skeptical about government intervention economic activism.

Today, every economy accepts some economic activism by its government. If there is no true laissez-faire economy any more, the issue is of the relative share of the public command sector and the private market sector in our mixed economies.

Fruit of the rise becomes the seed of decline

The smallest economy is the easiest to coordinate. A few producers are most able to determine the range of goods and services desired by a few consumers. If producers know in advance that consumers want their goods and services, they are willing to hire the households to perform the work. This simple system is self-coordinating.

Alternately, even a large but centrally planned economy can be coordinated in a similar manner. The central planner simply requires households to devote their labor to certain activities. In the aggregate, the central planner can ensure that there is a sufficient amount of human capital, physical capital, and earth's capital devoted to produce the goods and services the central planner deems necessary.

The central planner also distributes this production of goods and services as necessary to satisfy its consumption criteria on behalf of its residents.

Both the simple self-coordinating economies and the centrally planned economies are stable, if not particularly innovative. These economies work best when there is little change. What they may lack in innovation or dynamism they make up in predictability and invulnerability to the vicissitudes of the business cycle.

On the other hand, the free market system is innovative because it is fueled by the ingenuity of a myriad of entrepreneurs, each hoping to discover that product every consumer wants. The free market system also permits households to choose from a wide range of goods and services, something which neither a simple economy nor a centrally planned economy can provide.

If the measure is innovation, efficiency, and the ability to produce the goods and services consumers desire at the best possible price, the laissez-faire system typically outperforms the other systems by a wide margin. The diversity of production and the efficiency of economies of scale is a hallmark of the free market system.

However, an economic empire that fuels its substantial growth because it subscribes to the free market system is also more vulnerable to economic shocks, recessions, and depressions. A larger economy also requires a more robust and sophisticated system of regulatory oversight, especially with regard to the money supply and other monetary policies.

In addition, an economic empire, both dependent on and strongly linked to other global economies, affects and is affected by the success of its trading partners. The global financial meltdown that began in 2008 painfully demonstrated this reality. The meltdown also demonstrated how the fortunes of an economic empire can change dramatically based on the same global trade interactions it fostered to generate its economic greatness.

18
Herding Cats and Chaos Theory

A great civilization is not conquered from without until it has first destroyed itself from within.

(William James "Will" Durant, historian, 1885–1981)[70]

Edward Lorenz, a quiet assistant professor of meteorology at the Massachusetts Institute of Technology, once demonstrated that a seemingly innocuous change in one of twelve weather parameters, and of a magnitude well less than one part in a thousand, could change his model predictions dramatically. His observation, entitled "The Butterfly Effect" demonstrated that a butterfly flapping its wings in Brazil could cause a tornado in Texas.[71]

Lorenz was describing the Achilles heel of complex systems – small changes can result in huge oscillations or shifts over time. With the possible exception of the earth's biological systems and the weather, there are no systems more complex as the modern economy. A national economy that is made up of those hundreds of millions, if not more than a billion, actors, each pursuing his or her own self-interest, has the richness that only a system made up of billions of separate entities can muster.

A basic result of chaos theory states that the potential divergence from a projected trajectory increases exponentially over time with minor differences in the initial conditions of a chaotic system. The Lyapunov exponent describes how minor deviations in a complex system can cause share divergence over time. In other words, a small shock can have surprisingly large effects in a complex and chaotic system.

Empires are prone to the Lyapunov exponent divergence. They typically grow in proportion to their population, the number of economic decisions made by their households, producers, and institutions, and the size of their institutions. However, this very size of their institutions generates economies of scale, bureaucratic chaos, and vulnerability to shocks.

From efficiency gains to bureaucratic paralysis

Sufficiently small organizations need no burgeoning bureaucracy. It is not difficult for these organizations to coordinate its activities. However, such ad hoc management techniques or relatively simple procedures and policies prove inadequate as organizational systems increase in complexity.

Dating back to the very first empires and continuing through the Qin Dynasty of Confucius and all dynasties and empires since, the bureaucracy is a necessary but often maligned element of all institutions. From the root "bureau," meaning "office," a bureaucracy is the collection of functions necessary to execute the policies and organize the administrative resources for complex organizations. The various institutions of large for-profit, not-for-profit, and government require such a structured organizational model to track and coordinate their internal resources and manage its external relations.

Part of the maligning of bureaucracies is a consequence of the great number of vastly diverse institutions that must employ bureaucratic methods. For instance, the tax collector is a necessary element for the funding of government. To minimize corruption, tax collectors must follow rigid principles and policies that are designed for relatively objective valuation and collection. However, this necessary rigidity removes individual discretion and inevitably errs when rigid rules fail to anticipate every possible circumstance. Consequently, bureaucrats are often characterized as dehumanized, rigid, and insensitive.

Another aspect that leads to the maligning of bureaucracies is that the internal functions of an organization are not typically disciplined by external market forces. While every function of a small organization is buffeted by the needs of a market, a large organization internalizes many functions that may have previously been performed on an ad hoc basis or contracted out to the marketplace.

While such internalization of functions is typically designed to generate savings and economies of scale, lost is the economic discipline that efficient markets command. These transactions are measured by quantities, prices, and costs. Equivalent internal transactions are not contracted so strictly and objectively.

For instance, if a bookkeeping function is fulfilled outside the organization, contracts require accountability and explicit prices and costs. However, once this organizational function is internalized, it loses opportunities to contract out or request bids for services. Instead, the budget for an internal accounting office is periodically renegotiated internally. Lost is the accountability that, ironically, the company, and perhaps even the accounting department, would insist upon for most of its external transactions.

In a bureaucracy, the profit motive that drives efficiency is lost, replaced by an incentive of a department director to maintain and maximize revenue and staff. These alternative measures define how a bureaucratic department competes within the organization or is compared to other departments elsewhere.

A service sector

Organizations find it difficult to outsource those activities that are not easy to quantify. Consequently, enterprises often internalize such services. Conversely, goods producing activities within an organization can be more easily outsourced when it is not difficult to value and exchange these goods in the free market.

Efficiency of services-producing bureaucracies create even greater difficulties in measurement. Some measures, such as the number of clients served, the number of files reviewed, the number of employees hired, etc., belie meaningful qualitative measures of the quality of the tasks performed. Consequently, the familiar measure of a price, calculated by dividing total costs by the total quantity of services provided, is lost in the blur of bureaucracy.

None other than Karl Marx attacked the emergence of bureaucracies as a sub-market institution. In his *Critique of Hegel's Philosophy of Right*, Marx wrote in 1843:

> The bureaucracy is a circle from which one cannot escape. Its hierarchy is a hierarchy of knowledge. The top entrusts the understanding of detail to the lower levels, whilst the lower levels credit the top with understanding of the general, and so all are mutually deceived.[72]

Marx was concerned that bureaucrats did not produce in themselves. Instead, they oversaw and coordinated the production of tangible, market-destined goods and services. While this technocratic role was necessary, the technocrat attempted to maximize profits while minimizing its own effort.

This tension in the creation of an entity in itself rather than as a coordinating functionary causes bureaucracies to vie for larger budgets and greater organizational authority, just as would any product line within a diverse company. However, unlike market-oriented product lines, bureaucracies are not held to the discipline of market forces, except in the last resource when a company or agency must search for cost cutting opportunities.

The religion of production

Max Weber, a German political economist and politician, is often attributed as a father of modern sociology. He wrote a most influential set of comments on the economy in 1905. This collection of essays entitled *The Protestant Ethic and the Spirit of Capitalism* offered a religious underpinning to the pursuit of production and profit, as opposed to the Marxian belief that capitalism replaced religion. Weber argued that the pride of an entrepreneur could be likened to the religious devotion of a monk. Speaking from the Scottish Presbyterian perspective of work as a service to God and mankind, Weber's pro-capitalist perspective was in sharp contrast to Marx's perspective of the dehumanizing effect of capitalism.[73]

However, Weber could also be critical of the despiritualizing effect of bureaucracies when he wrote:

> The Puritan wanted to work in calling; we are forced to do so. For when asceticism was carried out of monastic cells into everyday life, and began to dominate worldly morality, it did its part in building the tremendous cosmos of the modern economic order. This order is now bound to the technical and economic conditions of machine production which today determine the lives of all the individuals who are born into this mechanism, not only those directly concerned with economic acquisition, with irresistible force. Perhaps it will so determine them until the last ton of fossilized coal is burnt.[74]

Weber's criticism was not one of entrepreneurship and enterprise. Rather, it was a condemnation of the frustrating effect organizations too large can impose on its laborers. He noted that human capital must feel attached to its production and organization, whereas bureaucracies and large-scale production frustrates this attachment.

Weber observed that bureaucracies fall into a number of unfortunate patterns. For instance, nepotism or political battles with an organization can replace competence and efficiency as the norm. He also feared that the increased specialization necessary for an increasingly large and complex organization breeds isolation and poor organizational information flows.

Such specialization can substitute rigidity and rules-based decision-making for creativity and innovation. Ironically, organizations become paralyzed by their own degree of specialization, with groupthink replacing a diversity of opinion and a marketplace for ideas. Ultimately, the system becomes more complex and less informed, and the coordinating effect of the bureaucracy actually diminishes.

This Weberian criticism of bureaucracy has been expanded by a number of writers and social commentators, including George Orwell in his books *Nineteen Eighty-Four* (1949),[75] and *Animal Farm* (1946),[76] and Joseph Heller in his *Catch-22* from 1961.[77]

A backward reversion

The effect of such dehumanization on human production has led large organizations to explore decentralization and the reversion back to simpler organizational hierarchies. For instance, in an effort to replicate the perceived advantages of a Japanese small car manufacturers, General Motors, then the largest automobile company in the world, decided in 1985 to create a "A different kind of car company, a different kind of car."[78]

The creative bud of a huge car production conglomerate was to produce a car in a small factory distinct from its Michigan roots that was to represent a new collaboration between management and unions. Union members would participate in managerial decisions and oversight, and workers were encouraged to learn as many processes on the assembly line so they could better understand a wider range of the production process.

Interestingly, GM was merely trying to repatriate the Japanese manufacturing philosophy that had originated with an American W. Edwards Deming. In the rebuilding effort of Japan following the Second World War, Deming was commissioned by the U.S. Department of the Army to assist in training Japanese corporate executives. Deming's philosophy of productivity and quality control was adopted enthusiastically in Japan. However, it took another 40 years before these same techniques met with widespread acceptance in his home country.

GM was one of the first to adopt the Deming model of quality control using Japanese manufacturing techniques. Within ten years of its inception, their new product, the Saturn automobile, was GM's biggest seller. However, less than 15 years later, their "different kind of car" company was on the chopping block. As GM faced bankruptcy in the onset of the Global Financial Meltdown of 2008 and was forced to reduce the range of cars it manufactured, it discarded the Saturn concept and mothballed the factory that was once argued to be its greatest symbol of a smaller, leaner, and more creative conglomerate.

Entrepreneurship versus herding cats

The ultimate frustration of large organizations is that any external market relationship is appropriately forced to justify its value on an ongoing basis. However, internal organizational politics holds internal functions relatively immune to regular scrutiny and accountability. Consequently, bureaucracies tend to creep up in size over time. Occasionally, an organization decides to decentralize and break itself up into smaller, more nimble and autonomous groups. However, this "smaller is beautiful" approach is rare and episodic.

The critique of bureaucratic organizations that have become too large and monolithic is not solely leveled at modern corporations. Indeed, corporations are held accountable in a marketplace that demands high quality product of good value. This constant check on corporate efficiency is not replicated in the bureaucracy of the public sector. Voters can withhold their support from a particular political party leadership on occasion. However, the public cannot regularly and effectively voice its discontent for public agencies and institutions and expect any tangible result. If the market only infrequently forces a corporation to reevaluate its bureaucratic structure, rarely are public agencies forced to retrench. Consequently, public institutions often grow at a rate that exceeds population growth or the general growth of economic activity.

A public sector bureaucrat suffers from a classic principal-agent problem. In economics, a principal-agent structure is one in which a principal, such as the shareholders of a company, the taxpaying public, or a client, engages an agent to pursue its interests. By doing so, the principal surmises that the agent can accomplish the principal's objectives with greater efficiency and at lower costs sufficient to justify the additional expense of hiring the agent.

Ideally, the agent internalizes this relationship to ensure it acts in the best interest of the principal, by maximizing value for the principal.

However, an ideal principal-agent relationship succeeds only if certain conditions are met. First, the method that compensates the agent must be directly tied to the agent's success in realizing the objectives of the principal.

Second, there must be sufficient transparency of information to permit the actions and effort of the agent to be easily observed by the principal.

Finally, the principal must have recourse to adjust the behavior of the agent if the agent's effort departs from the optimal effort that maximizes principal value.

While almost all hierarchical and employment relationships are principal-agent relationships by definition, few behave perfectly. This problem is most apparent in large organizations that balance a proportionally large number of competing objectives.

For instance, an employee in a department may view her responsibility to her immediate supervisor, rather than as a share of responsibility to a product. A professor believes his responsibility is to a department rather than to a collection of students. A police officer has a responsibility to a police chief rather than to the public he has taken an oath to protect. A politician may feel a responsibility to act in accordance with the goals of the leader of a political party rather than with the needs of her electorate. Alternately, a union worker may follow the edicts of the union shop steward before the pronouncements of the shop foreman.

As organizations grow in size, they find it increasingly difficult to align their organizational objectives, usually imposed upon an organization from an external and increasingly global marketplace, with the internal actions of myriad agents. Just as chaos theory suggests that divergence from a predictable path grows in proportion to size and exponentially over time, increasingly complex organizations diverge over time from the creative, innovative, and responsive structure necessary for maximum efficiency.

This disconnect often induces organizations to create elaborate, and often ultimately dysfunctional, sets of rules that will dictate their internal operations. This internal rigidity has caused some commentators to characterize bureaucracies as inherently inefficient.

For instance, Michel Crozier wrote in 1964 that the rationalization of the corporate organizational structure of Weber and Frederick Taylor has devolved in practice. In his book *The Bureaucratic Phenomenon*, Crozier complains:

> ... the slowness, the ponderousness, the routine, the complication of procedures and the maladapted responses of the bureaucratic organization to the needs which they should satisfy.[79]

He went on to add:

> A bureaucratic organization is an organization that can not correct its behaviour by learning from its errors. ... (It is) not only a system that does not correct its behaviour in view of its errors; it is also too rigid to adjust, without crises, to the transformations that the accelerated evolution of the industrial society makes more and more imperative.[80]

Crozier could easily have been commenting on a particular form of bureaucracy that was practiced in France. A recent bestselling book in France focused on the art of creating the illusion of work when little or no work was actually performed. *Bonjour Paresse* (*Hello Laziness*), variously subtitled *Jumping Off the Corporate Ladder*, or *The Art and the Importance of Doing the Least Possible in the Workplace*, was written by Corrine Maier in 2004.[81] This publication is at once an amusing and serious indictment on the modern bureaucracy and corporation.

While Maier's approach sounds anarchistic and destined to create the chaos that corporate rigidity strives to avoid, she nonetheless appealed to those who feel disconnected from their employer and use this disenchantment to rationalize a laziness that employees perceive of their direct supervisors. While she strived to be fair and to discover and emphasize a common goal for a less rigid corporate world, her book, and the comic strip *Dilbert*, nonetheless offer anthems to the organizationally disaffected.

Crozier goes even further than would Maier or *Dilbert*'s author, Scott Adams. From a sociological perspective, Crozier argues that bureaucracies are no different from the assembly of any group of humans in a social activity. He noted that all such assemblies yield those that would turn the objective of the group to his or her own advantage:

> Each group fights to preserve and enlarge the area upon which it has some discretion, attempts to limit its dependence upon other groups and accept such dependence only insofar as it is a safeguard ... [preferring] retreatisim if there is no other choice but submission.[82]

His conclusion is fundamental. While it would be ideal to assume that an organizational structure can somehow align the goals of the agent to those of the principle, ultimately these goals are most strongly aligned to the culture of a department. Crozier condemns group dynamics to a series of petty power struggles, and the dynamics of the larger group no different, with these struggles instead dictating inter-group interactions.

> ... the bureaucratic system of organization is primarily characterized by the existence of a series of relatively stable vicious circles that stem from centralisation and impersonality.[83]

Crozier believes such bureaucracies embody a number of organizationally dysfunctional principles. The first is the creation of impersonal rules, often recorded in elaborate procedures manuals, that govern individuals' relationship to the organization based on internal test scores, seniority, and perhaps nepotism.

This principle of rules creation inadvertently creates a system of centralized decision-making. Under such centralization, those who must impose the edicts of bureaucratic policy are protected by the claim that they are "only following the rules." As a consequence, creativity and responsiveness is lost, and so, too, is direct responsibility for decisions.

He also sees rampant policy-making in bureaucracies. Extensive and impersonal policies and the appearance of centralized decision-making create a sense of isolation and stratification within the organization. Individuals no longer internalize much influence or potency on the organization overall, are no longer surprised by the organizations' failure to recognize their contribution, and no longer believe they have much responsibility or obligation for organizational success. At this point, the principal-agent relationship has broken down and individuals begin to feel a stronger shared identity and relationship with their coworkers in their stratified departments rather than with the overall organization.

Finally, in the absence of a strong and unifying organizational objective that permeates all levels of the institution, workers define themselves within the stratified department and organize their activities to maximize their power within the strata. In this way, they can salvage an overall impotency in the organization with a political effectiveness that is much more substantial but is confined to the stratified department. From small fish in a big pond, some instead transform themselves into big fish in a small pond.

Ultimately, these parallel power structures compete for power within the organization. These parallel structures do not advance the effectiveness of the organization overall, but, rather, they compete for the resources of other departments. In effect, the very symbiosis and positive-sum-game aspects of an effective organization are transformed into a decidedly constant-sum-game competition among isolated departments within the organization.

Indeed, if this structure and competition between various departments divert energy that would otherwise have advanced the goals of the institution, the bureaucratic structure devolves into a negative sum game in which the whole is less than the sum of its parts.

When an organization reaches this level of dysfunction, value can be salvaged by breaking up the organization into its smaller parts. This devolution of the institution is part of the decentralization movement among many large corporations. Under such a strategy, individual units become semi-autonomous that report to a larger and overarching holding company.

Fruit of the rise becomes the seed of decline

Certainly, complex systems can increase diversity and uncertainty. They can also result in surprising and sometimes catastrophic perturbations because of their very complexity. On the other hand, small and carefully coordinated policies can create magnified and significant positive benefits to the economy. The art is in mastering and controlling such complex and decentralized systems.

Larger organizations run the risk of increased chaos and bureaucratic dysfunction. When this occurs, organizations often resort to a breakup of the organizational structure into autonomous parts that produce a product in return for clearer rewards.

However, there is a natural process of decay that results in organizational growth and dysfunction over time, followed by episodic decentralization. Institutions that can somehow prevent the rigidity that comes with size and encourage the creativity and principal-agent responsiveness of smaller organizations are the institutions most able to thrive.

19
Too Big to Fail

It is unconscionable that the fate of the world economy should be so closely tied to the fortunes of a relatively small number of giant financial firms.

(U.S. Federal Reserve Board Chairman Ben Bernanke in a public speech at the Independent Community Bankers of America conference in Orlando, Florida, March 20, 2010).

The economies of scale that give rise to economic empires can be substantial. Empires flourish through their ability to build better or more efficient mousetraps, or through natural endowments of various factors of production, often labor, that bestows upon them a comparative advantage over their global competitors. However, chaos theory predicts that economic uncertainty also increases with size.

Most problematic is when this economic uncertainty gives rise to economic contagion, recession, and depression. Ironically, when a strong and negative economic shock brings an empire to its knees, the empire is left, at times, with no choice but to bail out the dysfunctional institutions that caused the shocks in the first place.

Organizational theory gone awry

Bureaucratic theory and chaos theory taught us two things. From agency theory, we discovered that stratified agencies become politicized, and seek to maximize the benefits that accrue to the department. Within an organization, these benefits might include intra-organizational power. Agencies may also seek to increase their stature among all agencies by commanding greater resources, a larger number of staff, or a larger budget. In the absence of clear-cut and market-oriented rewards, these measures constitute agency influence.

Agencies can also seek external rewards. For instance, elected officials are use their position to enhance their prestige by adding out favors. This external prestige is proportional to the level by which the decisions of a public agency can most profoundly affect individuals or groups.

Such prestige seeking, in the absence of more tangible market-oriented rewards, would obviously lead to more agency representatives who have a strong effect on even a small number of external individuals or groups.

By contrast, a government agent that affects a large number of people to a lesser degree cannot command an equivalent amount of external prestige and reward. For instance, the manager who doles out a large number of welfare checks will not garner the same prestige as the bank manager responsible for originating a small number of high-value mortgages and bank loans. Greater economic complexity creates new avenues for such unproductive behavior.

One step ahead

We previously documented a series of recessions that punctuated the evolution of the world's first economic empire. Each major recession demonstrated how regulatory agencies had failed to create an environment that would manage the risk of an economy growing in complexity.

Chaos theory also tells us that, as the stakes become higher as organizations grow, so do the uncertainties and the significance of missteps. As the economic stakes grow, so does the possibility that an economic empire may find some of its constituent organizations too big to fail. Regulatory missteps become almost unavoidable. An economy grows by unleashing the creative energy of the producing class. If regulation is too conservative, growth is stunted. In addition, if regulation is too liberal, growth, too, is liberated. However, a relaxed regulatory environment will naturally prove inadequate, on occasion, to prevent serious economic failures.

History has shown that such regulatory failures often occur in waves. A period of deregulation is followed by economic growth that sometimes exceeds the boundaries of economic prudence. Occasionally, colossal failures occur. When they do, stewards of the economic empire must decide what to do with the failed organization or corporation and must develop a plan for the future to ensure the past does not repeat itself.

An unfettered market offers rewards to those most successful who grow with the size of the economy. Potential losses, too, increase. The issue confronting an economic empire is whether it can afford the mammoth losses that can occur in large economies. At times, economic leaders decide that these losses are just too much to bear.

The concept of too big to fail is a product both from chaos theory, that increasingly complex systems can experience increasingly large fluctuations, and from the network effect, that larger systems affect a greater number of stakeholders. With this confluence of forces, some economic institutions became so economically intertwined that they are too big to fail.

A history of bailouts

Economic history is riddled with bailouts and political favors doled out to organizations most politically connected to the leaders of economic empires. The corporate favors bestowed on the British East India Tea Company protected a few well-placed shareholders at the expense of British citizens forced to pay more for their tea and colonists forced into trades that advantaged the homeland. Indeed, this example of "too big to fail" gave rise to a political and economic revolution that would cause Britain's economic empire to be eclipsed, in just over a century, by its upstart former colony.

The American empire, itself, went through a series of bailouts and forced corporate marriages. Most notorious of these was a railroad industry bent on monopolization and, at times, destructive competition, contrary to the public interest. In the freewheeling era of the Gilded Age, economic power was never lost. Instead, it was often merged with or absorbed by other more powerful corporations. An economy reliant on an industry building its transcontinental railroad infrastructure could ill-afford backtracking in the investment infrastructure.

By the twentieth century, the economic infrastructure was well established. Still, major corporations remained too big to fail. For instance, while General Motors uttered, with some corporate arrogance, that what was good for GM was good for the country, it was Chrysler, one of the big three automobile makers employing hundreds of thousands of workers, that was deemed too big to fail. In the wake of the OPEC oil crisis, and after a long history of producing cars that could not compete with their fuel-efficient Japanese counterparts, Chrysler's corporate mistakes were forgiven through a loan guarantee of $1.5 billion in by taxpayers of the United States in 1979. Chrysler would be back at the bailout trough, requiring four times that amount just 30 years later in the Great Recession that produced a wave of the largest global bailouts in world history.

Just over a decade after the original Chrysler bailout, the private equity investment firm Long Term Capital Management (LTCM) exposed a threat to an economy that was increasingly dependent not on building a better mousetrap but on inventing a more complex financial instrument.

Big business and big government have always been closely tied. Wealth buys influence, and those privileged with the spoils of both enjoy common trappings and luxuries. Those who occupy the cradles of power, either political or economic, inevitably share a relatively lonely position at the top. LTCM tested this rarified world.

LTCM was founded in 1994 by a former executive of Salomon Brothers, then one of the world's largest investment houses. With winners of the 1997 Nobel Memorial Prize in Economics on its board, and with an investment strategy of its own creation, LTCM quickly rose to become the fastest growing major new power on Wall Street. Its growth was meteoric and the decline of this shooting star was equally astronomical. In 1998, it lost almost five billion dollars in four short months.

A better mousetrap?

LTCM's strategy was novel. It would scour the market for bonds that were thinly traded in at different locations around the world. It discovered that it could predict a large purchase of a security in one financial market that would soon translate into large and positive price movements in another market. By buying a security in one market and selling in another, similar to the actions of early tea and foreign exchange arbitragers in London and Amsterdam in the eighteenth century, LTCM booked billions in profits. They could move quickly and profit substantially well before the rest of the market could realize what happened.

Ultimately, LTCM created value for themselves, but at the expense of all others. There was no better mousetrap, no more innovative companies, and no new products. While there was a substantial wealth generated for LTCM that begot more wealth, the economy's pie was not growing.

These amazing successes for LTCM at the expense of other bondholders caused them to seek out more and more trading opportunities in more and more unfamiliar venues. By 1997, LTCM was increasingly using more conventional investment strategies in an effort to satisfy the increasing thirst by its principles for continued growth. Consequently, risk grew. This risk resulted in a spectacular failure that, because of the ever-broadening network effect, threatened the very confidence of Wall Street institutions that depended critically on that very confidence.

An operation so precarious that a few of the smartest people on Wall Street could bring down an entire industry was just too much for the sector to bear. First, the financial industry determined that it had to bail out its own, in recognition of their mutual strategic interdependence. Soon, though, these efforts and infusions from the likes of Warren Buffett and other proved insufficient.

Wall Street and its government regulators in the New York Federal Reserve Bank subsequently recognized that the sector could not bail itself out. The Federal Reserve coordinated an injection of four billion dollars, an amount that made the size of the Chrysler bailout in 1979 seem trivial. While the

LTCM bailout was colossal at the time, bailouts that are more recent make it seem like small change now.

Privatized profits and socialized losses

While the economy averted a failure that threatened the very foundation of markets dependent on market confidence, it also opened a Pandora's Box that could not be closed. An economic empire heralded in an era of "too big to fail" in which gains were privatized but losses were socialized.

In doing so, spectators of the economy were exposed to the term "moral hazard." Once used by economists who were concerned about the potentially dangerous effects of those insured so much that they behaved recklessly, the term moral hazard was soon applied to the financial institutions entrusted with the life savings of millions of citizens of an economic empire.

Beginning in 2008, a financial bubble that had benefited almost every financial investor on the globe suddenly burst. Moral hazard problems that began when millions of borrowers were offered mortgage packages well beyond what they could afford were soon exposed when people began to realize that these mortgage instruments were vulnerable if housing markets did not continue to rise in value. Within months, credit markets collapsed. Over a year, financial and real estate markets valued in the tens of trillions of dollars worldwide lost almost half of their value.

At first, regulators were willing to let the ruthless premise of economic Darwinism play out. However, as this contagion spread to other markets and significantly affected the wealth of hundreds of millions of consumers, a sober realism set in. With decreased wealth came increased economic conservatism and decreased consumption. Spending began to falter and with it the demand for goods and services. A noose was tightening around the circular flow of income that fueled the usually robust relationship between consumers and producers.

Consequently, consumers became cautious and delayed planned consumption, while producers fired workers and decreased their production. Unemployment grew, resulting in additional rounds of decreased spending and production.

Once this viscous global positive feedback cycle began, there was little to do but arrest its downward acceleration. The ultimate economic catastrophe had occurred. Nations around the world mounted a coordinated effort to stem the damage, at the cost of many trillions of dollars. Some of the world's largest investment banks disappeared overnight and others had to borrow hundreds of billions of dollars from taxpayers. After a year of economic carnage, the decline plateaued. However, the damage was done, even if the Great Recession narrowly averted the title of the Great Depression II. The economic repair will take years.

Perhaps the most significant result of the great global bailouts of 2008 was the heralding in of a new era in which global governments became the insurers of economic empires. The global economy discovered it had a stake in global enterprise, even as it did not have the tools to regulate global commerce. This deadly economic sin could not be put back into Pandora's Box. And, moral hazard was added to our lexicon, with government in the uncomfortable position of insuring foolhardy and irresponsible investment houses.

Global markets inextricably linked

How can a contagion in one market create a whiplash effect on the global economy? In one important way, global economics is a victim of its own success.

In the 1990s, the world suffered a great scare because of the Asian Contagion. Growing uncertainties in risk in foreign exchange primarily in Asia created a financial panic that enveloped the globe. Financial markets began to realize that an economic weakness in one region of the world can swiftly infect markets everywhere.

Since then, global economies have been increasingly networked. For instance, a scare in one global financial market can result in a flight of capital to a stronger market that may also be in decline, but not by as much.[84] The linking of two such markets can result in wild oscillations as money moves back and forth between the two, in search of better and safer returns.

Eventually, this oscillation back and forth between markets will settle down at a new and lower level that properly represents the economic shock that initiated these global reverberations in the first place. However, before they settle down, these global markets may fall much further and experience much more volatility than is justified. Such is one of the hidden costs of globalization and linked financial markets.

Fruit of the rise becomes the seed of decline

Networking theory tells us that an economic empire can create synergies that fuel sometimes-spectacular economic growth. Indeed, the positive sum game that is created as an economy harnesses and then capitalizes upon its economic potential is the common ingredient of all economic empires.

However, chaos theory also tells us that these very synergies also magnify uncertainty at a rate that can increase exponentially over time. A line blurred between the private institutions that give rise to the economic empire and the institutions that govern the empire creates even greater mutual dependencies and a greater expectation that government will bail out failing private institutions. With this implicit insurance comes even greater risk taking and moral hazard. In the end, this partnership of kingpins engenders public and private economic decisions that limit further growth and threaten economic growth elsewhere.

Wider networks in the best of times allow many to share in prosperity. However, these same networks in the worst of times create vulnerabilities and cause economic viruses to infect an increasingly networked global economy.

20
Private Property Gives Way to the Public Good

A right to property is founded in our natural wants, in the means with which we are endowed to satisfy these wants, and the right to what we acquire by those means without violating the similar rights of other sensible beings.

(Thomas Jefferson to Pierre Samuel Dupont de Nemours, 1816)[85]

We make no small point of the tendency of an economic empire to divert its attention away from private production and toward the more ethereal production of public goods. When governments fall into this trap, they, too, contribute to consumerism.

This tension between the private and public sectors is a reversal of economic philosophies. Private property is the underpinning of the capitalist system and is the innovation that allowed the United States to best leverage a Second Industrial Revolution to create the world's first empire derived from pure economic strength. The public interest of an affluent empire often compromises some of the private property protections that gave rise to the empire in the first place.

It is interesting to document the gradual transition of private property, fiercely protected in the Bill of Rights of the United States, into a regime that permits these property rights to be gradually eroded or subsumed into the public sector.

Protection of life, liberty, and property

Modern constitutions protect property in a number of different ways. This concept of the protection of property dates to John Locke, and others, in their belief that a natural law transcended the laws created by governments. This natural law must protect life, liberty, and estate (or property). Indeed, this sentiment was the basis for Virginia's Declaration of Rights, as drafted by

George Mason in 1776, which states: *"all men are born equally free ... [with] certain inherent natural rights, of which they cannot, by any compact, deprive or divest their posterity."*[86] Thomas Jefferson borrowed these words in his version of the Declaration of Independence, when he wrote:

> We hold these truths to be self-evident, that all men are created equal, that they are endowed by their Creator with certain unalienable Rights, that among these are Life, Liberty and the pursuit of Happiness.[87]

By recognizing Locke's natural law, which no government can abridge, and by enumerating the right to the pursuit of happiness as a substitute for Locke's right to estate (or property), Jefferson was reaffirming that property is a necessary element of the pursuit of happiness. He was preordaining the formation of a nation based on private property and free markets.

The United States Bill of Rights, ratified by the States in 1791 and appended to a U.S. Constitution written four years earlier, included the protection of property in its Fifth Amendment. This amendment abridged the federal government from taking private property for public use without paying just compensation. Later, the Fourteenth Amendment, ratified in 1868 as one of the Reconstruction Amendments following the U.S. Civil War, provided that same protection of due process for taking of property from private individuals by state governments.

The nation's attitudes have evolved since the Fifth Amendment was enacted in 1791, and the Fourteenth Amendment was enacted in 1868. First, the decision *Munn v. Illinois* in 1877 that permitted the federal government to abridge property rights through regulation.[88] When asked if a private company could be regulated in the public interest, the U.S. Supreme Court ruled that it could, and thereby established the framework for public regulation of private industry.

The court was no doubt troubled by the excesses and rampant capitalism of a burgeoning Gilded Age. In permitting public regulation of private enterprise, it declared that property rights of private entities could subsequently be abridged in the public interest, and taken with just compensation.

Such property rights were further eroded somewhat through a number of decisions. In *United States v. Carolene Products Company*, the U.S. Supreme Court decided in 1938 that while some rights are protected by strict scrutiny, economic rights shall only be protected based on the "rational basis" test.[89] This test offered deference to government in its determination of whether the costs of the abridgement of economic rights are exceeded by the benefits that would accrue in the public interest.

This threshold that would allow government to abridge economic rights, including property rights, offers the utmost deference to government. In effect, the Supreme Court was stating that it was in no position to second-guess the legitimate economic decisions of government. The courts would not intervene in such controversies unless it was clear that government was not exercising its authority legitimately. In other words, government is presumed to behave constitutionally in its deliberations over economic issues.

This fettering of free markets came at the height of the New Deal. President Franklin Delano Roosevelt, frustrated by a conservative Supreme Court unwilling to cooperate in his efforts to have government pull an economic empire out of a Great Depression, threatened to increase the size of the Supreme Court and appoint New Deal–friendly justices. While he failed in his court-stacking strategy, he did nonetheless influence the court to support his agenda, and managed to name the majority of the court through subsequent retirements.

A more friendly New Deal–appointed court issued a ruling in the Carolene Products case that was far more significant for its fourth footnote. That note justified a public interest in the regulation of private companies and dramatically and instantaneously expanded federal oversight and control over commerce ever since.

The Takings Clause

Overreaching government aside, the original purpose of the "Takings Clause" is justified. There is a range of legitimate government takings that enable government to further collective interests unambiguously. For instance, if interstate commerce is more efficient when state-constructed highways have a more direct route, the ability to appropriate land to allow these rights of way is in the interest of the economy. However, this interest can be frustrated if landowners are able to extort this public interest for their own enrichment. By providing only for just, or market-based, compensation, the Takings Clause prevents such speculative extortion.

However, while most can agree that takings are justified to prevent profiteering at the public's expense, cases naturally arise that are not as clear-cut.

For instance, in *Hawaii Housing v. Midkiff*, in 1984, Supreme Court allowed government to expropriate land owned by one large landowner, with the intent of subdividing the land to create a large number of small landowners.[90] Alternately, in *Poletown Neighborhood Council v. City of Detroit*, the Supreme Court of the State of Michigan ruled in 1981 that one large private landowner, General Motors, could use the eminent domain apparatus of the city council for Detroit to expropriate land from a large number of small landowners residing in the Detroit neighborhood of Poletown.[91]

This trend continued until it incurred the wrath of voters. In 2005, the U.S. Supreme Court determined, in *Kelo v. City of New London*, that eminent domain could be used to transfer land from one property owner to another whose project was deemed to afford the community economic growth through redevelopment.[92] This further example of forcing one set of private landowners to sell their property, at fair market value, to another set of private landowners created a backlash, with 43 out of 50 states subsequently passing legislation to redefine their eminent domain statutes.[93]

Economic growth through intellectual property

While property rights to land are predominantly local affairs, the protection of intellectual property has global implications. Just as real property rights offer an individual monopoly rights to the use of their land, intellectual property principles extend monopoly rights to patents and industrial design rights, copyrights, and trademarks.

We have observed that an economy will transcend through labor-intensive production and into capital-intensive production that employs increasingly sophisticated technology. A sophisticated economy will also increasingly rely on intellectual property.

The World Intellectual Property Organization recently reported that a study of six Asian countries found a positive correlation between the protection of intellectual property and economic growth.[94] The protection of intellectual property is an issue of most significant importance for the most developed nations worldwide. Given the observation that such developed countries capitalize on intellectual property to a far greater degree than do their aspiring nation counterparts, this should come as no surprise.

The global debate over intellectual property began with the Trade Related Intellectual Property (TRIPS) protocol. Trade related aspects of intellectual property rights was a package of rights negotiated in 1994 as part of the Uruguay Round of ongoing meetings for the General Agreement on Tariffs and Trade (GATT). This aspect of ongoing global trade principles embraced by GATT's member nations was advocated by the (then) world's three largest economies: the United States, the European Union, and Japan.

The protection of intellectual property is entirely consistent with the free market principle of protection of all kinds of property. However, as we noted earlier, the Protestant value of production and property is not a universally accepted culture.

For instance, my former University of Alaska colleague, John Lehman, recently wrote:

> Western attempts to obtain Chinese compliance with intellectual property rights have a long history of failure. Most discussions of the problem focus on either legal comparisons or explanations arising from levels of economic development, based primarily on the example of U.S. disregard for such rights during the 18th and 19th centuries. After decades of heated

negotiation, intellectual property rights are still one of the major issues of misunderstanding between the West and the various Chinese political entities. (An examination of)…the sources of this problem from the standpoint of traditional Chinese social and political philosophy, specifically Neo-Confucianism, (demonstrates)…. that the basic assumptions about the nature of intellectual property, which arose during the 17th and 18th centuries in Europe, are fundamentally at odds with the traditional Chinese view of the role of intellectuals in society.…(P)olicies which do not take these differences into account, but which attempt to transfer Western legal concepts without the underlying social constructs are responsible for much of the lack of success in the area of intellectual property rights.[95]

Lehman suggests that cultural differences in the protection of intellectual property rights go beyond mere differences in relative stages of economic development. There may be important cultural differences that dictate why economies of developed and aspiring nations differ in this, and, likely, other fundamental economic values.

Fruit of the rise becomes the seed of decline

The protection of property as a natural law dates back to the Magna Carta. It is a fundamental underpinning of free markets. However, this same right that permits the formation of markets also frustrates the public interest, at times. An economic empire is inevitably pressed between the competing interests of private property holders pursuing their own happiness and the greater public interests of all.

As these public interests are expanded in proportion to the growing role of government in economic empires, the same property rights that gave rise to dramatic economic growth are often curtailed. While this curtailment is a natural result of an emerging public interest, it can only frustrate the economic growth of the private sector as original engine of the economic empire.

We have argued that diffusion and imitation will result in a convergence of economic systems. While it is certainly true that the dominant economic system of free markets was facilitated by a political system of democracy, there is more to society than economics and politics. Embedded in every society are certain notions of equity, morals, and religion that also help determine cultural norms. These norms inevitably influence economic values as surely as economic values influence cultural norms over time.

While the economic innovations we take for granted have flourished for less than three centuries, strong cultural norms have prevailed in some societies for millennia. Inevitably, these norms of property, cooperation, and the role of government will influence the way dominant economies evolve.

There is also a looming conflict with regard to competing notions of property and competing economic systems. The protection of property rights is consistent with Western civic and economic principles. However, these principles so fully incorporated into the traditional economic empires are not fully embraced or shared by the aspiring nations that may vie for economic empiredom.

21
The Winner's Curse

Don't let your special character and values, the secret that you know
and no one else does, the truth – don't let that get swallowed up by the
great chewing complacency.

(Aesop, ancient Greek philosopher, 620–564 BC)[96]

There is a winner's curse that affects all but the most vigilant and disciplined.
When one is ahead, especially far ahead, there seems little need to look back.
A racer in a comfortable lead does not need to attend to her rear view mirror.
Those racing behind are most aware of the leader's advantage, and of other
up-and-comers. The winner's curse actually bestows an advantage on the up-
and-coming who recognize winners' complacency is their Achilles heel.

Lumbering giants

Occasionally, an up-and-coming competitor fires a shot across the bow that
awakens the lumbering giant. The Soviet era Sputnik satellite was one such
shot for a complacent U.S. empire still relishing in their success following
World War II. However, with the fall of the Iron Curtain and the end of the
Cold War, there have been other shots of similar significance to recalibrate the
economic discipline of the world's only remaining superpower.

It is hard to underestimate the blow to a national psyche that had grown
accustomed to its status as an economic empire. Coming off the First Industrial
Revolution, Britain continued to thrive through the era of Queen Victoria and
the first half of the Second Industrial Revolution. It was not until just before
the end of Queen Victoria's reign in 1901 that the United States overtook Great
Britain as the world's largest economy. Since then, the United States has not
looked back, until now.

There are lessons that Great Britain learned as its role as an economic empire
unwound over the twentieth century.

Certainly, Britain realized the great cost of maintaining an empire of such vast geographic expanse. To maintain the security of a far-flung empire is costly when that security is challenged on more than one front. For instance, wars with France and with the American colonies almost bankrupt Great Britain at a time when no other nation could otherwise challenge in for economic dominance.

Costly arrogance

The advantage of a far-flung economic empire is that it provides a continuous flow of income from the hinterland to the heartland. Of course, the cost of this flow is to maintain colonies or dependencies in subservience. An empire is not intrinsically benevolent, despite the best efforts of its citizens to assume it is so. The maintenance of economic power is costly if it is necessarily accompanied by coercion.

There is a self-deceiving tendency for economic and political leaders and citizens alike to rationalize that their influence on another people is based on higher ideological principles. One should never underestimate the penchant for humans to rationalize the ideology they find most convenient. This is not to say that there is not some higher ideology worthy of universal adoption. However, a subservient nation that does not also share in the benefits of its empire will fail to see the wisdom of this higher principle, no matter how logically compelling the ideology may be.

Consequently, empires often "invest" in sufficient military power as a necessary vestige of its empire status. While sharing in the wealth of the empire may be more effective in spreading the ideology, it is often more expensive. It also drains resources from the homeland in a way that is domestically less palatable than use of the military.

Nor is the empire's relationship to its dependents monolithic. Just like siblings, each international economic relationship is different and has different needs of the parent country. To further each of these relationships in a way that does not conflict with its other relationships is an impossible task.

As an economy begins to recognize its mortality, it can demonstrate an arrogance and denial that is not entirely unknown. Like the actor behind his prime or a middle-aged man recalling the glory days of high school sports, an empire past its prime may redouble its efforts to live in a false reality. When one does not receive laurels any longer, it is intoxicating to rest on past laurels.

At the same time, recalibrating the expectations of its citizens who have come to expect the prestige of the economic empire is difficult. A British Home Secretary was reported to have once said that his job was to "supervise the orderly decline of the British Empire." While political leaders must come to reckon that their role as emperors is over, it takes much longer for a nation steeped in such a culture to shake its self-image. Empires form over decades, if not centuries. They do not unwind quickly.

An empire may also lack the perspective to know when it can dictate foreign policy and when it must deal in it. A prevailing and domestically dominant culture drowns out all others. However, other aspiring empires, not so wed to a dominant culture, are better able to triangulate, and to take advantage of the best of many worlds.

A margin too comfortable

Part of the slow demise of an empire is that the trappings and symbols only decay slowly. They are part of the economic and cultural fabric, and so they erode slowly. Moreover, while the awareness of a people on a trajectory toward empiredom is acute and is fanned with nationalism and an increase in wealth, attainment of such a status becomes a low-key affair. One who is running fast to catch up has that carrot on the end of a stick. One who is ahead only rarely looks back.

Fruit of the rise becomes the seed of decline

Empire building is an exciting era for any aspiring nation. The nationalistic zeal of a nation that has come to vie for the ultimate economic prize is only comparable to the sense of satisfaction and pride once the empire arrives. At that point, it is all too easy to be carried solely by the momentum that brought it to that point. After all, it is all but unseemly to continue to strive for greatness once greatness has been bestowed.

However, the very arrival at the apex of an economic trajectory is the point at which an economy transitions from the chaser to the chased. What must follow are periods of reinvention and reflection that can allow a more perfect economy to continue to innovate. This, perhaps, is the greatest challenge of all.

Part VI
A New Economic Order

Despite its best efforts to reorient terms of trade to create freer markets of its goods and services, the affluence of an empire past its apex shifts away from a production emphasis toward a consumption emphasis. This shift also has a mercantilist tendency because affluence easily satisfies the need for goods.

An affluent economy increasingly becomes service-oriented and these services are typically provided domestically and locally. Consequently, gross domestic product becomes highly levered to consumption, the service sector expands, and export industries are deemphasized. These effects combine to sustain growth for a time, but at the expense of investment in its own physical capital. This lack of production and innovation-oriented investment in export-oriented sectors can lead to the end of growth.

22
The Politics of a Consumption Economy

> Conspicuous consumption of valuable goods is a means of reputability to the gentleman of leisure.
>
> (Thorstein Veblen, *Conspicuous Consumption*, 1902)[97]

Just as surely as an economy can move from production of machines on Main Street to the production of wealth on Wall Street, so, too, can an economy at the apex devolve toward economic isolation. An economic empire that enjoys the luxury of constant inflows of capital from abroad is doubly vulnerable to this isolation. Meanwhile, aspiring empires are all too happy to reinforce a complacent sense of well-being characterized by a consumer-based economic empire.

The circular flow

Economies create wealth through two avenues. The first avenue is through injections directly into the economy, from purchase of its goods and services and its factors of production by other nations.

This avenue is particularly important for aspiring nations. Such purchases create domestic demand and employ its factors of production, especially its human capital. This inflow of foreign currency can then be used to purchase capital goods from other nations. The importation of capital goods allows the aspiring nation to increase its capital stock and make its labor more productive. It also aids in the nation's modernization and technology transfer. Consequently, nations such as China and India are using their large trade surpluses to build their economic infrastructure in this way.

The second avenue to increased domestic wealth is to ensure that the income earned domestically by all factors of production is reinjected into the domestic

economy. Aspiring nations may use tax revenue and savings to fuel the creation of government sponsored infrastructure and private capital investment.
Both pathways create jobs and further income. However, to be successful, this
strategy requires that the economy has the capacity to absorb and effectively
channel infrastructure spending and capital investment into areas that can be
productive and offer strong public and private rates of return.

This process can continue until all the various factors of production are
fully employed. With a strong capital stock, a skilled entrepreneurial class, and
a stock of human capital hungry to get ahead, the resulting per capita gross
domestic product will rival that of developed nations.

The end to growth?

However, once factors are fully employed and the productive capacity is
reached, further growth can be achieved only from greater efficiency improvements, technological advances, and increases in factors of production, most
notably skilled labor. An economic empire that gained its status by optimiz-
ing its productive capacity will typically expand based on innovation and on
its ability to attract new financial, physical, and skilled human capital from
abroad.

Once this domestic capacity is reached, growth is no longer fueled by
unrealized potential. Instead, the stock of wealth and the rise of consumerism substitute for an export led economy and ambitious investments in new
capital. The nation has inevitably moved from a production to a consumption economy.

Maslow's Hierarchy of Wants and Needs also sets in. A nation that moves
from producerism to consumerism has a wealth sufficient to easily meet its
basic needs of food, clothing, and shelter. Consumers instead begin to devote a
greater share of their income to services. Sectors such as banking and finance,
entertainment, medical and education services, and food and travel take on a
much larger share of income.

This emergence of a dominant service industry differs from the traditional
goods producing industries in a number of fundamental ways. With the exception of some services such as health care, the service industries are typically
relatively low technology and require little capital. Also, because these industries are less capital-intensive, they are also typically low wage. Finally, the service sector is contemporaneous. Haircuts and doctor's appointments cannot be
inventoried. Services generally fuel consumption now and are difficult to set
aside as investments in consumption tomorrow.

These labor-intensive, low-wage, consumption-oriented characteristics ultimately mean that wealth is created less rapidly. An economic empire accustomed to spectacular growth must instead settle for a growth rate roughly

equal to the sum of the growth in the size and skill of the working population, and technological improvements.

Few countries can grow the domestic labor force very quickly. Some nations, most notably Germany, expand the labor force through increased immigration. Countries also manage to continue to grow in this mode by embracing education and enhancing the value of their human capital. Still others expand the value of their capital stock through ambitious research and development programs.

A shrinking productive sector

Frustrating sustained growth is the very nature of Maslow's Hierarchy of Wants and Needs as income rises. Not only does the hierarchy dictate that individuals increase their relative preferences toward services and away from goods. Individuals also prefer to translate their wealth into the purchase of additional leisure and into their benevolent regard for others. These effects will translate into a withdrawal of some from the workforce, to pursue more leisure, or to work flexible hours in settings that are more comfortable. Human capital moves further away from manufacturing and more labor-intensive industries and into service-oriented industries.

Individuals also increase their concern for others and develop an increasing taste for income redistribution. Lost in the transformation is the march toward greater productivity and higher gross domestic product. In its place is a greater emphasis on the distribution of the economic pie rather than on the creation of the economic pie.

Growth of government and consumption by the majority

This transformation of an emphasis from production to fair distribution should not be viewed as a regression of economic principles. Indeed, democracy itself is a highly valued principle that other economies may ignore. The wealth and affluence of an economic empire dictates that such democracy is a luxury it can afford. This luxury is one that satisfies Maslow's higher wants – of benevolence, actualization, self-determination, and even spirituality, for some.

Like every economic decision we make, with democracy we must balance benefits and costs. The benefits of democracy may include the security derived from social welfare nets democratic governments offer its citizens. Access to public education, a police force and military responsive to the wishes of the majority, freedom of association and expression, and the protection of civil liberties are all enhanced with democracy.

If these rights and freedoms, for liberty, security, and self-determination, are the benefits that satisfy the higher wants an affluent society can afford, these services come at a price. With a progressive income tax regime, the price rises with income and wealth, under the presumption that the wealthy can better afford, and are willing to pay a higher price, for these products of democracy, just as they are willing to pay a higher price than the less affluent for any other luxury.

These public goods and services, offered and maintained by government, are different from market-oriented goods in one important aspect, though. With the other goods and services we consume, each of us can make individual choices. With the services of government, the majority makes the choices for us all. With democracy comes some public goods and services that would not otherwise be provided by private markets. For instance, a private corporation would not be trusted to provide for a nation's defence or police force. Our social bargain for these goods and services of government is that we subjugate our personal preferences for these forms of consumption to that chosen by the majority through the ballot box.

An awkward bargain

An affluent society devotes proportionately more of the gross domestic product to the provision of these public services. For instance, government represented 7.84% of spending and production in the United States in 1909. By 2009, this share of gross domestic product spent by government had risen to 46.22%, a rise of 489%.[98] Many of these new government-provided services and income redistributions could not have even been contemplated a century earlier.

Government increasingly also provides for an economic infrastructure and a regulatory structure that enhances and maintains the integrity of the economic empire. As spending in the year 2009 demonstrated, government, at times, provides for fiscal policy that can be used to stabilize an economy in the depths of a recession.

However, the rise of big government, and the simultaneous decline in big business, also shifts our collective emphasis from those activities we can export to those government services and government-provided largesse that we can all enjoy. Our economy inevitably moves away from wealth growth toward wealth grabs.

In a wealth-grabbing world, we find it advantageous to form associations with those who share our interests. These special interest groups are better able to petition government to advocate for the government favors that will best advance its interests. Just as government leaders inevitably discovered they had more in common with business leaders, government leaders too found a convenient affinity with special interests most closely aligned with their interests, or with the best ability to advance the political fortunes of the government leaders. Inevitably, the peoples' interest, which motivated democracy in the first place, is subjugated by the best-organized special interests.

This shift away from production-driven growth and toward special interest grabs causes the productive class to grow less rapidly, or perhaps even to decline, and the unproductive special interest classes to grow more rapidly.

The rise of consumerism

Another aspect of an affluent economic empire is its emphasis on consumerism. Recall our discussion of Veblen and his description of consumer decadence in his book *The Leisure Class* In the parlance of Maslow's Hierarchy of Wants and Needs, consumerism for consumption's sake served to satisfy an individual's need to signal wealth to others. In the absence of other signals that work well in smaller communities, an individual can derive esteem from others in a larger and more anonymous community through opulence and consumerism.

This shift away from production of capital goods and of knowledge that will generate economic growth, and toward consumerism and leisure, stimulates consumption and the circulation of domestic income. However, it also increases the level of imports from other countries and biases economic decisions away from growth for the future and toward consumption for the present. Ultimately, the shift is not an economically healthy one, at least if sustainable economic growth remains the goal of the economic empire.

The bias toward the measurable

However, we should not elevate high growth to an all-consuming national goal for an economic empire. For instance, with affluence comes a greater regard for quality of life, in the present and in the future. This increased inclination translates into greater concern for the environment and its sustainability, greater insistence on human rights, and a greater awareness of injustice. Each of these qualities has redeeming aspects for the global society.

In addition, growth for growth's sake has its own unfortunate bias. The value of an economy, defined by the gross domestic product of the goods and services an economy produces in a given year, also embodies a number of assumptions, some seen unrealistic on face value.

For instance, measurement of the gross domestic product assumes the price of a good or service is an accurate representation of the value derived from the good. Some prices may well represent the underlying value. However, abundant supplies of some goods, such as water, may induce a low price, even though access to clean water is invaluable.

The gross domestic product also omits our consumption of goods and services that may be free or may be delivered outside of the market. One who enjoys nature and the out-of-doors may forgo traditional consumption and spend time, which he or she would otherwise devote to working, in the wilderness. Their very decisions to forgo consumption and production of market goods and services to enjoy natural services point to a serious flaw in national income and gross domestic product accounting.

This omission of non-market activities from our GDP becomes even more problematic as income and affluence rises. These very economies may appear to be stagnating by traditional measures, but may be growing substantially in other measures of human quality of life.

Some authors have attempted to capture these non-market activities. The authors Betsey Stevenson and Justin Wolfers also demonstrate that there is an imperfect correlation between a nation's per capita income and quality of life.[99] Their work demonstrates only a rough correlation with overall quality of life and per capita purchasing power. They find that countries such as Denmark, Finland, Canada, Israel, Spain, New Zealand, Ireland, and Norway typically have a higher quality of life than the United States, despite their lower per capita incomes.

Similarly, the United Nations regularly produces a quality of life ranking in which it publishes in an annual Human Development Report.[100] This index includes factors such as life expectancy, access to education, the standard of living, and immigration rates, as measures of overall attractiveness of a nation's quality of life.

If we plot the United Nations human development index against the purchasing power per capita for the nations of the world, we see only a loose correlation between the quality of life and the income of a nation's citizens. We find that some nations have a high human development index without a correspondingly high purchasing power. We also find some nations with very high income levels but with a human development index that is on par with some of the world's poorest nations (as shown in Figure 9).

Other similar measures of quality of life are only roughly correlated with gross domestic product. Unfortunately, the tabulation of national income and gross domestic product is the yardstick by which economies are most often compared. If conspicuous consumption is one way by which consumers in an affluent and impersonal society can garner esteem, nations remain fixated on this simplest measure of gross domestic product to rank economic power. Just as humans remain tied to relativism in their affluence vis-à-vis each other, so do nations vie for their relative positions as economic empires. Such comparisons are as inevitable as nationalism itself.

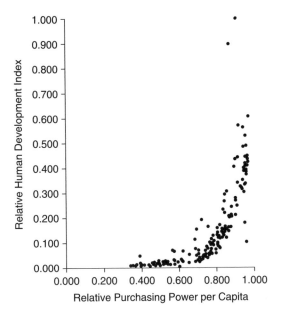

Figure 9 A Comparison between the HDI and PPP GDP

Fruit of the rise becomes the seed of decline

An affluent economic empire inevitably shifts its emphasis from production to consumption and from private production to the production of government-provided goods and services. This inevitability is a natural consequence of affluence combined with Maslow's Hierarchy of Wants and Needs.

One fundamental problem with the premise of growth for growth's sake is that an affluent economic empire begins to either shift its consumption away from market activities and more toward activities, such as leisure and nature, that are not included in our measures of gross domestic product or subtracted from them.

Affluence and Maslow's hierarchy gives rise to democracy, growth of government, and goals redirected from expanding the economic pie to dividing the economic pie. With this tendency comes an association with special interests that cater to meeting its constituents' needs by viewing the world as a constant sum game. In the process, good effort toward making things is diverted toward taking things, and the world actually becomes a negative sum game.

23
Gradual Economic Marginalization

Glory is fleeting, but obscurity is forever.
(Napoleon Bonaparte, French general and politician (1769–1821)[101]

Hegemony, from the Greek hēgemonía, English: "hegemonic" for "leadership" or "hegemon" for "leader", refers to the ideal representation of the interests of the ruling class as universal interests.[102]

It is natural for any leading entity to try to convert its status into influence that will advance its own interests. It is also compelling to rationalize that these interests are universal. However, it is tragic when a leader fails to understand that others do not accept the hegemonic assumptions.

There is an urban tale that a frog, when dropped into a hot bowl of water will struggle to escape. However, a frog left in a bowl that is slowly warmed will not struggle at all and will finally die. The politics of economic power that suffers from complacency is no different. Arrogance and complacency act as a great leveler that ultimately leads to the decline and fall of an economic empire.

The Roman Empire devolved into decadence and a corruption of purpose. However, the devolution of an economic empire does not typically arise out of decadence in its leadership. Instead, economic empires over time are characterized by mounting inefficiencies, a diversion of emphasis from production to taxation and the distribution of the spoils, and a prevailing faith and unrealistic optimism based on memories of past glories. In essence, economic leaders are leading into the future but by looking back through the rear view mirror.

A shifting emphasis

A significant force that stimulates growth in one economic era but decline in another is the changing dynamic between expansion of an economic pie and efforts to secure a larger share of that pie at the expense of another. When the emphasis becomes the division of the pie rather than the creation of more pie, everything becomes relative. These relative comparisons of the size of one slice versus another are at the core of hegemony.

This shifting emphasis can eventually yield economic marginalization vis-à-vis global trading partners. We can define marginalization as a deteriorating economic position relative to the average. If we measure this worsening position based on relative per capita incomes, marginalization can occur if there is a regression of an economic empire's fortune toward the global mean. A failure to grow at the same rate as its global competitors will then result in marginalization, even for the economic empire at its apex.

While domestic politics should mandate healthy per capita growth, empires are unavoidably measured against each other by their aggregate size and not by their per capita income. In other words, global power is proportional to economic influence, or the market share of a nation's purchasing power vis-à-vis other nations.

The marginalization of economic influence may appear only slowly. Once dominant stock exchanges merely become one of many exchanges. The market capitalization of a country's largest firms is rivaled by firms elsewhere. An export led economy becomes import dependent. Domestic investors begin to look to aspiring empires for investment opportunities. Finally, in an effort to maintain government spending, an economic empire finds itself borrowing substantially from rival nations.

This process leads to a marginalization, in which an economic empire is gradually absorbed into, or falls in the shadow of, a larger aspiring empire. This very process of descending the economic ladder removes the hegemonic influence that helped the former empire establish and maintain superiority.

Recall our previous calculations. In 1999, China's GDP was $1,083 trillion, at seventh place among nations. The United States' GDP was first among nations at $9,216 trillion.[103] In one decade, China moved from seventh to second, at $4.6 trillion, while the U.S. remains first among nations with a GDP of $14.261 trillion.[104]

The average, nominal (non-inflation adjusted) growth over that last decade was 14.5% in China versus 4.4% in the United States. If each nation maintained these rates of growth, China will have overtaken the United States as the world's largest economy around the end of the year 2021. China may have moved from just outside the world's ten largest economies in 1991 to the world's largest economy in just 30 years.[105]

Robert Fogel, director of the University of Chicago's Booth School of Business' Center for Population Economics, won the 1993 Nobel Memorial Prize in Economics (with Douglas North) for his use of quantitative econometric techniques to explain economic and institutional growth and change. Lately, he has devoted his research to the study of China's spectacular economic growth. In his article "$123,000,000,000,000: China's Estimated Economy by the

Year 2040. Be Warned",[106] he explains why he thinks the Chinese economy will be almost three times the size of the U.S. economy in just three decades.

Fogel arrived at this conclusion by noting that other commentators fail to take into account a number of subtle influences. For instance, the rate of population formation in the Western world has fallen below replacement. The analysis of economic growth also tends to be underestimated in China because it holds its currency at artificially low levels. With such currency distortions, it is more accurate to look at an alternative measure of economic influence, called Purchasing Power Parity (PPP).

If one looks at purchasing power parity measures of national output over the modern economic era, and tacks on Fogel's prediction of global market share in 2040, the graph shown in Figure 10 can be constructed.

The graph speaks volumes. If economic empiredom is measured by its size and economic power relative to other nations and the advantage that hegemony permits, empires naturally come and go. Even within their domestic economies, Fogel points out that by the year 2040, China's population may have a per capita income of $85,000 (in today's dollars), which will be more than double that of the European Union.

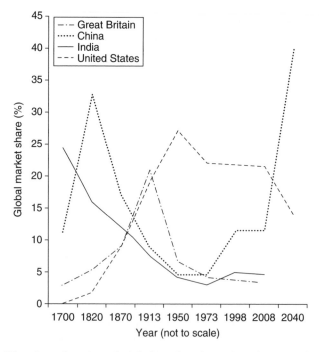

Figure 10   Historic and projected global market shares based on Purchasing Power Parity

While it is not difficult to imagine the effects of ascendancy of a new economic empire, in terms of global influence and power, it requires more imagination to comprehend the meaning and implications for those declining empires.

Fruit of the rise becomes the seed of decline

Data show that economic empires are transient. In just over a century and a half, from 1860 to 2021, China, Great Britain, the United States, and China again had, have, or will hold the mantle as the largest economy in the world. With the largest economy label comes an advantage to assert more than proportional control over the definition of global terms of trade.

However, while we can graphically observe the measurement of relative economic power, equally obvious is that this power falls just as often as it rises. Such an empirical observation does not substitute for rational explanations. Nonetheless, the pattern remains powerful evidence of the shifting sands of hegemony.

It is the sentiment of Reinhold Niebuhr that any economic empire must exercise power even though the exercise of power will eventually corrupt it. In his classic 1952 book entitled *The Irony of American History*, Niebuhr wrote:

> We take, and must continue to take, morally hazardous actions to preserve our civilization. We must exercise our power. But we ought neither to believe that a nation is capable of perfect disinterestedness in its exercise, nor become complacent about particular degrees of interest and passion which corrupt the justice by which the exercise of power is legitimized.
>
> Our lack of the lust of power makes the fulminations of our foes against us singularly inept. On the other hand, we have been so deluded by the concept of our innocency that we are ill prepared to deal with the temptations of power which now assail us.[107]

24

An Almost Empire

> If the American people ever allow private banks to control the issue
> of their currency, first by inflation, then by deflation, the banks and
> corporations that will grow up around them will deprive the people of
> all property until their children wake up homeless on the continent
> their Fathers conquered.
>
> (Thomas Jefferson, President of the United States, 1801–1809)[108]

If one attempting were to predict the next economic empire just a few decades
ago, most all indicators pointed to Japan. Paul Kennedy in his book entitled
the *The Rise and Fall of Great Powers,* published in 1980, documents the military history of empires to date. In this highly recommended book, Kennedy
noted that Japan was in its ascendancy.[109] Yet, Japan was overtaken by China
in December of 2009 as the world's second largest economy. What happened
to Japan's ascendancy then?

Japan and Germany both benefitted from the rebuilding of their economic
infrastructure by the allied victors in World War II as part of the Marshall
Plan. Until China's dramatic ascendancy, these two nations represented the
second and third largest economies in the world, after economic ruin just a
half-century earlier.

In the 1970s, Japan's dramatic ascendancy toward economic empiredom
was called "The Japanese Miracle." Japan succeeded in ways that other countries would soon try to emulate. Their success was attributed to a new form of
capitalism that married large holding companies, called "zaibatsu," with new
management techniques, based on a premise of total quality management. As
described earlier, these new techniques of total quality management actually
originated with W. Edward Deming. These same techniques would not be fully
appreciated in the United States until almost a half-century later.

These post-war management techniques created worker harmony by engaging
workers in management decision-making and offering them long-term

employment security. The government also created incentives for its citizens to save, so these savings could be reinvested into new physical capital for corporations. Finally, Japan's Ministry of International Trade and Industry coordinated industrial research and development that would benefit its major corporations.

Because of these novel management policies, Japan's economy grew spectacularly. In the dozen years between 1953 and 1965, gross domestic product grew by almost 10% per year as advances in agricultural productivity allowed workers to move to the industrialized cities. In the latter half of the 1960s, manufacturing and mineral production grew at the fantastic rate of 17%. While these growth rates moderated somewhat in the 1970s, average growth still hovered just below double digits.[110]

Japan's innovative industrial structure, emphasis on quality, and ability to anticipate rising oil prices by producing fuel-efficient automobiles set it up perfectly for the challenges of the 1970s. Very quickly, Japan shed its reputation for low priced and low quality manufactured goods and created a new reputation for high quality and high technology production of electronics, machinery, ships and steelworks, and vehicles.

At the same time, the U.S. style economic model was beginning to lose its luster. The American automobile industry, once the envy of the world, was facing heavy losses. U.S. steel production was being overtaken by Japan and Korea.

Engaged in labor strife and the usual national debates about global competition, industrialized countries worldwide were looking to Japan and their new economic model. As Japan's success was based on certain cultural practices enjoyed in that nation for decades, replication of these practices was only partially successful in other countries unaccustomed to Japan's sense of pride and cooperation.

Paul Kennedy documented these economic successes over two decades[111]:

In just two decades, Japan's share of global production had doubled. By 1987, Japan's trade surplus was so large that it had little choice but to recycle its surplus of U.S. greenbacks into the purchase of U.S. government securities. In essence, Japan was the underwriter of the U.S. military buildup designed to bankrupt any empire-building aspirations of the former Soviet Union.

Table 1   Shares of Gross World Product (%) 1960–1980

Year	1960	1970	1980
United States	25.9	23.0	21.5
U.S.S.R.	12.5	12.4	11.4
Japan	4.5	7.7	9.0
China	3.1	3.4	4.5

However, by the year 2000, Japan's share of gross world product had fallen to 7% while the U.S. total rose slightly to 22% and China's share rose dramatically to 12%.[112] The Japanese Miracle had become a nightmare. Japan was thrust into a recession in 1991 that continued through the next decade.

Japan's lost decade arose from the very sort of asset bubble that has also troubled the United States repeatedly, ever since both countries devoted a large share of savings to financial capital rather than physical capital. Despite sluggish rates of investment in private physical capital and public infrastructure, stock markets and real estate markets grew dramatically and disproportionately. In addition, with each rise came an increased probability of a calamitous decline.

In turn, real estate values dropped by as much as 80%, and the Nikkei stock market, once the envy of the world, dropped from a high of 40,000 in 1989 to 10,000 in 2010.

Unfortunate imitation

The U.S. economy, too, began to falter in the 2000s. After reaching a high just shy of 12,000 early in the presidential election year of 2000, the Dow Jones Industrial Average Index stood at 10,000 a decade later. The employed labor force was little changed over the decade, with 137,270,000 employed in the civilian sector in April of 2000 and 137,792,000 employed in December of 2009.[113] Over the same period, the population had increased by ten million people. The United States and Japan both lost a decade of economic progress.

These lost decades in the United States and Japan are interesting principally because they are not universally shared phenomena. While the United States faltered and Japan was unable to maintain the same growth rate it had supported for decades, China continued to grow. It is this phenomenon, the ability of China to continue to grow while other nations faltered, that we consider next.

Fruit of the rise becomes the seed of decline

The two economic superpowers – United States and Japan – maintained their grips on global economic power for decades. The United States achieved its economic stature over half a century corresponding to the Gilded Age and held this vaulted position for a century. Japan achieved its status in just a few decades and overtook the United Kingdom and Germany as the second largest economy in the world in 1967.[114] It just as quickly shed this status by December of 2009. Meanwhile, China's economic stature began to grow in the 1970s and accelerated through the 1980s and beyond.

The chart constructed from Kennedy's data demonstrates that China would attain a gross domestic product of $5.06 trillion (in 1980 dollars) by the year 2020.[115] If we adjust 1980 dollars to 2010 dollars based on the GDP deflator, this projection would be equivalent to $11.5 trillion by 2020, in 2010 dollar values. Projections we have made elsewhere demonstrate that China has accelerated its growth. At the same time, U.S. and Japanese growth has faltered under the weight of recessions and lost decades.

These examples suggest that a nation with sufficient economic capacity, especially in its labor force, can sustain spectacular growth for many decades. However, once a nation exhausts its excess labor supply and its low hanging fruit of productivity gains, it is vulnerable to economic shocks that detract from sustainable growth.

Nations at the apex are also much more vulnerable to those economic shocks that threaten the consumption sector. Too often, economic empires preserve their dominance though an overreliance on consumption-sustained growth, which in turn emphasizes financial growth over production growth. Meanwhile, aspiring empires fuel their growth through new investment in productive economic infrastructure. These aspiring empires can continue to grow through even the most debilitating global financial meltdowns, as China demonstrated during the global financial meltdown that began elsewhere in 2008.

25
A New Economic Order

Our greatest glory is not in never falling but in rising every time we fall.
(Confucius, China's most famous teacher,
philosopher, and political theorist, 551–479 BCE)

While repeated patterns in history would suggest that, eventually, any economic empire will be replaced by another, it is more difficult to predict which empire will replace it. Even if we can at best make an educated guess about future contenders for a dominant empire, we can nonetheless predict the qualities a successful contender will need. These are the same qualities, of innovation and production, vision and leadership, that have allowed every other aspiring empire to attain the mantle in another time.

What are these qualities?

Certainly, memories of a bleak or uncomfortable past, a present that forces individuals to rely on their own efforts, and a taste of a better future have motivated individuals and people throughout history. However, the defining ingredient for success must be foresight and willingness for an emerging economic empire to invest in its own future.

Without such investment, it is too easy to rest on national laurels and to veer toward a system of rights to happiness rather than the shared privilege to pursue happiness. While we have documented in this book the ways in which one economic empire has evolved over time, it is interesting to discover how another nation is trying to establish a more perfect empire.

The year of the Tiger

As an empire contemplates its glorious past, challenging present, and uncertain future, it is difficult at the same time to observe emerging successes elsewhere.

Ironically, we need not look too far. For it is the same characteristics that lead any modern country to the economic apex. To best illustrate this pattern, let us look for a moment at what China is accomplishing.

An education revolution

Any educator in Australia, Great Britain, Canada, and the United States can tell you the same thing: "Many of our top students are now from China."

China and its people are investing in human capital at a rate unprecedented for them. This investment is both in very affordable domestic schools and in parents' subsidization of student study abroad. Of course, this investment is designed to yield productivity improvements and to encourage the transfer and development of technology for China.

An interesting aspect of this investment is the significant investment that average middle-class households are willing to make in their children. In a country without a strong and generous retirement system, the productivity of children is viewed as an investment in the extended family's financial security. This truly is an investment, not only for the nation but also for families.

If China is able to replicate the success of high school and college participation that has been realized in other developed nations, the nation should be able to sustain double-digit economic growth for a generation to come. This substantial growth arises not merely because their individual human capital is proportionally more productive. The ability to study abroad and bring technology and knowledge home, the synergies that are created when a workforce is vibrant and well educated, and the emergence of many Chinese universities as world-class research centers bodes well for economic empire-building.

The United Nations Education, Scientific, and Cultural Organization's Institute for Statistics (UNESCO UIS) reports that 13% of government spending in China was devoted to education in 2007.[116] In the same report, China boasted a literacy rate of 99.3% of its youth. Moreover, while only 24% of China's students received post secondary education in 2007, this number has quadrupled in just one decade. Such growth will allow China to easily attain Western levels of post secondary education in a few short years. With 1.329 billion Chinese residents in 2007, China is already graduating more scientists, doctors, engineers, and business people each year than any other country in the world.

It is true that many of China's residents remain rural. However, just as agriculture in the United States fed its population by employing 40% of its workforce in the early twentieth century and less than 2% of its population by the early twenty-first century, China too is experiencing rapid modernization in its rural sector. From 1978 to 2002, China's rural population has fallen from 82% to 73% of its national totals.[117]

By comparison, the United States, a nation of not vastly different land mass, has a rural population of only 21%, according to the 2000 census. If China urbanizes at the same rate in the future as it has in since 1978, it would not reach the level of urbanization in the United States within the next century and a half. Clearly, there are decades of urbanization remaining for China.

As gross domestic income and wages rise, modernization will accelerate. China has the luxury of replicating methods used elsewhere rather than the necessity of developing the technologies in the first place, as the United States had to do. It is now much more efficient to purchase and replicate well-developed technologies than invent them.

Consequently, the conversion from a rural to an urban economy should be more rapid in China than it was in the United States in the nineteenth and twentieth century or in the Great Britain in the seventeenth and eighteenth century. In the process, China's rural population will become more productive by orders of magnitude, which will augment the rapid growth of productivity in the urban sectors.

China, too, is establishing a political system that allows the economy to grow. China's system is an interesting mix of extremely free markets and tight political control. Chinese leaders have taken a liberal approach to that economic growth in return for tighter control of domestic politics. Many Chinese citizens accept this bargain. If given a choice between economic progress combined with tighter political control, or political liberalism with an attendant more chaotic economic development path, most Chinese will accept the former. Its citizens may understand what Western countries too have learned. Higher income and quality of life typically force changes that ultimately result in greater political liberalism over time. However, the converse is not always true.

Why has this dramatic transformation largely escaped observation by Western nations? After all, anyone who has travelled to Shanghai or Beijing recognize that the pace of construction, infrastructure improvement, and commerce exceeds what one would find anywhere else on the planet.

While the gross domestic product per capita has not yet reached Western levels, the income and quality of life in urban centers is every bit what one would expect in many European cities. A currency held back somewhat by its Central Bank, low costs for services that translate into a correspondingly high purchasing power, and a failure to account for the activity of millions of entrepreneurs or the underground economy obscures the true wealth of the nation.

Once the combination of these effects is unleashed through a rapidly growing middle class that is just as rapidly adopting Western consumption preferences, China will surely emerge as a diversified and self-sustaining economic engine. For instance, the dynamism of the Chinese economy has permitted it to sustain near double-digit economic growth even as the rest of the developed world has been thrust into the greatest recession since the Great Depression.

We should actually not be too surprised. Except for the period from the middle of the nineteenth century to now, China has consistently been an economic empire. The world's best-kept secret is a secret no longer.

Fruit of the rise becomes the seed of decline

I typically end each chapter by documenting how the very forces that give rise to economic power ultimately reach their apex and can no longer sustain their potency. Undoubtedly, China too will be challenged by other nations, such as India, that are richly endowed with human capital and have a zest for education. However, it is clear that China's run has long legs, just as Great Britain had for almost a century and the United States maintained for more than a century.

26
Convergence

> They must often change, who would be constant in happiness or wisdom.
>
> (Confucius, China's most famous teacher,
> philosopher, and political theorist, 551–479 BCE)[118]

As inevitable as death and taxes is the tendency for those behind to run faster, and for those up ahead to slow down. This tendency must inevitably result in a convergence of the First and Second Economic Worlds. We will discover that an economic empire may need the Second Economic World more than it may think.

The First, Second, and Third Economic worlds

At one time, nations were divided into the three categories: the developed, the developing, and the undeveloped world. In these times when there is little to distinguish the developed and the developing world from each other, it may make more sense to modify our descriptions based on economic power and international influence.

Let's recall that the First, Second, and Third Worlds are a throwback to the Cold War. In the First World was the set of capitalist countries aligned with the United States and the free market economic principle, while the Second World included those countries aligned with the former Soviet Union that broadly subscribed to communism. Nations that did not belong to either block were considered the Third World.

Now that almost all the former Second World practices the free market economic model rather than the communist economic model, it is perhaps more helpful to view the world in economic terms. Let the First Economic World (FEW) be defined as those countries that have moved through the rapid development stage and reside on the right-hand side of the Kuznets'

Curve (recall figure 8), with sustained and moderated growth, well-developed financial markets, the maintenance of property rights, and a relatively narrow income distribution.

The Second Economic World (SEW) are those aspiring empires that are enjoying rapid economic growth enabled by redefined property rights, rapidly developing financial markets, and an eye on attaining First World affluence and innovations. Meanwhile, the Third Economic World (TEW) continues to struggle with ineffective property rights and government, and incomplete or corrupted markets.

Each of these categories shares a number of important characteristics. The primary characteristic is their respective growth rates.

A changing demographic

This differential growth rate arises for a number of reasons. First, Third Economic World development is often frustrated by an insufficiently small educated middle class and suffers from a lower level of economic activity that is unable to allow its labor force to develop fully. Often, these nations are unable to meet the basic needs of food and shelter, health and safety that other nations take for granted. Until these challenges are addressed, these nations perennially suffer from low and stagnant economic growth.

On the other hand, the First Economic World sustains higher but also unspectacular growth because they have a level of affluence that reduces the motivation for population and economic growth. Indeed, while the Third Economic World often suffers from excessive population growth and high mortality, the First Economic World suffers from negative population growth and a growing life expectancy because of superior medical technologies.

Indeed, the population growth of First Economic World nations often arises through immigration from Second Economic World nations. This immigration to the FEW fuels one of the two necessities for growth, but also accelerates the transfer of technologies to the Second Economic World and hastens their growth. Indeed, it is this population growth from SEW nations in combination with technological innovations that allow the FEW to continue to grow past the peak of the Kuznets' Curve.[119]

If labor were perfectly mobile, growth rates would converge rather rapidly. The tragedy of the Third Economic World is that it cannot contribute to the growth of the global economy until it can establish the property rights and rule of law so necessary for economic development. Almost all of the dynamic then occurs in the relative growth of the population and the economies in the Second Economic World.

Table 2   World population (in millions) 1750–2150

Region	1750	1800	1850	1900	1950	1999	2050	2150
World	791	978	1,262	1,650	2,521	5,978	8,909	9,746
North America, Europe, Oceania	167	212	314	496	732	1,066	1,066	966
Asia, South and Central America	518	659	847	1,021	1,569	4,145	6,077	6,473
Africa	106	107	111	132	220	767	1,766	2,307

Source: As projected by the United Nations Population Division, http://www.un.org/esa/population/publications/sixbillion/sixbilpart1.pdf, accessed February 7, 2010.

Population patterns between First, Second, and Third Economic Worlds are arranged roughly along the lines of North America and Europe, Asia and South America, and Africa, respectively. We see some strong patterns over the past couple of centuries and into the next century. The United Nations Population Division regularly projects world populations. In their most recent report, they projected the following:

We see that global economic power may be reaching a tipping point, with First Economic Worlds in North America, Europe, and Oceania declining since their 1999 peak, while the Asian, South, and Central American countries of the Second Economic World increase in population along with the growth of a Third Economic World concentrated primarily in Africa.

These population dynamics will have profound effects on relative economic power, financial flows between increasingly global stock and capital markets, and the balance of political power that follows economic power.

These population projections have been the focus of economists since the eighteenth century. Economist Thomas Malthus observed that the geometric growth of population would eventually outstrip the linear growth of its food supply. While he estimated that this dismal prophecy would occur by the middle of the nineteenth century, advances in agricultural technologies delayed his inevitable projection.[120] Nonetheless, economics has been labeled "the dismal science" ever since.

The tendencies are more striking when presented as a table, with the dark bank showing the relative size of the First Economic World, the gray band showing population growth in the Third Economic World, and the lightest band depicting the size of the rapidly developing Second Economic World. The graph in Figure 11 also indicates the emerging political and economic power that follows their spectacular growth over four centuries.

We see that the First Economic Worlds of North America, Oceania, and Europe have grown relatively slowly, while the continents that represent

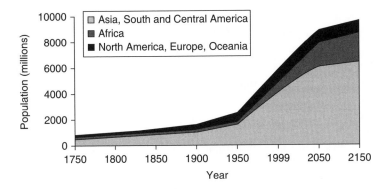

Figure 11 Population growth in three Economic worlds

Source: As projected by the United Nations Population Division, http://www.un.org/esa/population/publications/wup2007/2007WUP_ExecSum_web.pdf, accessed February 7, 2010.

the Second and Third Economic Worlds have grown rapidly. As the Second Economic World converges with the First Economic World beyond 2050, we see that its population growth, too, begins to falter relative to the Third Economic World.

Convergence

Figure 11 demonstrates that the First and Second Economic Worlds to converge. By the year 2050, we can expect both of these worlds to increasingly turn their eyes toward the Third Economic World in a shared effort to sustain economic growth. By 2100, the world will likely be divided into a combined First Economic World and a newly aspiring Second Economic World.

The primary force that is accelerating these tendencies is the aging of the First Economic World. Those nations in the current Second Economic World are youthful. The young people in the aspiring empires of China and India create a substantial and valuable bank of human capital. Moreover, as their human capital is developed, they will likely begin to make similar economic decisions as their counterparts in the traditional First Economic World.

This convergence of economies thus gives rise to a convergence of values as well. The human capital-rich youthful class will insist on a greater share of political power commensurate with their growing economic influence. Empires dominated by a middle class under 40 years of age will expect a level of dynamism from government that has heretofore been absent. Governments will need to cater to the unique demands of this cohort growing in size, wealth, and stature.

These individuals will demand that their property be protected, that they have a more egalitarian access to education, and that their higher technology needs are satisfied. Lower crime, better telecommunications, safer streets, a higher quality of life, and a new sense of community are values that this powerful cohort will expect.

This youthful class will also push up property values and prices, making it difficult for those on fixed income in an elderly class to survive. The very young may also have a more difficult time attaining the quality of life the youthful class comes to demand.

An urban and rural divide

We will also see a dramatically accelerated urbanization. In the past 60 years, we have seen rapid urbanization worldwide that will be sustained over the next 20 years:

Never before has the world's population been primarily urban. This accelerating urbanization will raise property values very rapidly in Central and South America and parts of Asia. This accelerating urbanization will require modernized and conveniently located housing but at much higher costs when compared to these nations' rural areas.

As we discussed earlier, economic theory tells us that new wealth mostly flows to an economy's most fixed and scarce factors of production. The factors

Table 3   Urbanization and global population (in millions) 1950–2030

Region/World	1950	1975	2000	2030
North America, Europe, Oceania – Urban	398	641	802	930
Asia, South and Central America – Urban	302	772	1,760	3,266
Africa – Urban	33	103	295	748
North America, Europe, Oceania – Rural	334	300	273	203
Asia, South and Central America – Rural	1,263	1,948	2,440	2,331
Africa – Rural	188	305	500	650

Source: As projected by the United Nations Population Division, http://www.un.org/esa/population/publications/wup2007/2007WUP_ExecSum_web.pdf, accessed February 7, 2010.

of land and resource that cannot be renewed will command the greatest share of the new surpluses these aspiring economies will create.

Less scarce factors include educated workers and their intellectual property. These factors can be created but it takes perhaps a generation to be replicated. The modest ability to replicate these factors over time confers upon them modest rewards. Those nations that are rich in commodities and human capital will be best positioned to capitalize on this global economic transformation.

Economic theory then allows us to predict that convergence between the First and Second Economic Worlds will result in rapidly growing land and commodity prices and fast growing income for young professionals in Second Economic World countries. Those who own property will benefit, while the manufacturing sector will grow increasingly competitive.

Some stark demographics

As these aspiring empires join the league of First Economic World nations, they will find themselves responding to demands for social welfare nets now commonplace in the First Economic World. A child born in 2010 in a country like Japan can expect to live to the next century. In comparison, when President Franklin Roosevelt passed the social security pension system in the United States in the midst of the Great Depression, the life expectancy was only 63 years old.

Now, a child who becomes a doctor may only be in the labor force for less than 40 years after completing medical school and residency and before retiring at 65 years of age. Well less than half one's life may be in the productive sector. In effect, less than half of the population in the productive sector will be supporting those either in pre-school, school, or retirement. If population growth continues to be negative and life expectancy continues to rise, it may well be that one-third of the population is supporting the consumption needs of two-thirds of the population.

This reality in the converged First Economic World may necessarily accelerate development of the Third Economic World. This TEW may be nudged into the SEW for the convenience of the FEW. The United Nations estimates show that, by the year 2050, the over 60 years of age cohort will represent more than 32% of the population in North America, Europe, and Oceania. The converged SEW from Asia, and Central and South America will contain a little more than 23% of the population over the age of 60. In contrast, the elderly of the Third Economic World will represent fewer than 11% of their population by the year 2050.

Meanwhile, only 17% of the population of North America, Europe, and Oceania will be under the age of 15 by 2050, while the converged Second

Economic World will have 28% of their population under the age of 15. At the same time, Africa will have a relatively large and growing population under the age of 15.

Will these factors continue to widen the gap?

We are now familiar with the Law of Diminishing Returns that states that any activity eventually will find it increasingly difficult to make additional economic gains. The driver of diminishing returns will be access to scarce resources. Once the rural population has become primarily urban, further growth becomes more difficult. With an urbanization rate of 82% in the First Economic World, and a rate of 53% in other nations, there remains a great capacity for the creation of wealth in the other economic worlds.

The most abundant factor of production will be entrepreneurial capital. Their tools of business and management are relatively easily created, imitated, and replicated. Similarly, financial capital comes from the surpluses accruing to households and not spent on consumerism. These surpluses end up in financial markets. Such markets will thrive only to the extent that the converged First and Second Economic Worlds are willing to emphasize saving over consumption.

As always, there are forces that tend to mitigate economic power over time. Retirees may be just one such force. As their share increases with the convergence of the First and Second Economic Worlds, there will be a decline in the wealth redirected to financial markets. An optimal retirement plan requires the retiree to slowly wind down saving rather than augment the savings as they may have done in their middle ages. As we move from the economy of the mid-twentieth century in which four in five people work to an economy in which one in two or one in three people work, the level of financial capital could well begin to decline.

This modern interpretation of the dismal prophecy may take some time to emerge, though. The population pyramid in the First Economic World may be inverted now, but there remains a solid youthful population boom in both the Second and the Third Economic Worlds.

The wild card

If extended longevity in the converged First and Second Economic Worlds and a reduced rate of family formation in the Second Economic World stacks the non-producing population against the producing cohort, is there any salvation on the horizon? Certainly, medical advances will continue to exacerbate this effect. Some argue that technological advances will allow physical capital to take care of more of the needs of the aging human capital. Other reforms include an increase in the normal retirement age from 65 perhaps to 67 and then 70 and 75 years old. Already, some countries, most notably in Europe, are moving toward reduced workweeks. Unless combined with delayed retirement, this trend will further reduce the output from the producing class.

We can hope for the theory of economist Joseph Schumpeter to come to the rescue. The Schumpeterian Growth Theory states that waves of innovation and technological improvements have permitted the First Economic World to advance in quality of life steadily over time.[121] His hypothesis is in spite of the evolving demographic tendencies, at least until now. And while we have seen some significant advances that have made food and housing cheaper, and have brought down the price of manufacturing, telecommunications, information, and computer processing, we have seen many more developments in the medical field that have prolonged life still further. While the former forces help us address the dismal prophecy, the latter forces may actually exacerbate the prophecy.

It would be more comforting, though, if Schumpeter's theory were instead a law.

Fruit of the rise becomes the seed of decline

There is an interesting dance between demographics and development. A less developed nation sees the size of its pool of human capital as a strategic economic asset. The aspiring empire that invests in the productivity of human capital is able to create a huge stock of an asset differentiated from the masses of unskilled labor found elsewhere. The productivity of this stock of productive human capital is often a nation's best resource.

The increased productivity of this valuable asset raises national incomes for the aspiring empire. However, as income rises, economies develop a taste for a higher quality rather than a larger quantity of labor. With further increases in income and quality of life, and with a shifting emphasis toward dividing the economic pie rather than creating it, developed economies begin to offer social welfare nets that provide alternative financial security for the family.

Once a nation shifts its focus from production to the politics of the division of the economic pie, spectacular growth tapers off. No longer is a fast growing labor force the norm – rather, the most developed nations rarely provide for replacement population.

In this sense, economic empires may again sow the seeds of their eventual demise. The necessary importation of labor, through immigration, supports population led economic growth, but at the expense of a dilution in the population and cultural homogeneity that acted as a vehicle for nationalism and economic growth.

Part VII

From Where Have We Come, and Where Will We Go?

We will conclude by summarizing the significant factors that determine the evolution of an economic empire. We will then look at various ways in which an empire can get back to its roots so that it may sustain its economic strength. This discussion is framed within an environment of optimism. After all, the lessons learned offer insights for a new and sustainable form of development that does not repeat the past but instead remakes the future.

27
From Producer of Ideas to Protector of Interests

> Nations, like stars, are entitled to eclipse. All is well, provided the light returns and the eclipse does not become endless night. Dawn and resurrection are synonymous. The reappearance of the light is the same as the survival of the soul.
>
> (Victor Hugo, French poet and novelist, 1802–1885)[122]

Economic empires form when a number of different forces come together at one time. A disproportionately large endowment of an important factor of production, usually resources or labor, is a common element of all economic empires. These endowments may come through conquest and colonization, or discovery and domestic population growth.

An economic empire also requires the protection of property rights necessary to allow efficient markets to form. The most progressive economic empires are also willing to invest in the public infrastructure that will allow these markets to be as efficient as possible. Highways, airways and seaways, power, and telecommunications are the networks that modern commerce requires.

A successful economic empire must also be willing to invest in its human capital. Without a well-trained labor force, a nation is relegated to produce goods and services that can be produced everywhere and, hence, do not command a premium anywhere. Primarily by creating highly productive labor, a country can generate greater surpluses.

A nation must also be able to motivate its creative and productive sectors. An economic empire must ensure that inventors, innovators, and producers receive a sufficient share of the surpluses they create, at least while it charges toward its apex. We have seen that a mature empire will begin to divert increasing shares from the productive to either the public or the distributive sectors.

However, we have seen that an empire near its apex often becomes less concerned about production, and devotes more energy to consumption, redistribution of income and public production. Such mixed economies sacrifice the efficiency of free markets by providing its citizens with more goods as deemed necessary through democratic institutions.

Ultimately, though, for all economies that rely on the factor of labor, the productive sector shoulders the responsibility to produce the goods and services consumed by all. An economy with a greater share of those in the workforce over those without will be more successful in meeting these needs, assuming the antecedents above are met.

To measure this balance between those in the productive sectors and those who will consume without producing, we can compare the relative populations of three cohorts. Typically, measures of the labor force assume that the population under the age of 15 does not work. The statutory age of retirement in most countries is between 60 and 70 years of age.[123]

Consider the underage cohort and the retired cohort worldwide. The United Nations' Population Division of their Department of Economic and Social Affairs regularly publishes historical and projected population figures for its member nations.

Using their estimates and graphs (Figure 12), we see that the world's working age population has been increasing dramatically for the past 40 years, and

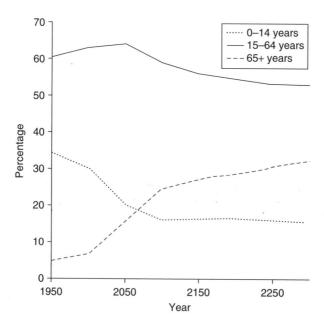

Figure 12   Total world population by age, 1950–2300

is expected to continue growing rapidly until about 2030.[124] After that, the growth will begin to taper off somewhat.

We observe that the working age population is peaking, and is expected to converge to a little more than half of the population by the next century.

At the same time, we see a more profound young population leveling off around the year 2000, and the growth of the world's elderly population accelerating after the year 2000.

The growing elderly population arises from advances in medical care. The last figure shows that approximately two billion people will be 60 years of age or older by the year 2050, and this number is expected to continue to grow. Meanwhile, the youthful population will have declined to about two billion by that date. While there will be over five billion individuals supporting almost four billion out of the workforce, the dramatically increasing elderly population and a level youthful population will worsen this ratio after 2050 as the working population peaks out.

Canada and the United States show a similar, but even more pronounced challenge (as shown in Figure 13).

However, the picture in Europe is more pronounced yet (as shown in Figure 14).

We see that the working age population in Europe is estimated to have peaked in 2005, and is predicted to fall precipitously by the year 2050. Meanwhile, the

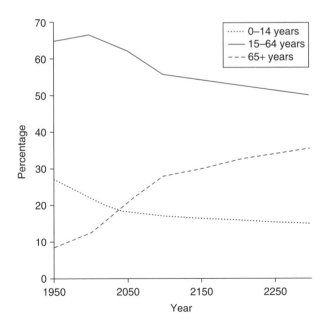

Figure 13   Total North America population by age, 1950–2300

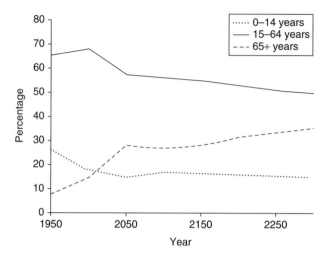

Figure 14   Total Europe population by age, 1950–2300

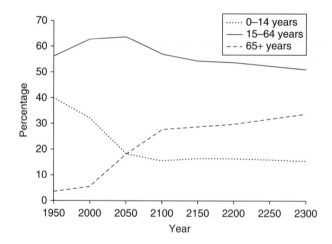

Figure 15   Latin America population by age, 1950–2300

elderly population continues to grow even as the youthful population that normally supplements the working population remains relatively flat after 2005. By the year 2050, there will be about as many people of working age as there are underage or retired. At this point, each worker is producing for himself or herself, and for one other person.

Those nations that aspire to converge with the First Economic World are only marginally less vulnerable. For instance, in Latin America, the very strong growth in the working age population will level off as well in about 2040, while the youthful population will decline, and the elderly population will rise, albeit from a lower level. By 2050, about 450 million working age individuals will be supporting themselves and another 375 million youth and retired individuals.

Asia, the other set of nations in the Second Economic World, shows a similar leveling off of the working population, at about three billion people, in 2050, and will be supporting about 2.1 billion people (as shown in Figure 16).

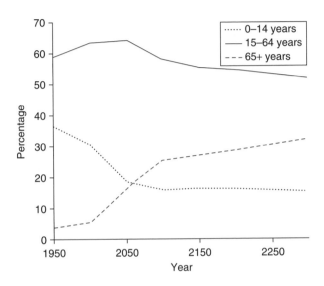

Figure 16   Asia's population by age, 1950–2300

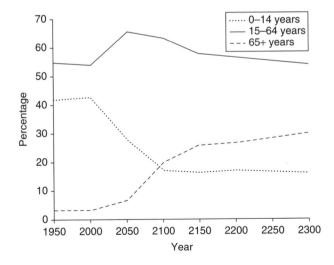

Figure 17   Africa's population by age, 1950–2300

The Third Economic World nations of Africa fare better, with a working age population projected to continue to grow through 2050, and with a strong, but also leveling off, youthful cohort and a relatively small elderly population. By 2050, about 1.25 billion people will be supporting themselves and another 750 million people who are elderly or below the age of 15 (as shown in Figure 17).

A more useful way to look at this problem of producers and consumers is to measure directly the number of unproductive consumers who are supported by working age producers. Without judging the various reasons why a nation would manipulate this ratio through their decisions to support retirees or encourage, or discourage, domestic procreation, there is an unforgiving economic reality that tells us working age producers will have to work harder, or consumers enjoy less, if this ratio of workers to dependents is disproportionate.

Worsening these dependency ratios is the trend among First Economic and Second Economic World nations to delay the onset of graduating into the workforce. While the age of 15 may not be considered too young to enter the workforce in a Third Economic World nation, the age of 20 (or more) is more typical for First and Second Economic World nations. If we measure the number of consumers who will be supported by each working age individual in five representative nations, we find the dependency ratios shown in Figure 18.

We see that the United States in 1970 typically had a low of 1.1 working age individuals for each person younger than 20 or older than the age of 65, which

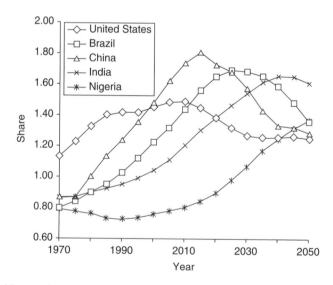

Figure 18   Non-working age populations, 1950–2050

is a common retirement age in the United States. The working age to non-working age population will have stabilized at about 1.25 by the year 2025.

However, in 2025, only the Third Economic World country of Nigeria will have a lower number of working age individuals also supporting non-productive age individuals. In 2025, China and India will have 1.5 such workers for each non-working age consumer, while India will still have almost 1.7 such workers.

We also see that China will have peaked in about 2015, with almost 1.8 working age individuals for each non-working age consumer. China's decline after that apex is due to its one child per family policy, implemented in 1979 over concerns that a rapidly growing population would outstrip its agricultural capacity and hinder its social and economic development.[125]

Wealth and fertility

There is a striking correlation between the average purchasing power of a nation's residents and the number of children women have, on average. From data gathered on the CIA Factbook (2009), I compared the fertility rate of women based on their national per capita purchasing power parity income.[126]

Figure 19 represents the stark correlation between wealth and fertility. On average, women from nations with a per capita purchasing power of under $15,000 per year have 2.76 children. In comparison, women from countries with an income over $15,000 per capita each year have 1.67 children on average. We see that higher income nations do not attain the replacement population

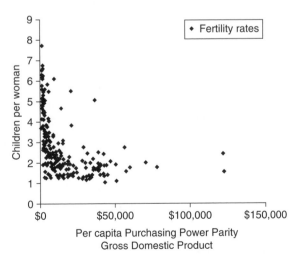

Figure 19   Fertility as a function of per capita Purchasing Power Parity, 2009

of 2.0 children per woman. We also see that families in lower income nations are 65% larger than their higher income counterparts.

Economists classify our choices depending on whether the rate we make these choices fall, rise, or rise significantly as income increases. Choices we make relatively more often at low incomes are labeled inferior goods. The data suggest that the rate of family formation is one such inferior good. We choose smaller families as our income rises.

There are various explanations for this phenomenon. As we discussed earlier, a higher rate of urbanization is correlated with higher incomes. Urbanization creates space challenges for families, and obviates the need for more children to tend the farm.

In addition, wealthier nations offer greater career opportunities for women. Affluence often demands greater attention to human rights, of which women's rights are an important component. Such an increasing preference for women's rights is what economists label a "luxury good." These are things we prefer in much greater proportion as our income rises. With this greater regard for women's rights often comes greater autonomy for women to control their reproductive choices, and, often, to have fewer children.

Also, with these higher incomes comes a greater opportunity cost for women to have children. My research demonstrates that higher incomes for women cause both a delay in child bearing and a lower probability of child bearing.[127]

A third reason is the greater use of birth control methods and contraceptives in the First Economic World. Nations with a well-developed legal system that permit oral contraception yield a lower rate of family formation.

Some low income nations also suffer from high rates of infant mortality. Such a high rate of infant mortality may reduce the effective rate of family formation in poorer nations.

Finally, most world religions encourage family formation. As we have discussed earlier, conversion from a non-secular to a secular state is a common consequence of the adoption of free market principles. In turn, the de-emphasis on religion may result in a lower rate of family formation.

Infant mortality aside, the net effect is a tendency for more affluent nations to drop below the two-children-per-woman replacement population level. Once a nation falls below this replacement level, the population pyramid will invert. Such a declining rate of family formation results in a greater share of the population in the older cohorts than in the younger cohorts. The population pyramid will remain inverted until the rate of family formation rises above two children per couple, unless immigration is encouraged to reverse this trend.

Consequently, an affluent empire without a liberal immigration policy is destined to shrink, in the absence of the encouragement of immigration, unless there is a successful policy of domestic family formation. Such a nation will therefore have a disproportionate number of elderly residents, compared with its youthful population.

These growing elderly population and declining youthful population create a strain on the various public services and social welfare nets an affluent empire comes to expect. It is this tension between production and consumption we take up next.

The FEW needs the SEW

Some argue that an affluent empire can thrive even with a dramatically reduced population and rate of family formation. In some sense, it is true that accumulated wealth will allow the wealthy to purchase the product of others.

An analogy is that a wealthy neighborhood can survive without production. A wealthy retirement community will spend its accumulated savings to support itself. This wealth allows it to purchase production made elsewhere. However, the wealthy retirement community cannot survive without that production made somewhere else. In that sense, an affluent non-producing community is not self-sufficient or sustainable. Once their wealth is consumed, there remains no productive base in the community.

Consequently, a nation, too, is unsustainable if it does not produce itself and instead consumes products made elsewhere. While it might be compelling to rationalize that an affluent nation can support such an imbalance, this rationalization is not supported by the evidence in the long run.

In this era of globalization and technology transfer, financial capital flows to those areas that can offer the greatest return. With the financial capital comes physical capital that makes this production even more efficient. It is likely that the next few decades will demonstrate a great leveling of labor productivity worldwide. Once such a leveling of productivity occurs, wealth will again follow production. The nations that can create new wealth will have the distinct advantage over those draining their old wealth.

If such a convergence of productivity and worker wealth occurs, the measure of a nation's per capita consumption will then track the ratio of working age producers to non-working age consumers. If the same tendencies of reduced family formation and increased longevity become universal among the converged First Economic World, the advantages most pronounced in India, and to a lesser degree in China and Brazil, may be reduced as they converge with the FEW. However, these countries do not typically have the same traditions of generous state-sponsored pensions for their elderly. Consequently, there may be a widening gap between growing worker incomes in these countries, and only modest retirement incomes.

Europe may have the opposite challenge. In the year 2009, the Organisation for Economic Co-operation and Development showed that state-sponsored

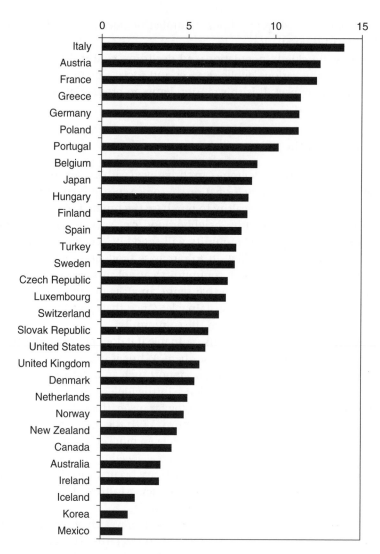

Figure 20   Retirement entitlements among developed OECD countries

pensions in Europe are already funding a significant share of production (as shown in Figure 20).[128]

If medical care support is removed, the level of social security spending in the United States in 2009 represented 4.45% of the gross domestic product, lower than all the OECD European nations except Ireland.[129]

Because the working age population of most First Economic World nations is declining so rapidly, while their elderly population is growing, the share of the gross domestic product will have to increase even more dramatically in the future, or the generosity of these pension plans will have to be curtailed. Either choice will be politically difficult in societies that have come to expect generous pensions and believe they have been paying into this social benefit for their working lives.

The mechanisms that transfer income between the producing and the non-producing sectors of an economy are most varied. Public pensions, typically, are taxes on the income generating class that are transferred to those receiving public pensions. Governments find this opportunistic. For instance, the United States collected $949.4 billion in social security and payroll tax revenue, but only paid out $644 billion in social security payments in 2009. Almost every nation relied on a growing working age population to collect abundant pension taxes, and a smaller retirement population that would draw upon these funds. The difference is a public surplus that can support other public programs.

When President Franklin Roosevelt instituted social security as a Great Depression–era social welfare net, all workers had to pay into social security until they began to collect their pension at the age of 65. However, the first recipient was not eligible to retire and collect her first social security check for another three years.[130] At the time, the life expectancy in the United States for a male born in 1936 was only 57 years, and for a female it was only 61 years.[131] FDR had succeeded in creating a tax that provided revenue to fund the New Deal while it passed the burden of social security to subsequent generations.

Fruit of the rise becomes the seed of decline

Only a share of any economy contributes to the production of the economic pie. This working age population must provide the production enjoyed by all. In a steady-state equilibrium, the wealth and surpluses they generate confer upon a nation its economic power.

Perhaps more importantly, it is this productive pie that must be divided among all the citizens of a nation, producing and non-producing alike. While each nation develops conventions that will dictate these divisions between producers and non-producers, the average level of consumption is ultimately related to the average productivity of workers, and the share of workers compared to non-workers. This is simple math.

However, also important is the incentives offered to workers to produce. If economic leaders make decisions that divert a greater amount of income from producers to non-producers, the incentives for workers to produce are reduced.

In addition, while a family's support of young people is a decision within the family's consumption autonomy, the compelled support of others is considered a tax and not an obligation. Obviously, the politics of these transfers is more emotionally charged. However, the reality that fewer producers cannot maintain the support of a growing number of dependents is difficult to escape.

Further exacerbating this phenomenon, a family can respond to an economy's social welfare programs by relying less on their extended family and more on the social largesse they support over their working lifetime. Perhaps as a consequence, the citizens of the First Economic World have fewer children. This fertility rate is correlated closely with per capita income, indicating that children are what economists call an "inferior good." Such goods are enjoyed relatively more by those of low income than those of high income.

At the same time, the reduced family formation rate compounds the challenge of a population that can replace those who retire from the workforce.

28
A Tear in the Social Fabric

> At his best, man is the noblest of all animals; separated from law and justice he is the worst.
>
> (Aristotle, ancient Greek philosopher, scientist, and physician, 384 BC–322 BC)[132]

The last two centuries brought unprecedented wealth and affluence to the group of the First Economic World. In a few decades, the majority of the planet will have access to that same affluence brought about by free markets and our competitive juices. This convergence will create some challenges arising from size and affluence that must nonetheless be overcome.

As we have seen, this affluence was brought about because of a number of seemingly small, but nonetheless significant, innovations.

First, constitutions around the world have imitated the constitutions of the United States, and then France, that adopted the right to "life, liberty, and the pursuit of happiness." Now, even the United Nations' model constitution has adopted the premise that each of us is permitted to further our own lot. This economic principle was a vast departure from economic systems of the past that functioned at the pleasure of the elite royalty.

Second, the rule of law is more than just the pursuit of order. With lawlessness comes too much effort in vigilante justice and in protecting one's own property. The effort to protect one's life, liberty, and happiness is too costly if done individually. An essential role of government must be in the creation of laws that protect citizens and promote commerce.

Third, the rule of law must be employed to protect something the world's affluent population takes for granted. There can be no commerce if there is no sense of private property. Imagine a world in which you could not claim your possessions that truly belonged to you. Not only would one have little allegiance to maintain the stuff one cannot own, but one would also be thwarted from engaging in commerce that is, in essence, the exchange of ownership.

And, fourth, we need markets that provide the incentive to produce and to consume, to allow producers access to consumers who desire their wares, and to allow consumers the opportunity to buy from whomever they choose to and who can offer them the best value.

These four innovations seem small, but the totality of their effect may well surpass the benefits of democracy itself. After all, every successful political system has adopted these premises, more or less, and every failed political state has also failed to provide for free markets, the rule of law, property rights, and the pursuit of happiness.

From these innovations have flowed a wealth of commerce and a plethora of transactions. The Internet has certainly multiplied these opportunities many fold. There was a time when the goods and services you bought were locally made, or at least locally retailed. These transactions were simple primarily because you know with whom you were contracting. A handshake and a sense of honor were the most important ingredients of a successful trade. One who did not possess honor could not find willing traders.

Regional, interstate, and now global commerce has multiplied the scope and competitiveness of the marketplace. In turn, it has magnified wealth and affluence, but at a subtle cost. Regionalization and globalization has torn the social fabric.

With greater size comes anonymity. When we no longer know our trading partners with whom we contract or exchange, and once reputation and character are more difficult to discern, we discover the unseemly underbelly of expanded commerce.

This anonymity of commerce has its parallels elsewhere in an increasingly complex economy. An unethical company's mission could devolve from what will enhance its reputation to how it can skirt the laws. With greater anonymity, individuals think less about what we can do to benefit others, and more about what we can get away with without being caught. And, we all look at those who succeeded by damaging others, and somehow rationalize that, if they can engage in such abuses, well, we too can.

It is precisely this tear at the social fabric that is the Achilles heel of increasingly large and global economies. When citizens do not know with whom they are dealing, trust deteriorates, people factor in the chance of unscrupulous traders when they make their offers, and much more cost and effort must be devoted to contracting. A world where one's word is good enough and one's honor was important was also much more efficient in trade.

When commerce becomes so geographically diverse that we never quite know the quality of the goods we receive, nor even if we will receive the goods we bought at a distance, commerce reaches its limit. The market for quality is replaced by a market for lemons. Various middlemen may spring up to match anonymous buyers with essentially anonymous sellers. However, if the dominant corporate model becomes one of protecting unscrupulous sellers at the expense of unsuspecting buyers, commerce of all sorts, everywhere, suffers. Such a business strategy may work for one company in isolation. Unfortunately, its poisoning effect extracts a toll on all commerce.

It would be interesting to calculate this cost of market complexity and the frauds and lack of trust it can engender. I expect that these costs may be substantial. To avoid these costs, consumers may increasingly buy goods that have been commodified and packaged by the largest corporations. The erosion of trust will eventually reduce, rather than enhance, choice and prices.

What can we do to buck this tearing at the social and commercial fabric? The rule of law must enforce fair play. On one hand, regulatory agencies must address the damage that can occur when traders begin to distrust the marketplace en masse. On the other hand, our trade will only be as geographically diverse as is the reach of our consumer protections. Ultimately, it may be as costly to work with a new consumer protection bureaucracy as it has been to work with unscrupulous sellers.

Regionalization and globalization that has brought about unprecedented affluence also has some subtle and hidden costs that must be addressed. However, it seems equally difficult to create a consumer protection organization that can span jurisdictions, protect buyers, and punish unscrupulous sellers wherever they may be.

In the meantime, we have to hope that those intermediaries who bring together buyers and sellers will place greater value on protection of buyers and show more zealousness in weeding out unscrupulous sellers. Unfortunately, it is not always in their interest if they gain their revenue from sellers that pay the commissions.

We have seen this story before, as we saw the global economy unravel under the weight of failed credit and financial markets. Consider those ratings agencies that would rate any collateralized debt instrument highly – for a price. We all know how that story ended. These ratings agencies, whose advice we trusted in choosing the right financial instruments, have left a legacy that will continue to cost us all for decades.

Indeed, until we figure out how to weed out and expose bad actors, commerce may never be the same. A few bad apples have the ability to rot the entire barrel. We must have the will to police shady commerce if we someday expect to sew up that tear in our social fabric.

Fruit of the rise becomes the seed of decline

As global economic pies have grown, so have the scope, diversity, and efficiency of global commerce. However, this global commerce diverts us away from a system in which we well knew our trading partners to one in which transactions are impersonal and at a distance. Dishonest and unscrupulous traders flourish in such anonymity. But, while this anonymity is profitable for them, it is much more costly for the rest of us. If we lose our trust in the integrity of markets, the entire economic system fails to live up to its potential.

This effect is exacerbated when trade becomes increasingly global. Humans more easily rationalize taking advantage of others who are not "their kind" or cannot easily avail themselves of justice in faraway jurisdictions. But, without recourse that forces the fairness that local trade can provide, we are limited in our enjoyment of economies of scale and regionalization/globalization. Granted, some firms will still step up and provide the guarantees we need to trade at a distance. However, they will do so only for a price that removes value from wary consumers.

29
Steady State and Sustainability

Now, the choice we face is not between saving our environment and saving our economy. The choice we face is between prosperity and decline. We can remain the world's leading importer of oil, or we can become the world's leading exporter of clean energy. We can allow climate change to wreak unnatural havoc across the landscape, or we can create jobs working to prevent its worst effects. We can hand over the jobs of the 21st century to our competitors, or we can confront what countries in Europe and Asia have already recognized as both a challenge and an opportunity: The nation that leads the world in creating new energy sources will be the nation that leads the 21st-century global economy.

(President Barack Obama, 2009)[133]

Keynes convinced us that the economy could settle on any number of equilibria, some of which are worse than others. A nation aspiring to join the First Economic World will grow at a rate that is not sustainable, if history is any indication. Meanwhile, the Third Economic World languishes in corrupt government and inadequate protection of property. The steady-state equilibrium remains unchanged until property rights and good government are forthcoming.

An interesting issue is the sustainability of the steady-state equilibrium that keeps the economies of the First Economic World at a steady, if unspectacular, growth. Let us spend some time describing what it means to be sustainable.

Some definitions

A discussion of sustainability inevitably relies on jargon unfamiliar to many readers. Let us begin with a definition of equilibrium.

An equilibrium is simply the description of a state in which the forces that might move a system in one direction are balanced by forces that would bring it in another. An equilibrium occurs when the system is balanced. This balance does not imply stagnancy. Rather, in equilibrium the forces are balanced so that an economic outcome is sustained.

For instance, a well functioning First Economic World nation may maintain growth at 2–3% and can maintain its cross section of population, public and private institutions, and various forms of capital over time. The system is in equilibrium because the various economics forces are in balance, even as the economy grows. This equilibrium is steady state because the observables that describe the equilibrium, like the demographic mix, the rate of growth, and the mix of private and public institutions, remain constant over time.

An economic system must be in steady state. Herman Daly, one of the founders of the notion of sustainable economies, defines a steady-state economy as one with:

> ... constant stocks of people and artifacts, maintained at some desired, sufficient levels by low rates of maintenance "throughput", that is, by the lowest feasible flows of matter and energy from the first stage of production to the last stage of consumption.[134]

Such a steady-state equilibrium can provide for the needs of its economy with an efficiency that produces little waste and a flow of energy and resources just sufficient to maintain the desired economic measures.

The notion of a steady-state economic equilibrium goes back to Adam Smith in *The Wealth of Nations*. Smith noted that, while the efficiencies of the free market are realized, an economy could grow spectacularly. However, once an economy transitions from a command economy to an efficient market-oriented economy, it will press upon its limits of growth. Smith believed that efficiency improvements would give rise to economic growth, which would, in turn spur population growth for the same sort of reasons Thomas Malthus postulated. Increased abundance supports a population that will grow until it meets the limits of available resources. As this population grows, the growing labor supply will earn a steadily declining wage until it too is barely supported. Meanwhile, resources necessary to support the larger population will become increasingly scarce until a low wage, high population rebalance is obtained.

Almost a century later, John Stuart Mill argued that:

> It must always have been seen, more or less distinctly, by political economists, that the increase of wealth is not boundless: that at the end of what they term the progressive state lies the stationary state, that all progress in wealth is but a postponement of this, and that each step in advance is an

approach to it. We have now been led to recognise that this ultimate goal is at all times near enough to be fully in view; that we are always on the verge of it, and that if we have not reached it long ago, it is because the goal itself flies before us. The richest and most prosperous countries would very soon attain the stationary state, if no further improvements were made in the productive arts, and if there were a suspension of the overflow of capital from those countries into the uncultivated or ill-cultivated regions of the earth.[135]

Smith and Mill agreed that the world's most prosperous nations must necessarily reach a steady state in which, absent technological improvements, the earth's resources are used to their full carrying capacity.

Even John Maynard Keynes weighed in on the limits of growth. In his *Widow's Cruse*, Keynes argued that, at the limit of growth, savings of the wealthy would dominate all investment to the point that the interest rate is driven to zero and thus the savings rate of the middle class would likewise fall to zero. At that point, the working class is held in a condition in which their consumption would equal their income and they would, in essence, be held in a "miserable condition." He noted:

> ... the natural degree of populousness is likely to exceed the ideal. ... It is not in accordance with Malthus' position to suppose that a day will actually arrive either in the near future or at any time when population will have become so dense that all the inhabitants of the world will live on the margin of starvation. Before that happens, some check is likely or certain to intervene. But such an admission does not affect two judgements of pessimism, – that, even as it is, the maintenance of a proper equilibrium generally involves misery; and that in most places the material condition of mankind is inferior to what it might be if their populousness were to be diminished.

Smith, Mill, and Keynes were not as sanguine as Malthus, with his dismal prophecy that economies are doomed to a pattern of feast followed by famine. However, absent the technological improvements supposed by Schumpeter, affluent economies do come to rest.[136]

But are they sustainable?

The issue is, though, whether these steady-state equilibria can be sustained over time. In 1971, in *The Entropy Law and the Economic Process*, Nicholas Georgescu-Roegen argued that there are physical limits to an economic development. The very nature of consumption of earth's resources requires that these resources be moved from an organized and concentrated state to a dispersed state. In this dispersion, entropy is increased, and this entropy cannot be reduced without energy. In the absence of plentiful energy, consumption becomes limited by the increasing scarcity of resources. Moreover, increased consumption and growth will require ever-increasing amounts of energy and natural resources, driving up their prices to the point that growth is limited.[137]

Ultimately, sustainability requires that resources and energy be available in a manner that present levels of consumption can be perpetuated and energy can be sustained to permit the recycling of resources in perpetuity.

In such a steady-state and sustainable economy, the profile of production, consumption, and population would change only if there were gains in technology that allow for even greater consumption without further taxing resource usage.

Obviously, this notion of a sustainable and steady-state equilibrium presumes that all the earth's resources are used sustainably. If combined with John Rawls' notion in *A Theory of Justice*, sustainability requires that all the earth's citizens have an opportunity to enjoy a similar level of affluence.[138]

With convergence of the First and Second Economic Worlds, it is foreseeable that each nation will someday consume resources with similar intensities that can be maintained in perpetuity. However, before that happens, there are a number of antecedents.

First, all resources must be priced at a level that properly reflects their ultimate scarcity and cost of recycling. With global markets for commodities, it is likely that there can be geographic price convergence. However, it is less likely that these prices will reflect the true long-run costs of the resources. After all, the goal of establishing the proper scarcity of resources with perpetuity in mind is more elusive when these pricing decisions are made by mortal individuals.

Second, sustainability requires convergence. An aspiring empire levels a legitimate complaint that it should not be expected to respect the pricing needs of a more affluent economic empire that garnered its affluence by disregarding the scarcity of commodities in the past. An economic empire is often built on its access to underpriced resources, abundant land, and fresh and clean water and air. If their subsequent affluence has been fueled by the under-pricing of earth's resources, an aspiring empire can make some claim on a transfer of ill-gotten wealth from the affluent to the aspiring as an inducement to embrace the value of sustainability.

Third, a steady-state and sustainable equilibrium would need to offer intergenerational equity if it is to ensure a constant and stable mix of populations. In other words, each generation, in each nation, can claim an entitlement to the degree of affluence and comfort afforded to other generations, across all countries. Even if nations could establish a compact that equalized the appropriate pricing of commodities, it would likely take generations to see affluence evenly distributed. Until there are no less fortunate generations coveting the affluence of a more senior generation, sustainability will be elusive.

Finally, steady-state economic sustainability will require complete convergence. If the First and Second Economic Worlds converge within this century, it may take another century before the Third Economic World is fully integrated. As long as any nation can rationalize that it too should share the fortunes of others, the politics of sustainability will be difficult to overcome.

Fruit of the rise becomes the seed of decline

The goal of a sustainable and steady-state economic empire is laudable. However, these values lack meaning in a global world if they are not values shared by both affluent and aspiring economies. To obtain global economic sustainability requires a convergence of the global economies. While it is likely that the Second Economic World will join the First within this century, sustainable development of the Third Economic World may prove more elusive.

30
Dinosaurs and Economic Darwinism

> I met a traveller from an antique land
> Who said: "Two vast and trunkless legs of stone
> Stand in the desert. Near them on the sand,
> Half sunk, a shattered visage lies, whose frown
> And wrinkled lip and sneer of cold command
> Tell that its sculptor well those passions read
> Which yet survive, stamped on these lifeless things,
> The hand that mocked them and the heart that fed.
> And on the pedestal these words appear:
> "My name is Ozymandias, King of Kings:
> Look on my works, ye mighty, and despair!"
> Nothing beside remains. Round the decay
> Of that colossal wreck, boundless and bare,
> The lone and level sands stretch far away.
>
> (Percy Bysshe Shelley (1792–1822), *Ozymandias*, 1818)[139]

While there are various theories that try to explain why the dominant species of dinosaurs became extinct, the theory of a sudden and cataclysmic event has gained the most currency. This theory of a major climatic disturbance arising from the crash of a meteor into the Gulf of Mexico did not kill off all living things. Rather, certain species suffered when their strengths in normal times became weaknesses once adaptability to a rapidly changing environment was essential.

At the same time, species that could eke out, survival in the periphery of mightier animals found themselves most agile and adapted to a new environment. Organisms that were more nimble and opportunistic prevailed over a lumbering giant that consumed more than its proportion of resources. Economic empires are no different. Every advantage eventually becomes a disadvantage that must be overcome.

Ten prevailing themes in the rise and decline of empires

In a number of dimensions, we have documented how these advantages become disadvantages. I would like to take a moment to summarize these artifacts of empiredom from our various chapters so that we may, in turn, formulate strategies that can turn challenges into opportunities. I summarize our results so far along ten broad prevailing themes.

Theme 1 – Repeated patterns of economic empires

Early economies moved more or less quickly through similar stages. In the beginning, an agrarian revolution and early barter economy permitted a dramatic expansion in the scope of goods that humans could produce. The invention of money accelerated this expansion. The economic revolution freed time for humans to pursue higher-level activities beyond meeting the basic needs of food and shelter. In turn, culture and civilization were born.

The resulting economic bounty produced incentives to organize into larger groups and tribes. Some of the spoils were diverted to maintaining a ruling elite that organized these early economies. These surpluses allowed the elite to support armies even as it maintained the basic needs of the farmers, the carpenters, the bakers, and the potters. In turn, the armies could extend the geographical reach of emperors so their empires could absorb ever more agricultural lands, control more peasants, and generate even greater economies of scale.

As the empire grew, though, it had to contend increasingly with rivals who would vie for power. In addition, while markets permitted empires to trade with other regional economic powers, these same markets allowed peasants and rivals to divert a share of production destined for the economic commander. Parallel underground economies emerged to challenge, and eventually frustrate, the leaders of the empire.

While markets at first allowed empires to take advantage of larger economies of scale through increased efficiency, these economies of scale eventually turned into diseconomies. Once the economies of scale were exhausted and the optimal scale was reached, any further growth simply drove up costs and forced an empire to the brink where it could break under its own weight.

While most enterprises recognize that growth for growth's sake is sheer folly once its efficient size is reached, empires often know no such bound. Their leaders begin to expect growth as an indicator of continued success. At some point, though, encouraging and forcing growth beyond the point of diminishing returns simply makes an empire more vulnerable and less nimble.

These invulnerabilities and inflexibilities can eventually lead to the demise of even the mightiest empires. Military might often had to be employed to hold together geographically disparate empires. Such empires based on markets and the military came and went over millennia.

Meanwhile, there came along a rapid succession of innovations that forever changed the social balances that were created and sustained over centuries. In this First Industrial Revolution, dramatic economies of scale from steam engines and waterwheels induced profound changes in the very ways labor was employed. The combination of innovations created growth and wealth that had been unprecedented in the course of the human experience. And, the changes in industry forced a redefinition of the social contract.

Theme 2 – A social contract

Most economic empires that adopted free market economics and benefited from the First Industrial Revolution also flirted with colonialism and mercantilism. These new models of economic colonialism differed substantially from the model of military dominance they replaced.

For the first time, an empire could cultivate colonies that would provide factors of production. In turn, the empire also secures a steady demand for the finished goods of the heartland. Likewise, colonists of the hinterland contributed to the sustained growth of the empire in return for its access to secure and sustainable trade.

This economic model of symbiosis permitted the heartland to sustain rapid growth, but at a cost. The gains from trade were often lopsided. The colonies that served the empire gained little from the relationship, while the empire gained a lot.

To sustain growth in the heartland over time as heartland diseconomies of scale set in, the hinterland colonies were afforded ever-worsening terms of trade. Just as earlier emperors gradually increased taxes to maintain their quality of life as their empire subsided, colonial empires increasingly distorted their terms of trade and, in doing so, disenfranchised the colonies they had hoped would sustain the growth of the empire. When this exploitation and disenfranchisement became too much for colonists to bear, some would declare their economic independence.

Rousseau argued that government should be viewed as a party in a mutually advantageous social contract. Likewise, a colony's membership in an empire can be viewed in a similar way. The empire would provide its allied colonies the protection of property and the rule of law, and access to markets for finished goods. In return, the colony provides the empire with markets for its goods and sustained growth. When the junior trading partner perceived its returns exceed the cost of membership in the empire, its citizens were content to support the economic system. When terms of trade tipped the balance too far toward the empire, economic revolution is almost inevitable.

While we now take for granted the mutually advantageous aspect of our membership in society, the notion that we make a conscious choice to accept the authority of our leaders, in return for the bounty the economy provides, is a relatively new concept.

If the health of an economic system ultimately required that its citizens voluntarily support the system, it would be a surprising coincidence if all enjoy equal benefits. The empire inevitably had some who would benefit a lot, and others who would benefit just enough to maintain their support of the empire.

In the colonial model, those citizens with immediate proximity to the heart of the empire were the likely big winners. Meanwhile, those citizens in the periphery were more likely to challenge the economic system. These marginalized citizens who were disaffected by the system, or those who felt abused by the system, were the empire's harshest critics.

Even a geographically compact empire had some citizens that felt alienated from the broader nationalistic fervor that supported the empire. In a far-flung empire that was inevitably more responsive to the citizens closest to the heartland, many residents at its periphery felt economically marginalized and nationalistically alienated. This alienation was an almost unavoidable consequence of a growing colonial empire.

Some colonial systems offered sufficient benevolence toward the hinterland to delay this natural tendency toward marginalization of the periphery. Most empires, however, met the sense of alienation from its most far-flung participants as a sign of disloyalty and a lack of appreciation and character. The issue became one of political pique and hubris rather than a sober consideration of legitimate tensions between differing economic interests and perspectives.

Almost inevitably, this growing sense of alienation was the fatal flaw for an empire that had become too diverse to support a common economic vision. When combined with an inability to mount sufficient coercive force to maintain the authority of the empire, revolution becomes unavoidable.

The animosity colonialism created in the hinterland eventually forces a redefinition of the social contract. The American Revolution was one such renegotiation. A new United States was the first country to forge a new political system on decidedly economic grounds rather than on the principles of power and politics.

Theme 3 – A nation formed on a new economic premise

Some countries, most notably England, had used common law principles to secure similar protections afforded by the U.S. Constitution on all its citizens. The United States was the first country, though, to enshrine a comprehensive new set of rules for a new economy as a set of founding principles. It was also the first country to offer economic protections through the arbitration of an independent judiciary.

Even the preamble that declared a new nation's economic independence made bold statements about a new economic premise for a new nation. Their words have reverberated ever since:

> We hold these truths to be self-evident, that all men are created equal, that they are endowed by their Creator with certain unalienable Rights, that among these are Life, Liberty and the pursuit of Happiness. That to secure these rights, Governments are instituted among Men, deriving their just powers from the consent of the governed, That whenever any Form of Government becomes destructive of these ends, it is the Right of the People to alter or to abolish it, and to institute new Government, laying its foundation on such principles and organizing its powers in such form, as to them shall seem most likely to effect their Safety and Happiness.

It is apparent from even a cursory reading of the Declaration of Independence, the U.S. Constitution, and the Bill of Rights that a new economic order was not only based on the realm of the possible, but also bounded the influence of government in the affairs of private individuals and private markets.

Despite the best efforts of a set of founding fathers determined to limit the scope of government, some of the most strident declarations of individual sovereignty over an oppressive state would be renegotiated under the constant and unrelenting force of new and special interests. Even a quarter century of brilliant insights by a new nation's founding fathers could not be expected to anticipate every possible scheme designed to separate fair-minded women and men from their surpluses. Laws would need to develop to prevent, or at least ameliorate, new abuses of an evolving economy.

Theme 4 – Spectacular growth gives way to special interests

These sentiments of economic individualism enshrined in a revolutionary U.S. constitution would eventually fall victim to the same sort of market failings and monopolizations that gave rise to revolutionary fervor in the first place. The price rigging of the British East India Company in factor and goods markets of the eighteenth century was replaced by the antics of railroad tycoons who rigged financial markets and monopolized many other markets in the nineteenth century.

The Gilded Age, fueled by a Second Industrial Revolution, soon eclipsed the brilliance of the First Industrial Revolution that transformed England just a century earlier. An empire founded on democracy in politics and in commerce, and a meritocracy that did not confine one to a station in life, created both a new set of opportunities and challenges.

Unfortunately, it has always been a natural proclivity of emperors and industrialists alike to covet the chattels of others as an easier path to amass great wealth than through their own production. After all, it is sometimes easier to gain by seeking the gains of others than to innovate oneself.

While a rising tide lifts all boats, a few soon realized that some boats could always be made to rise more than others. When other groups in society saw their position and economic status worsen in comparison to other groups, they challenged the economic status quo and demanded redistribution of the surpluses.

However, in the absence of an industrial model that would create partners of those who owned the financial and physical capital and the laborers who owned their human capital, government often found itself wedged between the two competing groups. The greater the economies of scale and the surplus these economies would create, it seemed, the greater the size of government necessary to redress the imbalances that arose under unfettered capitalism.

Unfortunately, government does not typically produce the goods and services that contribute to the economic pie. Instead, government assumed the role of a regulator of the private sector and a redistributor of economic surpluses and wealth. Its regulation and redistribution, primarily on behalf of the middle class, ultimately limited the efficiencies of industry and led to a decline in competitiveness of the economic empire. In turn, an empire resorted to neocolonialism or mercantilism in an attempt to sustain economic growth and support the expectations of their subjects.

Certainly, opportunities abounded as protection of property and the creation of free markets uncorked creativity and enterprise at a rate never seen before. However, there can only be so much economic creativity and explosive growth. Unchecked growth required new and broader markets. If growth outstripped the ability of markets to absorb the newfound bounty, or if it was impossible for people to work more hours to purchase the goods of others, growth would inevitably begin to stagnate. A country that initially rallied around a growing economic pie increasingly began to focus on how the pie was sliced.

The democratization of opportunity also led many to believe that they too could be the next millionaire. While many new millionaires were created, most of the rest subscribed to an American Dream that may have been more fiction than reality for the vast majority.

For a government formed by the people and for the people, economic stagnation and growing concerns about redistribution created political dilemmas. An economy accustomed to double-digit economic growth would run the risk of economic panic if growth fell to a still strong, but much more sustainable, 2% or 3% growth rate. A government that understood its responsibility in the social contract understood the political repercussions of anemic economic growth. However, double-digit growth must inevitably falter. As it did, the weaknesses of an economic empire became much more apparent.

In an effort to maintain growth and prosperity, empires often resorted to a new focus on paper wealth rather than real wealth. Indeed, U.S. and European economic empires regularly experienced bouts of speculation in which the production of paper profits substituted for the production of real goods and services. Even more recently, in the year 2006, fully one-third of all profits in the United States were "made" in the financial industry. Two years after the most profitable year in history, a breakdown in the U.S. financial industry led to the greatest global economic collapse in history.

We have since discovered that the de-emphasis of production and the celebration of speculative bubbles had played a major role in every economic panic since the onset of the Second Industrial Revolution. Part of the reason is the interplay between greed and special interests increasingly focused on capturing bigger pieces of an economic pie. Government could not typically stay ahead of the next financial ploy designed to secure for its creator a greater share of a fixed pie.

We should not have been surprised at this economic tendency, though. Mercantilism itself was based on the premise of lopsided trade. Speculative investors were merely taking the lead from the strategies of empires and their beggar-thy-neighbor polices. Just as empires would redefine terms of trade over time, financial and industrial capitalists alike tried to expand what was theirs by coveting another's share of the pie. Meanwhile, firms could expand their surpluses by monopolizing markets and charging higher prices, or by depressing wages of workers. In turn, workers could unionize and demand a greater share for themselves by limiting producers' access to labor and driving up wages. Everyone was catching-as-catch-can.

Caught in the middle was a hapless government that subscribed to laissez-faire economics and tried to stay ahead of a rapidly evolving economic landscape.

There is an end to every speculative cycle. When the bubble burst and paper profits were erased, people clamored to find scapegoats in these most challenging of times. A new set of special interests formed, as each group argued that another was to blame and demanded, through whatever political channels it could tap into, a greater share of a shrinking economic pie.

Indeed, this regression into special interest politics can become downright destructive. The focus shifts even further away from production and into renewed calls for redistribution of wealth. Political coalitions form that are adept at peeling off just enough of the disaffected to win an election and skew the balance into its constituency's favor, at least until another coalition can form.

These lessons from the Gilded Age are just as relevant today as they were poignant in the 19th century. As the social upheaval of the Gilded Age demonstrated, it is exceedingly difficult for government to anticipate and control every misguided attempt of free enterprise to innovate in less than economically healthy ways. Almost as quickly as an unhealthy economic innovation is kindled and subsequently extinguished, another new scheme is hatched. Even an aware and enlightened government often has the unpopular responsibility of curbing such unhealthy economic practices when they inevitably occur, and of taking the blame when unhealthy practices go too far.

A free market ideology that raised an empire to new heights may need to be reined in at different times. With millions of individual actors, each pursuing their own self-interest in virtual anonymity, and with the increased urbanization that breaks down community, it is a testament to our economic system that it is as robust and affluent as it has proven to be. Only rarely does our economic system find itself at the brink of collapse. Consequently, it should come as no surprise that government is typically slow to respond to problems that arise periodically.

Nor could government easily direct a decentralized economy that could find itself shifting away from the production of ideas and innovation and toward the protection of self-interests and the promotion of rampant consumption.

Theme 5 – The Achilles heel of conspicuous consumption

An economy that is growing in prosperity is often also growing in population and diversity. In an effort to create community, participants increasingly align themselves with the special interests that are so caustic to a shared economic vision. While prosperity allows the vast majority to meet their more basic needs, growing fragmentation of all elements of our society makes it more difficult to realize the equally important human needs for social respect and esteem.

Some in society have always been able to transcend this frustration and attain self-actualization. However, many more have resorted to the purchase of market icons that can communicate to the greater community that they had "arrived." The yardsticks in this race for esteem were accumulations of wealth, home size, the quality of our vehicles, the exclusivity of our children's schools, and other such luxuries. Ultimately, conspicuous consumption or the accumulation of wealth rather than the pursuit of happiness became unproductive activities that drained the economic resources of a nation.

This shift from production to consumerism was a great leveler that frustrated economic growth. In the short run, the impetus to consume in such a manner could sustain an economy. However, consumption for consumption's sake does not create the efficiencies and innovations that are associated with growing economic power.

Consumerism, though, is a fickle thing. A consumer-oriented economy becomes dependent on the psychology of consumers rather than on the optimism of entrepreneurs. Once this entrepreneurial optimism is lost, the slightest economic downturn can cause rampant pessimism and induce its capital to flee to safer or more productive economies.

An affluent society that transcends into conspicuous consumption rather than efficient production should remember similar lessons from its past. The world has, time and time again, repeated a now familiar development cycle. This cycle is a natural consequence of institution formation and increasing returns to scale, followed by decreasing returns to scale, a democratization of production and institutions, greater decadence, and an increase in consumerism. It would be folly to imagine that spectacular growth, of a kind demonstrated in aspiring economies, can continue unabated indefinitely.

The spectacular growth that arose from positive economic feedback loops eventually diminish, often to be replaced by processes that constrain growth.

The spectacular growth occurs when those that enjoy the surpluses are sufficiently confident of the continuation of growth. They will reinvest their surpluses to ensure future growth. Particularly, when the surpluses are concentrated in the hands of a few who easily meet all their consumption needs, they will likely reinvest their surpluses into greater future productive capacity. Moreover, a growing and optimistic economic empire will keep this investment capital at home. Effective government policies can even be designed to promote domestic investment and encourage such domestic investment.

However, once the surpluses are spread among many, they increasingly employ these surpluses in their attempt to raise their level of consumption. This shift away from reinvestment and toward consumption reverses the positive feedback loop. More affluence and greater consumption results in decreased savings and investment, and reduced growth. Government, too, often reflects the actions of its voting public by emphasizing equity over efficiency and short-term goals at the expense of long-term debts.

The resulting decline in savings and the drain on loanable funds leads financial capital to flee elsewhere. Fortunately, for aspiring nations, financial capital is mobile. It can easily transcend borders and flow into emerging nations that protect property and encourage investment. Unfortunately, for an economic empire, the positive feedback loop that allowed for spectacular growth and the attainment of an apex of economic power is reversed through conspicuous consumption and capital flight. This reversal acts as another great economic leveler.

Theme 6 – Globalization and corporation-driven colonialism

Economic theory has long recognized that financial investment flows toward its greatest return. Globalization now permits financial capital to flow anywhere in the world, almost instantaneously. Just as a middle-class household can now choose to invest anywhere in the worlds, it is equally obvious that well positioned and sophisticated companies can move its resources anywhere within the global economy.

While national policies may, at times, try to thwart the economic autonomy of its corporations, it is futile to try to bar corporations from conducting commerce across borders. A company from an economic empire has too many global tools to maximize its multinational profits. Efforts to avoid high domestic wages or organized labor, or to take advantage of lower wages elsewhere or tap into new markets induce corporations to develop subsidiaries in other countries.

To some extent, a nation, too, can be complicit in furthering these corporate interests in global trade. A nation would rarely do so through military power, but can still exert economic influence for its corporations through other, more subtle, means. It can influence terms of trade, apply political pressure on foreign nations to support its companies, or can foster treaties or trade pacts that benefit its multinational corporations.

Under an onslaught of lobbying by foreign corporate interests, only a most determined and enlightened trading partner can discern and embrace the best opportunities for its own economic development, disregard the rest, and create sustainable economic activity that permits greater diversification and increased independence for its citizens.

However, while a nation can and should advocate free trade and global commerce, it is ultimately torn between two forces. Its own corporations within the empire grow by fostering and maintaining monopoly or monopsony power in their cross-border strategies. However, an empire does not thrive in isolation. Membership of an economic empire in a community of nations implores it to pursue international partnerships rather than international paternalism. Good international citizenship clashes with the very forces that give rise to economic empires. Instead, empires find themselves asserting global principles that may thwart economic development elsewhere.

This tension is perhaps most striking in efforts to preserve and protect the intellectual capital and technologies that sustain an economic empire.

Theme 7 – An inevitable diffusion of information and technology

Economic empires increasingly rely on technology and intellectual capital to maintain their comparative advantage. However, multinational companies must let their technology and intellectual capital flow to foreign subsidiaries if they are to provide the best return to their shareholders. In addition, as an economy and empire grows, population grows, processes must necessarily involve more people, and ideas that once gave rise to monopoly profits become increasingly difficult to protect.

Further accelerating the great leveling power of transfer of knowledge and the dissemination of information is the Internet. Indeed, we may discover that the Internet has been the greatest leveler of all time.

In the 20 years from 1989 to 2009, the Internet grew from a tool employed primarily by university researchers who held 100,000 host sites,[140] to a tool employed in commerce and social networking by 1.73 billion users.[141] This works out to compounded growth of 49% per year for 20 years. This exponential growth in Internet usage occurred in an era that also saw China move from outside of the ten largest nations in the world to the world's second largest economy.

At the rate of growth demonstrated in China over the decade 1999–2009, I extrapolate that the size of China's economy will surpass that of the United States by the end of the year 2021. Such dramatic growth could not have occurred without technology transfers and the democratization of information.

In addition, the rate of capital flows, technology transfer, information exchanges, and global trade are at levels never before seen and only few could have imagined. If the British Empire dominated global economics for two centuries and the United States dominated commerce for a little more than a century, China's expected ascendency may be short-lived, though. Economic empires find it increasingly difficult to maintain superiority through their traditional tools of monopoly and secrecy in this era of instant communications and global competition.

Theme 8 – Complex systems and coordination failures

Many political and economic systems have come and gone in the past century. Modern history has demonstrated that no economic system has performed as efficiently and as resourcefully as has the free enterprise system. Economic empires and aspiring empires alike have universally adopted the free market system that has proven so productive in various empires' golden ages. The challenge, then, is to manage the great engine of production that free enterprise can provide, while still manage potential weaknesses that can bring the free market system to its knees.

All economic empires eventually realize that size does matter. For instance, the smallest economy is simple to coordinate. A few producers can easily determine the range of goods and services desired by a few consumers. If producers know in advance that consumers want their goods and services, they are willing to hire the households to perform the work. Such a simple system is almost self-coordinating.

Alternately, even a large command economy can be coordinated in a similar manner. The central planner can ensure that there is a sufficient amount of human capital, physical capital, and earth's capital devoted to produce the goods and services that government deems necessary. Such a centrally planned economy can distribute production of goods and services as necessary to satisfy its consumption criteria of its citizens.

Both the simple self-coordinating economies and the centrally planned economies are stable, if not particularly innovative, anticipatory, or efficient. These command and control economies work best when there is little change.

What they may lack in innovation or dynamism they make up in predictability and invulnerability to the vicissitudes of the business cycle.

On the other hand, the free market system is innovative because it is fueled by the ingenuity of a myriad of entrepreneurs, each hoping to discover the new product that every consumer wants. The free market system offers consumers a choice of the widest range of goods and services. Neither a simple economy nor a centrally planned economy can provide such a diversity of choice combined with efficiencies that only perfect competition can create.

If the appropriate measure is the innovation, efficiency, and ability to produce the goods and services consumers desire at the best possible price, the laissez-faire system outperforms other systems by a wide margin. The diversity of production and the efficiency of economies of scale are hallmarks of the free market system.

However, an economic empire that fuels its substantial growth based on the free market system is also more vulnerable to economic shocks, recessions, and depressions. A free market economy requires more robust and sophisticated system of regulatory oversight and monetary and fiscal policies that may exceed the capacity of governments' regulatory bodies.

In addition, an economic empire, both dependent on and strongly linked to other global economies, affects and is affected by the success of its trading partners. The global financial meltdown of 2008 poignantly demonstrated this painful reality.

The free market system may well be one of the most complex systems created by humankind. Such complex systems increase both diversity and uncertainty. They can also result in surprising and sometimes catastrophic perturbations because of their very complexity. On the other hand, small and carefully coordinated policies can create magnified positive benefits to the economy. The art is in mastering the control of complex and decentralized systems.

Just as large, free market economies are susceptible to economic shocks as a consequence of their complexity and decentralization, large, complex organizations can also be susceptible. Every large corporation must divine a balance between a size that offers sufficient economies of scale and one that prevents the rigidity that comes with size.

Moreover, just like an economic empire, when an organization becomes too big to fail, it gives way to groupthink, its vision and ethics can become challenged by its blinding pursuit of growth, and it loses the creativity that allowed it to grow in the first place.

Any economic entity also functions best when it can sustain a superior flow of information that is not drowned out in a cacophony. These networking effects create synergies. However, if these same networking synergies subsequently cause an economic entity to grow too large, chaos theory predicts that the entity again becomes increasingly vulnerable to uncertainty at a rate that grows exponentially with its size. With the diversity of size also comes increased uncertainty and a growing difficulty to coordinate a complex economy.

Theme 9 – Cultural differences and economic advantages

The path of development, for economic empires and aspiring nations alike, is one of nuance. Principles that work for one nation at a given time may be entirely inappropriate for another at a different stage of development. Differences in the size and skills of the labor force, incomes and capital in the nations, and even the cultures that govern each country's evolution, make it difficult to impose on all nations the types of solutions advocated by global conventions like the World Trade Organization or climate change talks.

In a rapidly evolving global economic environment, empires understandably try to protect their franchise and exercise their economic influence. Typically, economic superpowers play a disproportionately large role in formulating the rules that govern global economic interactions. However, these understandable, if not misguided, attempts of economic empires to set global trade standards that best suit their needs may be unproductive for all concerned. In the process, economic empires may marginalize aspiring nations.

The aspiring nations have an advantage, though. A large and populous nation, or a nation able to mobilize a hardworking and motivated workforce, has great opportunity for growth. Such a nation can produce labor-intensive goods and services comparatively cheaply. This production puts income in the hands of the owners of human capital, creates a strong and sustainable middle class, and helps fuel rapid economic growth. Moreover, the free flow of global financial capital ensures that aspiring nations that can guarantee the rule of law and protection of property will have the physical capital they need to augment their other factor endowments.

Consequently, as we saw in China and Japan in the past 40 years, economic success can rapidly shrink the gap between what a nation's income was and what it could be.

Such rapidly growing nations are wise to remember certain economic lessons. As an aspiring empire nears its apex, this capacity to grow still further is mitigated. Production based on human capital shifts toward production based on physical and financial capital.

However, physical and financial capital can easily transcend borders, and will always flow to those countries that have the basic economic infrastructure, a lower cost and motivated labor force, and the capacity to grow rapidly. In turn, as an aspiring empire arrives at its apex, it too will discover consumers prefer to invest in other aspiring nations that offer the spectacular growth an economic empire at its apex cannot sustain.

It is the motivation of workers, the unrealized capacity for economic growth, and the natural development cycle that act as a great opportunity for growth in aspiring nations. These factors also serve as a leveler of growth in economic empires that have fully realized the potential of their underutilized resources. This leveling effect is unavoidable and is simply a consequence of success, combined with the Law of Diminishing Marginal Returns.

While the inevitable diffusion and imitation will result in a convergence of economic systems, every ascendancy has subtle differences. Embedded in every society are individualized notions of equity, of morals, and of religion that determine cultural norms. These cultural norms inevitably influence economic values as surely as economic values influence cultural norms over time. However, while the economic innovations we take for granted have flourished for less than three centuries, strong cultural norms have prevailed in some societies for millennia. Inevitably, these norms, with regard to such economic values as property, cooperation, and the role of government will influence the way all economies evolve.

Cultural norms are also challenged as global commerce flourishes. Local transactions are by their nature personal and based on integrity and reputation. Increased regionalization and globalization allows unscrupulous traders to engage in commerce in near-anonymity. Dishonest commerce has a poisoning effect on all consumers and on those producers who remain honest even when trading with those they do not know. As trust is eroded, the entire economic system cannot live up to its potential.

Instead, large and reputable firms can take advantage of their reputation to commodify goods of quality that is difficult to discern. This commodification of goods and services reduces diversity and also extracts value from otherwise trusting consumers. Either way, the global economic system suffers from its sheer size and its growing anonymity.

Theme 10 – History repeats itself

While the dominant economic system can typically dictate broad economic principles, economic empires are transient entities. In just over a century and a half, from 1860 to 2021, China, Great Britain, the United States, and China again, have or will hold the mantle as the largest economy in the world. On average, a new economic empire ascends as the dominant economy every half century. With dominance comes economic influence and an advantage to assert more than proportional control over the definition of global terms of trade, for a while.

Each of these empires over the past few centuries exhibits an interesting dance between demographics and development. An aspiring empire regards the size of its pool of human capital as a strategic economic asset and seeks to optimize the return on its asset. As income subsequently rises with its economic success, an economy develops a taste for a higher quality rather than a larger quantity of labor.

With further increases in income and quality of life, and with a shifting emphasis toward dividing the economic pie rather than creating the pie, an economic empire begins to offer social welfare nets that provide alternative financial security for the family. No longer is a fast growing labor force the norm. Rather, the most developed nations rarely provide for replacement population. In this sense, economic empires once again sow the seeds of their eventual demise. The necessary importation of labor, through immigration, supports population led economic growth, but at the expense of a dilution in the population and cultural homogeneity that acted as a vehicle for nationalism and economic growth.

Undoubtedly, China too will be challenged by some aspiring nation that we can only today imagine. Perhaps India, richly endowed with human capital and have a zest for education, will be the next nation to aspire for the apex of economic dominance.

While we may be able to chart various measures of relative economic power, equally obvious is that economic power eventually falters just as surely as it is created. While this consistent empirical observation is no substitute for informed analysis, the pattern remains powerful evidence of the shifting sands of hegemony.

This chapter summarized one side of the coin that gives rise to an economic empire, and another side in which forces frustrate the economic empire's growth and, eventually, brings about its decline. The art of empire building is to applaud the first set of forces and prevent the latter set. Pathways for sustainable growth of an affluent empire's quality of life are the subject of our final chapter.

31
Fifteen Policy Prescriptions for Relevance

> The wave of the future is not the conquest of the world by a single dogmatic creed but the liberation of the diverse energies of free nations and free men.
>
> Change is the law of life. And those who look only to the past or present are certain to miss the future.
>
> (John F. Kennedy, President of the United States, 1961–1964)[142]

We can take this study of the economic history of empires and prescribe certain qualities that will dictate ascendancy and predict a subsequent decline. The path of empiredom and subsequent decline may sound like a dismal prophecy. However, I view an understanding of patterns repeated as an opportunity to avoid repeating the past. Knowledge allows one to determine a course that may slow the pace of decline, and may perhaps even reverse it.

In closing, I offer some prescriptions for innovation and economic relevancy, even at the height of economic power.

Acknowledge the end game

It is understandably difficult to acknowledge the fleeting nature of economic power. However, acceptance of the inevitability of convergence is essential if an economy is to develop a strategy that is proactive and forward-looking rather than reactive. Such a strategy must realistically recognize the strengths and weaknesses of the economic empire, as well as the strengths and weaknesses of those aspiring economies that could either compete or cooperate with the empire.

Economic superpowers accustomed to the hegemonic power they wield are reluctant to forego or acknowledge an end to this power. For instance, it has been said that superpowers dictate foreign policy while less powerful nations deal in foreign policy. This privilege is difficult to sacrifice.

However, if an empire does not forge international relationships as an equal partner, potential trading partners may participate less than willingly and with a jaundiced eye toward a long-term relationship. Relationship building is best pursued in an atmosphere of mutual advantage. Lopsided and hegemonic relationships are forced marriages that cannot be sustained. Such imbalanced relationships may have consequences as these aspiring nations ascend and the economic empire descends.

Better economic management

Economic leaders face a quandary. Certainly, no electorate is more ruthless than one facing significant unemployment or inflation. The subjects of an economic empire come to expect good economic stewardship. Stagnant growth also frustrates voters. A slipping economic position in a global world strikes a nationalistic cord that can be exploited by opposition parties.

Economic leaders well understand this dynamic. However, the challenge of leadership is that every decision, good or bad, is scrutinized and remembered. Those that have the luxury of opposition do not face the same accountability.

The Global Financial Meltdown that began with the Credit Crisis of 2007/2008 illustrates the paralyzing effect of global economic leadership. At that time, a financial problem that originated in the United States had created a global credit crisis. This crisis came on the tail end of a global commodity bubble fueled by the demand for factors of production by aspiring nations like China and India.

The United States was placed in the position of either slowing down a commodity-driven global boom to ameliorate inflation, or remedying the credit crisis through stimulus. Every major central bank around the world was watching its every move. As the acknowledged economic leader of the time, the pressure on Ben Bernanke, the chair U.S. Federal Reserve was immense. He decided to do nothing, for fear that anything he did might solve one problem but make the other worse.

Had the United States instead sought a global consensus on a global strategy, its policy would have likely been more proactive and direct, its tools would have been more extensive and coordinated, and its outcome would have likely solved the credit crisis before it brought the global economy to its knees.

Actually, the United States did eventually act, somewhat belatedly. In a vacuum of effective policy, an increasingly frightened Europe began to take economic leadership. The former U.K. prime minister and finance minister, Gordon Brown, took unprecedented steps to shore up its credit markets. Similar efforts in Europe followed. Soon, the United States was forced into using its mammoth economic influence and capacity to do the same.

This coordination of global economic policy was effective, if a bit too late to avert the Great Recession. Although the tools were relatively well understood, the inability to swiftly employ these tools in a coordinated global effort, because of issues of national economic autonomy and pride, may have permanently reduced the global leadership potential of the world's largest economy.

Understand the motivations and aspirations of other nations

Sometimes we can learn about ourselves by looking at our children. We can share in their successes and enjoy their energy and experiences by looking at the world through their eyes.

An economic empire can likewise learn by viewing the world through the eyes of those who aspire to affluence and financial security. This situational reality check is valuable. Indeed, law students are taught not only to develop a strategy to advance their case, but also to develop a strategy their opponent might employ. The exercise of looking at a contest for economic supremacy through an opponent's eyes is most instructive.

This ability to be reflective is hardest for the economic empire. As an example, the United States and Canada have historically been the two largest mutual trading partners in the world. Canada, with an economy a tenth the size of the United States, is obviously the much smaller trading partner. The United States looms large in Canadian eyes.

This asymmetry creates a dynamic that should not be surprising. Canadians understand almost every aspect of the U.S. culture, economy, policy, and politics. On the other hand, U.S. citizens know little about Canada. This pattern is common among asymmetric trading partners everywhere. Ultimately, economic or cultural arrogance is perilous for any economic empire.

Sufficient awareness is difficult, however. Empires, by their very diversity, self-sufficiency, and envy by others, are understandably self-absorbed. However, a greater emphasis of an education system on global issues, an encouragement of more international trade and travel, and foreign policies that endear other nations to the philosophies of the economic empire can reverse this self-destructive tendency. Such internationalization sacrifices hegemonic power by instead building toward the end game.

Recognize the chief asset

Every empire begins with some underutilized factor of production. Often, but not always, this factor is labor. England had its colonial labor and resources, the United States had its burgeoning immigration, and the United States, Japan, and China all had agricultural sectors that could realize significant efficiency improvements.

By enhancing agricultural production and creating the economic infrastructure that could move the freed labor to the manufacturing sector, each of these countries demonstrated double-digit growth that lasted for decades. Every seven years of double-digit growth resulted in more than a doubling of economic output. Three decades of such growth allows output to rise sixteen-fold.

It is possible that a country can simply bleed its agricultural sector into manufacturing without increasing agricultural productivity. However, almost every country considers agriculture as an essential industry for domestic security reasons. Consequently, an improvement in agricultural productivity is a strategy shared among economic empires.

Safety net for the least fortunate, accountability for all others

An inevitable conclusion of Maslow's Hierarchy of Wants and Needs is that with affluence comes a greater generosity for those less fortunate. The hierarchy also predicts that more affluent households will value financial security, self-actualization, and a broader cultural education. These values often translate into a measurement of the capacity of an empire based on how it takes care of those least fortunate.

However, this compassion can create unintended consequences. For instance, as income rises, most societies increasingly adopt systems of social welfare. Eventually, these mechanisms for compassion and financial security become regarded as entitlement programs.

The paradigm shift from a gift of compassion to one of entitlement naturally induces some recipients of social largesse to view such programs as a right rather than a privilege. In doing so, the social contract is renegotiated to include a new set of clauses that depart widely from its original premise of hard work in return for economic progress. Such a culture of entitlement defies the ethic that created original wealth for all economic empires in the first place.

This paradigm shift fundamentally reshapes the social fabric. However, it is not for the obvious reason that one set of values emphasizes production for others and the other emphasizes consumption from others. Rather, the paradigm shift moves an economy from its concerted efforts to create a larger economic pie and toward greater efforts to distribute a fixed economic pie. An emphasis away from a positive-sum-game and into a constant-sum-game mentality actually creates a negative sum problem.

This is problematic because a political system designed around redistribution rather than production ultimately expends a great deal of what would otherwise be productive activity into redistribution. While there are noble and self-actualizing justifications for some redistribution of wealth, once these redistribution efforts become an industry in themselves, our eyes are averted from the true economic prize.

In addition, an emphasis that shifts toward entitlements becomes overreaching. Some begin to see others succeeding by working less. This shirking, either partially or completely, tears at the fabric of any work ethic, and divides a culture into two competing cohorts – one that advocates hard work and self-reliance and another that justifies entitlements. This division inevitably diffuses into the political debate and dilutes a nation's centrality of focus.

Renew infrastructure investment

An aspiring nation invariably invests in itself. For instance, the level of infrastructure investment in China is reported by some experts to be somewhere between two and five times greater than that in the United States. However, the United States, too, invested in itself to a similar degree when it was growing by leaps and bounds in its golden age.

Without the steady influences of annual infrastructure investment and an emphasis on production over consumption, an empire is vulnerable to increasingly fickle consumers who believe they are king. However, an economic empire at its apex can use infrastructure investment as sound economic policy. When the economy begins to turn toward bust in the business cycle, fiscal policy through infrastructure investment can ratchet up. As the economy rebounds toward a boom, it can wean off this infrastructure spending and begin to save for the next rainy day. The art is in knowing when to invest and the wisdom is in knowing when to pull back.

Reduce size and shirking

Great economies are ultimately built on the shoulders of successful enterprises. However, while corporations are able to grow organically because of their size and economic might, they also suffer from their size. The cost of reduced loyalty from a large and increasingly anonymous workforce, shirking of those that can hide in a shadow of corporate anonymity, and an inability to coordinate, regulate, or even police themselves are all challenges to a burgeoning corporate empire.

The creation of companies too big to fail is also problematic. These companies can violate sound and ethical corporate management simply because management becomes unwieldy and disconnected. Because of their size, an economy can ill-afford the failure of these firms.

Consequently, when major corporations falter, the government and, therefore, the taxpayer are much more likely to bail them out and prop them up. In doing so, the very economic Darwinist forces that allowed these corporations to succeed are mitigated. Such a crutch cannot be healthy for the corporation or for the economy as a whole.

If we recognize the inevitability that corporations can grow too big to fail, our economic leaders must limit the size and exposure of such companies. Merger policy should be scrutinized still further and companies that become so large as to make an entire economy vulnerable must be broken up into independent units that are much less threatening to national economic security.

If an economy can mandate such strategic corporate breakups, problems of shirking, divided workforce loyalties, chaos, and coordination will also be solved.

Increase innovation and entrepreneurship

With affluence comes a less cohesive and coordinated economic path. A highly diversified economy has trouble articulating the message of entrepreneurship and innovation that is the hallmark of any rapidly growing economy. Indeed, entrepreneurs garner an almost second-class reputation as opportunists hoping to get rich quick. Ironically, the opportunity to get rich quick is often the same value so cherished in an aspiring nation trying to attain a national economic dream.

To succeed, every economy needs innovators and entrepreneurs. These rare and valuable individuals are in the business of change. In a nation aspiring to develop, change is not difficult. After all, change requires us to be willing to shed our past in pursuit of an unknown future. When the past is bleak, this bargain is not difficult. However, when our past and present are relatively comfortable, change becomes much more difficult to forge and manage. An economic empire that can successfully motivate and navigate change is the one that can improve quality of life and retain its global stature.

Pick some winners

There are sectors in the economy that we can confidently predict will play a role in sustainable growth in our quality of life. Every aspiring empire recognizes the role of science, engineering, technology, and research and development in creating high quality jobs, economic progress, and a higher quality of life requiring less human toil.

There are eras of great economic and social progress that ride on waves of optimism. This sense of optimism and excitement is often embraced and fueled by visionary leaders who understand the utility of identifying a few key sectors that can move a whole nation forward. Colonialism by Great Britain in the eighteenth century, the Transcontinental Railroad in the nineteenth century, the Space Race in the twentieth century in the United States, and China's modernization in the twenty-first century are all examples of an innovation vision that excited whole nations. It takes visionary leadership to have the courage to pick winners. Moreover, it takes highly skilled leadership to foster such innovations from infancy through fruition.

Be willing to pick the winners

When there are few opportunities vying to become a national dream, picking such winners is not difficult politically. However, leaders of a large and complex economy with many politically well-connected industrial interests find making such choices more difficult. If heirs-apparent to economic winners are christened, then those not chosen are considered losers, if only in a relative sense. Leaders are loathe to single out winners and losers in highly political systems, making it very difficult to put sufficient economic resources behind opportunities for future success.

Heckscher-Ohlin in reverse – a capital mobilization nation

Aspiring nations typically have some factor of production with sufficient excess capacity. The development of an economy's unrealized potential can fuel spectacular economic growth.

This growth has a multiplying effect. Typically, an aspiring nation leverages its excess labor to fuel the labor-intensive manufacturing sector. The economists Heckscher and Ohlin demonstrated that this leverage can yield a multiplier effect that can vault ahead an economy by employing its labor in the production of labor-intensive goods and services.

An affluent nation can similarly leverage its abundant endowment of savings and capital. This financial capacity can be leveraged if accompanied by a government willing to employ fiscal and tax policy. Research and development spending, manufacturing process innovation, and an expansion of technology training in science and engineering can allow a nation to take advantage of their capital asset.

However, this asset is often diverted into other less productive ways. If a nation's capacity to save and invest instead finds its way into greater consumption rather than investment, it may be able to create domestic jobs today, but only by increasing imports from abroad, and ultimately by sending jobs abroad. Consumption today sacrifices investment that would have generated domestic jobs tomorrow.

The maintenance of spending in a dysfunctional economy bent on consumption rather than investment is not a sustainable economic policy. A successful economy must create pathways to redirect spending from consumption into new investment in research and development, private physical capital, and public infrastructure.

Consumption deferred today will result in more consumption tomorrow. However, people are unwilling to make this trade if they only live for today. A consumption tax, levied as a small percentage of all consumption spending, can serve this purpose. It will at once discourage some consumption and create a pool of income to support physical capital investment.

It is also compelling to channel savings into financial investment rather than physical investment. Savings diverted to financial markets that encourage increasingly sophisticated financial instruments and increasingly dangerous speculative bubbles create only paper profits and economic vulnerability. We noted earlier that, in 2006, one out of every three dollars of profit earned in the United States was in the paper wealth-generating financial services industry. In 2008, this industry initiated what would become the greatest global decline of wealth in our planet's history.

The straitjacket of debt

There are very good reasons for a nation to incur debt. A strategic buildup of infrastructure that will subsequently fuel economic expansion is one such reason.

A balanced fiscal budget constrains such strategic use of government resources to foster and stabilize economic growth. A prudent economy will run a budget surplus when the business cycle is in a boom and can subsequently use this rainy day fund to support new infrastructure improvements when the business cycle moves through its periodic economic busts.

Government deficits that are used to fuel growth in good and bad times may appease the subjects of an economic empire in their need for constant and sustainable economic growth.

However, the creation of perennial deficits to support consumption but which gives rise to mounting debt becomes an economic straitjacket. Debt constrains a government from securing the funds needed for strategic investment at a sufficiently attractive rate. It also diverts private savings that could have gone to private investment into the public sector instead. If this diversion results in greater publicly subsidized consumption at the expense of private infrastructure investment, at ever-increasing interest rates, the economy loses doubly.

Be willing to tailor incentives to activities that promote growth

An economy must do more than merely identify winners. It must use incentives that promote growth in sectors that the private sector cannot sufficiently fund. While the hallmark of a free market system is confidence in an invisible hand that guides resources to those sectors that provide the greatest return, the free market can falter at times. For instance, development of an infant industry without any established economies of scale is a risky venture. Given the necessary scale to compete globally, few industries have the capacity to create global competitors quickly and easily.

For instance, a nation can help an infant industry get over obstacles, at first. A large social investment fund can help mobilize venture capital. Of course, it will inevitably pick some losers over time. This is acceptable if it can pick more winners than losers. However, few individual or corporate investors can risk picking a loser these days, without threatening the very survival of even large corporations. A pool of investment funds can better deal with a mix of successes and failures, and confers an advantage in a large economy willing to invest in itself.

Industries are also loathe to develop opportunities in which they can capture only a share of the returns. Those industries that simultaneously create broad economic spinoffs may require government participation. Government appropriately subsidizes higher education and research and development because it recognizes only a small portion of the benefits flowing out of major research centers will flow to a specific industry.

Even if these industries could capture the returns of all the various spinoffs that may flow from a broad research initiative, its business model would compel it to hold their innovations close. The patents that would remain in the private domain could be licensed out, but the recipients would be forced to negotiate with a monopoly holding the patents and innovations. The efficiency and deadweight losses when economic innovations are closely held translates into a market failure an aspiring economy can ill-afford.

A march toward efficiency (as if it matters)

Economic evolution is as ruthless and unforgiving as evolution is in the biological world. The pace of innovation in either system is strongest when the systems are permitted to work.

Ruthless biological Darwinism is not imitated in modern society, for very good reasons. A human being with a congenital biological problem is afforded medical treatments that can permit a healthy and often productive life. These same genetics that may have prevented procreation in a primitive world can be maintained and passed along in our technologically advanced world. The sustainability and viability of the species does not suffer so long as medical advances can ameliorate the consequences.

However, if economic evolution is artificially frustrated by propping up obsolete industries or corporations, for fear of temporary displacements of its workers or shareholders, we fail twice. First, we maintain an enterprise that demonstrated it cannot complete. Perhaps more problematically, we retain our valuable workers and capital in an unproductive industry when they ought to be transitioned to an industry that has a greater likelihood of success.

We offer this economic crutch because we are reticent to make the difficult choices that displace voters. However, if we could help in the transition and the retraining of these displaced workers, we could indemnify the worker, aid in the transition, and foster productivity in a new enterprise, all at the same time. This solution would require us to demand accommodation and change from those displaced. Considering the stakes, this responsibility, in return for our social investment, is justified.

Do not fall into the fallacy of growth of the measureable

Finally, it would be a mistake to judge that the growth of the gross domestic product of an economic empire should be our central goal. Economic growth ought not promote solely the industries that produce measurable products. The fallacy of growth for growth's sake must be considered.

For instance, if the goal of an economy is simply to expand the pie of economic activity denominated in dollars, euros, yen, or yuan, we neglect all those worthy activities that occur outside of markets. One could quickly expand a nation's output by 20%, simply by requiring all workers to work an extra day each week. Obviously, if a society wanted to work more, it could have put in place this innovation already. However, society also values leisure time to enjoy the fruits of economic success. Indeed, some of the world's most affluent nations have recently chosen to work less rather than more, even if their gross domestic product may suffer.

Instead, an economy must have the wisdom to foster the quality of life for its citizens. An affluent empire can maintain its relevance by working much smarter rather than working much more. Its ability to exercise its wisdom to generate a high quality of life is the truest measure of its economic strength.

Conclusion

> Britain's most useful role is somewhere between bee and dinosaur.
> (Harold MacMillan, prime minister of England, 1957–1963)[143]

Power based solely on economics is a relatively new concept. However, lessons learned from power derived from military prowess is little different. There is a certain inevitability to the decline of both. And, there are lessons to learn from each.

Many authors, so far, have explained why military and colonial empires have come and gone. However, the utility of militarism and colonialism is obsolete in today's global environment. Instead, economic empires are now able to extract the hegemonic power once the sole purview of military powers.

Just as these earlier empires, based on military or colonial power, have experienced spectacular ascendancies and subsequent declines, modern economic empires are no less fragile over time. Many of the same forces and arrogance that led to the demise of military or colonial empires have their analogies in economic empires.

We have described the various factors that give rise to economic empiredom and document how these same forces eventually lead to their downfall. By presenting the successes of these factors and the reasons why they faltered, we can gain insights into the ways to sustain economic relevancy. We also offered lessons to aspiring economies so that they may best leverage and manage their growth and avoid the problems that beset less carefully managed growth.

In doing so, we took what I hope was an interesting glimpse into the current global dynamic in which the United States, the world's first empire based primarily on economic might, struggles to maintain its global economic supremacy – in the face of a rapidly growing China that shall soon challenge the United States as the world's largest economy.

We find that the avenues to economic success for a nation like the United States are now replicated in aspiring nations around the world. Countries such as India and China are able to make their rural workforce more productive and move some of this workforce into their industrial sectors. With a rich endowment of labor, these aspiring empires can then capitalize on their endowments to create labor-intensive manufactured goods and intellectual services that have a competitive advantage in the global economy.

Other economies without such a huge endowment of labor may nonetheless have equally important endowments of other factors of production. For instance, affluent societies could easily divert conspicuous consumption into pools of savings that can be channeled into productive capacity in those industries that are physical capital-intensive. They can also invest in increasingly valuable and sophisticated human capital. If a nation can avoid the temptation of diverting savings into current consumption, with or without government as a partner, it can sow the seeds for a sustainable economic future.

The biggest challenge facing an economic empire also represents its greatest opportunity. Affluence is created when an economy offers incentives to produce. Developing nations often progressed because of an unwavering work ethic motivated by the desire for affluence and financial security. Unfortunately, once a nation realizes affluence, its focus changes from expanding the economic pie to distributing the economic pie. In other words, a nation transitions from a regime characterized as a positive sum game to one viewed as a constant sum game.

Complicating the dynamic is the gamesmanship that typically emerges when one special interest views it can more easily advance at the expense of others. This dynamic forces an empire to divert energy from the economic to the political realm. The work ethic is replaced by a sense of entitlement. As public discourse moves away from a shared national dream to a series of special interests, the economy is left poorer. The public dialog becomes focused instead on the politics of constant sum strivings for each other's share of the economic pie rather than in the creation of the economic pie in the first place. Productive effort diverted to the pursuit of special interests is an economic waste. In the process, the constant sum mentality actually becomes a negative sum game as the competition of special interests bleeds off resources.

My hope is that the recognition of the phenomena that give rise to economic empires and lead to their ultimate decline can create the wisdom that will allow a nation to avoid these trappings. A centrality of economic vision and the willingness to assert economic leadership emerge as essential ingredients for sustained economic growth.

However, few First Economic World nations seem able to muster the leadership that will put them on a path of sustainable economic development. Economies function best when entrepreneurship is encouraged, research and development and education is supported, those enjoying the largesse of a society are held accountable, and corporations are prevented from becoming too big to fail. These are the values that bring every economic empire to its apex, and can transition empires into a sustainable future.

Of course, each of these important tasks is politically difficult to accomplish in isolation. To engage an entire economic empire in an agenda for sustainability would require all citizens to do their part. In turn, we would be able to pass on to our great grandchildren a vibrant economy. While this bargain may indeed be more difficult than it sounds, the benefits are certainly worth the effort.

Notes

1. http://www.sciencedaily.com/releases/2008/09/080919075005.htm, accessed February 27, 2010.
2. http://www.sciencedaily.com/releases/2008/09/080919075005.htm, accessed February 27, 2010.
3. Veblen, *The Theory of the Leisure Class*, Penguin Twentieth-Century Classic (1994). Introduction by Robert Lekachman. New York: Penguin Books, 1899.
4. Smith, Adam, *An Inquiry into the Nature and Causes of the Wealth of Nations*. Edwin Cannan, ed. 1904, Book 1, Chapter 2.
5. http://en.wikipedia.org/wiki/Economy_of_Greece, accessed April 18, 2010.
6. Report on British Broadcasting Corporation news, morning of Friday, February 19, 2010.
7. Laffer, Arthur, *The Laffer Curve: Past, Present and Future*, http://www.heritage.org/Research/Taxes/bg1765.cfm, retrieved December 19, 2009.
8. Keynes, John Maynard, *The Collected Writings of John Maynard Keynes*. London: Macmillan, Cambridge University Press, 1972.
9. http://www.truthout.org/102508C, retrieved December 9, 2009.
10. Smith, Adam, *An Inquiry into the Nature and Causes of the Wealth of Nations*. Edwin Cannan, ed. London: Methuen and Co, 1904.
11. Edward Gibbon, *The History of the Decline and Fall of the Roman Empire*, London: Strahan and Cadell, 1776–89.
12. James, Lawrence, *The Rise and Fall of the British Empire*. New York: St. Martin's Griffin, 1997.
13. Shirer, W., *Rise and Fall of the Third Reich*. New York: Simon & Schuster, 1990.
14. Kennedy, P., *The Rise and Fall of the Great Powers*. New York: Vintage Books, 1989.
15. Smith, Adam, ed. *An Inquiry into the Nature and Causes of the Wealth of Nations*. Edwin Cannan, 1904.
16. This description is drawn from the excellent analysis of Kennedy, Gavin, *Adam Smith A Moral Philosopher and his Political Economy*. Palgrave-Macmillan, 2008, p. 101.
17. Dickens, Charles, *Hard Times*. Wordsworth: Printing Press, 1854.
18. Bradford, William, "Of Plymouth Plantation 1620–1647", Samuel Eliot Morison, ed. 1952, pp. 120–121.
19. Reid, T.R., and James Stanfield, "The World According to Rome." *National Geographic* (August 1997), pp. 54–83.
20. See for instance this interesting article http://americanhistory.suite101.com/article.cfm/indentured_servants, accessed February 20, 2010.
21. http://library.thinkquest.org/TQ0312848/quotes.htm, accessed February 27, 2010.
22. http://www.theamericanrevolution.org/hevents/bteapart.asp, retrieved February 20, 2010.
23. Corbett, William, "Cobbett's Parliamentary History of England: from the Earliest Period to the Year 1803," Vol. 17, T.C. Hansard, London, 1815, p. 1280.
24. http://www.constitution, accessed February 27, 2010.
25. http://www.constitution, accessed December 27, 2009.
26. Indentured Servitude in Colonial America, Deanna Barker, Frontier Resource.

27. http://www.nationalcenter.org/VirginiaDeclaration.html, accessed February 9, 2010.
28. http://www.gutenberg.org/dirs/etext05/trgov10h.htm, retrieved December 27, 2009.
29. *The Revolutionary Writings of John Adams,* Selected and with a Foreword by C. Bradley Thompson , Indianapolis: Liberty Fund, 2000.
30. Journals of the Continental Congress, 1774–1789, I, Washington, 1904, 63–7.
31. http://www.ushistory.org/declaration/, accessed February 9, 2010.
32. http://www.un.org/en/documents/udhr/, accessed December 27, 2009.
33. http://www.ushistory.org/declaration/, accessed February 9, 2010.
34. Twain, Mark, and Charles Dudley Moore, *The Gilded Age – A Tale of To-day.* New York: Harper and Brothers, 1924,p. 291.
35. Twain, Mark, and Charles Dudley Warner, *The Gilded Age: A Tale of Today.* Hartford, Connecticut: American Publishing Company, 1874.
36. http://us.history.wisc.edu/hist102/pdocs/carnegie_wealth.pdf, accessed February 10, 2010.
37. In fact, by the year 2006, the financial sector would earn one of every three dollars of profit in the United States.
38. Galbraith, Kenneth, *American Capitalism: The Concept of Countervailing Power.* Boston: Houghton Mifflin, 1956.
39. http://www1.bbiq.jp/quotations/fear.htm, accessed March 21, 2010.
40. Mettam, Roger, "Power, Status and Precedence: Rivalries among the Provincial Elites of Louis XIV's France," *Transactions of the Royal Historical Society,* Fifth Series, Vol. 38, 1988, pp. 43–62.
41. Mettam, p. 48.
42. Veblen, Thorstein, *The Theory of the Leisure Class: An Economic Study of the Evolution of Institutions.* New York: Macmillan, 1899.
43. Maslow, A.H., "A Theory of Human Motivation," *Psychological Review,* Vol. 50, 1943, pp. 370–396.
44. Stanley, Thomas and William Danko, *The Millionaire Next Door.* New York: Pocket Books, 1998.
45. Mill, John Stuart, *Principles of Political Economy with some of their Applications to Social Philosophy,* 7th ed. William Ashley, ed. London: Longmans Green, 1909.
46. Blake, William, *The Marriage of Heaven and Hell.* Facsimile edn. London: Dent, 1927
47. Kuznets, Simon, *"Economic Growth and Income Inequality,"* AER, March *1955,* pp. 1–28.
48. http://energyfarms.wordpress.com/2009/09/03/crop-yield-projections-miss-biofuel-report-target/corn-yield/, retrieved January 14, 2010.
49. http://www.ers.usda.gov/publications/eib3/eib3.htm, retrieved January 14, 2010.
50. Remarks by Edward P. Lazear, Chairman, Council of Economic Advisers at the Economic Summit of the Stanford Institute for Economic Policy Research, March 2, 2007, http://georgewbush-whitehouse.archives.gov/cea/lazear20070302.html, accessed February 26, 2010.
51. http://www.brainyquote.com/quotes/quotes/k/kinggeorge189273.html, accessed March 22, 2010.
52. https://www.cia.gov/library/publications/the-world-factbook/geos/ha.html, accessed January 23, 2010.
53. Bogdanich, Walt, and Jenny Nordberg, "DEMOCRACY UNDONE: Back Channels vs. Policy; Mixed U.S. Signals Helped Tilt Haiti Toward Chaos," *New York Times,* January 29, 2006.

54. http://thinkexist.com/quotation/sell_a_man_a_fish-he_eats_for_a_day-teach_a_man/151465.html, accessed February 27, 2010.

55. http://en.wikipedia.org/wiki/Fortune_Global_500, accessed January 23, 2010. The other top ten companies include a bank and an automobile company. The rest were oil companies in 2009.

56. http://www.telegraph.co.uk/finance/economics/6890189/Chinese-economy-overtakes-Japan, accessed January 23, 2010.

57. http://www.nationmaster.com/graph/eco_gdp-economy-gdp&date=1999, accessed January 23, 2010.

58. http://forecasts.org/gdp.htm, accessed January 23, 2010.

59. http://www.nationmaster.com/graph/eco_gdp-economy-gdp&date=1991, accessed January 23, 2010.

60. Friedman, T., *The World Is Flat*. New York: Farrar, Straus and Giroux, 2007. The sub-title for this book is *A Brief History of the 21st Century*, and first appeared in 2005, barely five years into the century. Friedman makes a compelling argument about the great leveling of economic power as a consequence of extensive global supply chains.

61. http://www.zakon.org/robert/internet/timeline/, accessed January 23, 2010.

62. http://www.internetworldstats.com/stats.htm, accessed January 23, 2010.

63. http://www.brainyquote.com/quotes/keywords/imitation.html, accessed February 28, 2010.

64. *Philipp von Hornick*, Chapter X in *Early Economic Thought: Selections from Economic Literature Prior to Adam Smith*, 1924, pp. 221–243 from McMaster University Archive for the History of Economic Thought.

65. Carey, Henry, "The harmony of interests agriculture manufacturing and commercial," reprinted by University of Michigan Library Ann Arbor, 2005.

66. Chang, H., *Kicking Away the Ladder*. New York: Anthem, 2002.

67. *Prolegomena* by Ibn Khaldun, translated in part by Reynold A. Nicholson in *Translations of Eastern Poetry and Prose*. Cambridge University Press, England, 1922.

68. George, Henry, *Progress and Poverty: An Inquiry into the Cause of Industrial Depressions and of Increase of Want with Increase of Wealth; The Remedy*. Kegan Paul, 1881. (reissued by Cambridge University Press, 2009; ISBN 9781108003612).

69. Say, Jean-Baptiste, (1803), *A Treatise on Political Economy, Or On the Production, Distribution and Consumption of Wealth*, translated by C.R. Prinsep, and reprinted by Augustus M. Kelley, Publishers, New York, 1971, pp. 139–140.

70. Durant, Will, *Caesar and Christ*. New York: Simon and Schuster, 1944.

71. Edward N. Lorenz, "Atmospheric predictability as revealed by naturally occurring analogues," *Journal of the Atmospheric Sciences*, Vol. 26, 1969, pp. 636–646.

72. Marx, Karl, *Critique of Hegels' Philosophy of Right*, Joseph O'Malley, ed. Cambridge University Press, Cambridge, 1972.

73. Weber, Max, "The Protestant Ethic and the Spirit of Capitalism," Parsons Talcott, ed. Scribners, New York, 1958, p. 181.

74. Weber, pp. 181–182.

75. Orwell, George, *Nineteen Eighty-Four. A novel*. London: Secker & Warburg, 1949.

76. Orwell, George, *Animal Farm*. London: Penguin Group, 1946.

77. Heller, J., *Catch-22*. New York: Simon and Schuster, 1961.

78. For instance, see the excellent discussion of Saturn's inception by Pil, Fritz, and Saul Rubenstein, "Saturn: A Different Kind of Company?" in *Between Imitation and Innovation*, Boyer, Robert, Elsie Charron, Ulrich Jurgens, and Steven Tolliday, editors, Oxford University Press, New York, 2004.

79. Crozier, Michel, *The Bureaucratic Phenomenon. An Examination of Bureaucracy in Modern Organizations and its Cultural Setting in France*, Chicago: Chicago University Press, 1964, p. 3.

80. Crozier, pp. 197–198.

81. Maier, C., *Bonjour Laziness*. New York: Pantheon Books, 2005.

82. Crozier, p. 156.

83. Crozier, p. 193.

84. Read, Colin, "Gyrations in Interlinked Financial Markets," unpublished paper, 2010.

85. Thomas Jefferson to Pierre Samuel Dupont de Nemours, from *The Writings of Thomas Jefferson*, Memorial Edition, Lipscomb and Bergh, editors, Washington, D.C., 1903–04, Vol. 14, p. 490.

86. http://www.lva.virginia.gov/lib-edu/education/bor/draftvdr.htm#2, accessed February 27, 2010.

87. http://www.ushistory.org/declaration/, accessed February 1, 2010.

88. *Munn v. Illinois*, 94 U.S. 113 (1877).

89. *United States v. Carolene Products Company*, 304 U.S. 144 (1938).

90. *Hawaii Housing Authority v. Midkiff*, 467 U.S. 229.

91. Poletown Neighborhood Council v. City of Detroit, 410 Mich. 616 (1981).

92. *Kelo v. City of New London*, 545 U.S. 469 (2005).

93. http://en.wikipedia.org/wiki/Kelo_v._City_of_New_London, accessed February 1, 2010.

94. http://www.wipo.int/portal/en/news/2007/article_0032.html, accessed February 1, 2010.

95 Lehman, John A., "Intellectual Property Rights and Chinese Tradition Section: Philosophical Foundations," *Journal of Business Ethics*, Vol. 69, No. 1, November, 2006, pp. 1–9.

96. http://thinkexist.com/quotation/don-t_let_your_special_character_and_values-the/222988.html, accessed March 22, 2010.

97. http://www.fordham.edu/halsall/mod/1902veblen00.html, accessed February 27, 2010.

98. http://www.usgovernmentspending.com/us_20th_century_chart.html, accessed February 1, 2010.

99. Stevenson, Betsey, and Justin Wolfers, "Economic Growth and Subjective Well Being: Reassessing the Easterlin Paradox", *Brookings Papers on Economic Activity*, Spring 2008, http://bpp.wharton.upenn.edu/jwolfers/Papers/EasterlinParadox.pdf, retrieved February 2, 2010.

100. http://hdr.undp.org/en/media/HDR_2009_EN_Complete.pdf, accessed February 2, 2010.

101. http://www.quotationspage.com/quote/995.html, accessed March 22, 2010.

102. Clive Upton, *Wiliam* A. Kretzschmar, Rafal Konopka: Oxford Dictionary of Pronunciation for Current English. Oxford University Press (2001); *Oxford Dictionary of Sociology*, John Scott, Gordon Marshall, ed. Oxford: Oxford University Press, 2005. eNotes.com. 2006. 2 Feb, 2010 http://www.enotes.com/oxsoc-encyclopedia/hegemony, accessed February 2, 2010

103. http://www.nationmaster.com/graph/eco_gdp-economy-gdp&date=1999, accessed January 23, 2010.

104. http://forecasts.org/gdp.htm, accessed January 23, 2010.

105. http://www.nationmaster.com/graph/eco_gdp-economy-gdp&date=1991, accessed January 23, 2010.

106. Fogel, Robert, "$123,000,000,000,000," *Foreign Policy*, January/February 2010.

107. Niebuhr, R., *The Irony of American History*. New York: Scribner, 1984.

108. http://wiki.monticello.org/mediawiki/index.php/Private_Banks_%28Quotation%29, accessed February 27, 2010.

109. Kennedy, P., *The Rise and Fall of the Great Powers*. New York: Vintage Books, 1989.

110. http://www.country-data.com/cgi-bin/query/r-7176.html, accessed February 7, 2010.

111. Kennedy, Paul, *The Rise and Fall of the Great Powers*, New York: Random House, 1987, p. 436.

112. http://www.visualizingeconomics.com/2008/01/20/share-of-world-gdp/, accessed February 7, 2010.

113. http://research.stlouisfed.org/fred2/graph/?chart_type=line&s[1][id]=CE16OV&s[1][range]=10yrs, accessed February 7, 2010.

114. Hitomi, Katsundo, "Historical Trends and the Present State of the Us Industry and Manufacturing," *Technovation*, Vol. 25, No. 6, June 2005, pp. 673–681.

115. Kennedy, Paul, *The Rise and Fall of the Great Powers*, New York: Random House, 1987, p. 454.

116. http://stats.uis.unesco.org/unesco/TableViewer/document.aspx?ReportId=121&IF_Language=eng&BR_Country=1560, accessed February 2, 2010.

117. http://www.china-profile.com/data/tab_rurpop_1.htm, accessed February 9, 2010.

118. http://www.brainyquote.com/quotes/quotes/c/confucius104507.html, accessed March 22, 2010.

119. Kuznets, Simon, "Economic Growth and Income Inequality," *American Economic Review* Vol. XLV, 1955, pp. 1–28.

120. Malthus, Thomas, and Antony Flew, *An Essay on the Principle of Population*, Harmondsworth English, Penguin, 1982.

121. Aghion, Philippe, *Schumpeterian Growth Theory and the Dynamics of Income Inequality*, *Econometrica*, Vol. 70, No. 3, 2002, pp. 855–882.

122. http://thinkexist.com/quotation/nations-like_stars-are_entitled_to_eclipse-all_is/263558.html, accessed March 22, 2010.

123. See The Organization for Economic Cooperation and Development's "Pensions at a Glance 2005." An executive summary can be found at http://www.oecd.org/dataoecd/27/27/43126151.pdf., accessed February 22, 2010.

124. Graphs were generated using data from *World Population to 2300*, United Nations Division of Economic and Social Affairs of the United Nations Secretariat, World Population, http://www.un.org/esa/population/publications/longrange2/WorldPop2300final.pdf, accessed April 18, 2010

125. "Family Planning in China," http://www.fmprc.gov.cn/ce/celt/eng/zt/zfbps/t125241.htm, retrieved February 22, 2010.

126. https://www.cia.gov/library/publications/the-world-factbook/rankorder/2004rank.html, accessed March 1, 2010.

127. Read, Colin, "Optimal Career Interruption and Duration – Family Planning in the Age of Careers, the Pill, and Dual Career Families," unpublished paper, 2007.

128. Graph constructed from date published by "Pensions at a Glance 2009: Retirement-Income Systems in OECD Countries," The OECD, 2009, http://www.oecd.org/doc

ument/49/0,3343,en_2649_34757_42992113_1_1_1_1,00.html, accessed April 18, 2010.

129. The U.S. budget can be found at: http://www.gpoaccess.gov/usbudget/fy09/pdf/budget/tables.pdf, retrieved February 22, 2010; http://www.bea.gov/national/index.htm#gdp, accessed February 22, 2010.

130. http://www.socialsecurity.gov/history/imf.html, accessed February 22, 2010.

131. http://www.cdc.gov/nchs/data/dvs/nvsr52_14t12.pdf, accessed February 22, 2010.

132. http://www.moralquotes.com/index.php/a?cat=191, accessed April 18, 2010.

133. http://www.whitehouse.gov/blog/09/04/22/A-Choice-Between-Prosperity-and-Decline, accessed February 27, 2010.

134. Daly, Herman, *Steady-State Economics*, 2nd edition. Washington D.C.: Island Press, 1991, p. 17.

135. Mill, John Stuart, *Principles of Political Economy with some of their Applications to Social Philosophy*, William J. Ashley, ed. 1909. Book IV, Chapter VI, Section 2., Library of Economics and Liberty, http://www.econlib.org/library/Mill/mlP61.html, retrieved February 21, 2010.

136. Toye, John, *Keynes on Population*, Oxford: Oxford University Press, 2000, pp. 60–61.

137. Georgescu-Roegen, Nicholas, *The Entropy Law and the Economic Process*, Cambridge, Massachusetts: Harvard University Press, 1971.

138. Rawls, John, *A Theory of Justice*, The Belknap Press of Harvard University Press, 1971.

139. http://www.online-literature.com/shelley_percy/, accessed February 27, 2010.

140. http://www.zakon.org/robert/internet/timeline/, accessed January 23, 2010.

141. http://www.internetworldstats.com/stats.htm, accessed January 23, 2010.

142. http://www.wisdomquotes.com/cat_future.html, accessed February 27, 2010.

143. http://www.quotesandpoem.com/quotes/showquotes/author/harold_macmillan/122700, accessed March 1, 2010.

Index